Psychoanalytic Objects Near and Far

Touching upon the most sensitive nuances of the analytic encounter, *Psychoanalytic Objects Near and Far* combines a far-reaching theoretical manifesto with an intimate clinical journal to express curiosity, skepticism and love towards the psychoanalytic clinic, theory and history.

Basic concepts and controversies that often become a conceptual ivory tower receive here a new and fresh vitality from the perspective of an experienced clinician, scholar and teacher, all while crossing the boundary of theoretical fantasy. While holding theory as central to the clinical act, Rolnik does not see it as a self-sufficient philosophy, detached from the free spirit of psychoanalysis as a practice and ethics. Rolnik has no need for iconoclasm. He is committed to the curative speech – his patients' and his own – as well as receptiveness to the unconscious space in the most Freudian sense of the word.

This volume will be of great interest to analysts in practice and in training, and to any reader interested in the analytic process.

Eran J. Rolnik is a board-certified psychiatrist, historian and training and supervising psychoanalyst at the Israel Psychoanalytic Society and the Frankfurt Psychoanalytic Institute (IPA/DPV). He is the author, contributor and editor of numerous books, including *Freud in Zion: Psychoanalysis and the Making of Modern Jewish Identity* (Routledge).

Psychoanalytic Objects Near and Far

Talking Cure

Eran J. Rolnik

Routledge
Taylor & Francis Group

LONDON AND NEW YORK

Designed cover image: Netta Lieber Sheffer, *Red Tent*, Pastel – pencil on paper, 2004.

First published in English 2025
by Routledge
4 Park Square, Milton Park, Abingdon, Oxon OX14 4RN

and by Routledge
605 Third Avenue, New York, NY 10158

Routledge is an imprint of the Taylor & Francis Group, an informa business

© 2025 Eran J. Rolnik

British Library Cataloguing-in-Publication Data
A catalogue record for this book is available from the British Library

ISBN: 978-1-032-86650-5 (hbk)
ISBN: 978-1-032-86649-9 (pbk)
ISBN: 978-1-003-52847-0 (ebk)

DOI: 10.4324/9781003528470

Typeset in Times New Roman
by Apex CoVantage, LLC

This book is dedicated to my students and to my patients.

Contents

Preface

Teaching psychoanalysis, that is: depositing words and thoughts in the hands of students, analysts in training or experienced colleagues, is an important part of my identity – as a training-psychoanalyst, a psychiatrist, a researcher and an author. As the Covid-19 pandemic broke out, I was planning on using the time freed by the first lockdown for writing. Life as we knew it stopped and the vacuum left by life's bustle was filled with the new presence of the Covid epidemic. It was threatening and oppressive, but it also filled me with a feeling of urgency and gratitude. It is not every day that a person is given the opportunity to feel historic time flowing through them, and that feeling was generously given to me by Covid. What happened then was something I did not expect: I found out I prefer to fill the free time during lockdowns with spoken, rather than written, words. I was missing the experience of thinking psychoanalysis while discussing it with colleagues.

In March 2020, I made the seminars I held in my clinic into video conferences. I called the series of digital meetings *psychotherapy under fire*, and shortly my Wednesday nights' Freud reading seminar had formed into a learning community of a few hundred therapists. The webinar drew students (not only of psychology), psychotherapists working in various approaches, psychiatrists, psychoanalysts, senior academics and lovers of psychoanalysis from different backgrounds. The discussion, which started with Freud for the most part, weaved through different issues and psychoanalytic positions. Each encounter was 90 minutes long, during which I spoke freely to the camera, stopping every so often to take a breath and review the dozens of heads staring at me from the screen.

And they were really there. Sitting in their homes, their clinics, now empty of patients, or the open air, whether in a kitchen in Tel Aviv, a backyard in a town up north, or a study in Philadelphia, London, Berlin or San Francisco. I discussed subjects that concern us even in normal times. I discussed ideas I think should interest new therapists, and hoped they still interest even experienced colleagues who took part in the seminar. I went back to old texts I read, or wrote, years ago. I described personal gut feelings and tested the audience's reaction to clinical and theoretical notions. Some lectures went by in a haze, just like dreamy hours of analysis, where the analyst is roused from their thoughts at the last moment, to end the hour on time.

Whether I directed my speech to an audience of psychotherapy instructors and training psychoanalysts, or to psychology students, who have only recently come across the notions of "primal scene" or "projective identification" – any theoretic thought, any clinical deliberation and any technical controversy carried, so I felt, the mark of the unique moment in history provided by the epidemic. Perhaps I imagined myself in the image of Freud, wading through the snow – at the height of World War I and the Spanish Flu – to the lecture hall at the University of Vienna to deliver his *Introductory Lectures on Psychoanalysis* to a diverse audience. Perhaps I was anxious this would be "the last lecture." Times of plagues also afford an opportunity to exaggerate.

Every talk focused on a particular subject – psychotherapy and anxiety during an epidemic, on-line therapy, the unconscious, transference and countertransference, interpretation, containment, listening, enactment, resistances, termination of treatment, a psychoanalytic worldview, and more.

All told, I held a couple dozen of these "psychotherapy under fire" Zoom encounters during the Covid-19 lockdowns. Some were dedicated to Freud's thought, and some dealt with the mutual relations between theory and technique in psychoanalytic thought. Unlike a university lecture or a conference talk, I let my thoughts wander, inscribing wide and far-reaching circles around the topic of each meeting. I dealt with fundamental issues of psychoanalytic psychotherapy practice, the history of concepts and debates, and also the current state of psychoanalytic knowledge and discourse. They were the free associations of a clinician, who is also a historian of psychoanalysis, on theory and technique and the philosophy and history of psychoanalytic thoughts, "interrupted" every few moments by colleagues asking, commenting, arguing. The result was a sort of "psychoanalytic beit-midrash" that combined theoretical musings and a close reading of selected texts from psychoanalytic literature with a "clinical diary" that included practical advice for therapists, given from a perspective which was, as described, personal, scholarly and deliberative at one and the same time. Little by little, I have become accustomed to my virtual discursive self, and waited for my next encounter with it and the group. I have come to think of these Zoom meetings as my own "talking cure."

Transforming the recorded encounters into text also allowed me to become more familiar with my own psychoanalytic palimpsest. I was not very surprised to discover the central place taken up by Freud in my lectures – that is one thing Covid did not impact – But I did discover to what extent my thoughts on psychoanalysis, as practice and ethics, as a lifestyle and form of being, have changed in recent years. More importantly: I discovered how much this experience, of speaking to the camera from within a space I share with patients, echoes into the way I teach, think and talk. Talking from within the treatment room allowed me to link the objective and subjective dimension in the psychoanalytic act and anchor our talks in praxis, in my vita activa as an analytical therapist. To muse and speak to a camera about psychoanalysis, live in front of a rather large audience of therapists, and do so from the room where, just moments ago, you concluded an analytic hour is a rather unique experience.

*

Ever since the publication of this book's Hebrew (2022) and German (2023) editions, I had the opportunity to present selected chapters of it as lectures in conferences and psychoanalytic societies in Tel Aviv, Rome, Munich, Berlin, Frankfurt, Oslo, Philadelphia, Chicago and New York.

I would like to thank the participants of these seminars for those exhilarating months of joint thinking, reading and study. My thanks also to this book's translator and editor, Tom Atkins, and my loving gratitude to Nili Lubrani Rolnik, who not only transcribed my lectures but also found, as always, ideas hidden from me in my own spoken words.

I hope that the psychoanalytic thoughts and questions that have found their way into this book bear witness not only to my psychoanalysis but also to that protracted, historic moment, that feeling of a shared fate, both professional and human, that allowed contemporary psychoanalytic thought to persist through a pandemic and war.

Tel-Aviv/Frankfurt am Main, Autumn 2024

"It is a pity that one cannot make a living, for instance, on dream interpretation!"
Freud, 1897

Chapter 1

Introduction

Calm throughout the storm

Once upon a time in America, psychoanalysts were popular speakers in various forums and symposiums. One star of that age was the Californian psychoanalyst Ralph Greenson (later known as Marilyn Monroe's analyst). In 1960, Greenson appeared before a crowded University of California auditorium. He was invited to discuss how psychoanalysis relates to religion and was joined on the program by three speakers with predictably differing points of view: A Catholic priest, a Protestant minister and a Jewish rabbi. It was a stormy night, and during the heated debate, a terrifying thunderclap was heard, and an instant power failure occurred. Fearful of some disaster, or maybe God's wrath, everybody jumped to his feet. However, when the lights came on again, Greenson calmly observed: "Please note, I am the only speaker still sitting down." His self-assurance has scored him a point for psychoanalysis (Greenson, [1960] 1992, p. 41).

There are various ways of interpreting this story. It seems reasonable to attach it to a time when American psychoanalysis experienced a certain feeling of superiority and uplifted itself to a religious status. It can also be interpreted via a question: Should the psychoanalyst be the last one sitting when darkness falls and panic strikes? Is that the analyst's social role? Greenson, it seems, took pride in staying in his seat, unlike the clergymen who bolted under the table.

I'm not certain that therapists today would see that as an ideal – be the one to remain calm and seated under any circumstance. But I do think we have a role in these times. Our role isn't only to treat individuals but also to keep "thinking under fire," as Bion (1979) puts it, even under conditions that make thought seem almost impossibly courageous. Psychoanalytic thinking is a worldview, a particular way of being in the world that the analyst puts in the service of the society and community they are rooted in. In the following talks, I would like to discuss questions beyond the technical, such as "How to perform psychoanalysis during lockdown?" Or "How can the therapeutic technique be adapted to a pandemic or other extraordinary conditions such as war and massive collective trauma?" These are important questions, certainly, but I am also interested in questions such as "What else can we contribute in these turbulent times?" I would like to use these extraordinary circumstances we experience during

DOI: 10.4324/9781003528470-1

which this book is written to think of things that concern us as analytic thera-pists also in normal times.

In many senses, our discipline, psychodynamic therapy, develops during times of crisis. We might not be aware of that, but a significant portion of the theories that guide us have been developed "under fire," so to speak, during various external shocks and attacks, which have accompanied the development of psychoanalytic thought in its 130 years. We would do well to remember the historical context in which our theories and techniques have been developing.

Freud developed his theory of anxiety in a time when anxiety was very present in Vienna's social and political climate. Viennese schools and universities were closed due to the Spanish flu, and Freud returned to the issue of anxiety, which had occu-pied him since he started his clinical work. In the 25th of his introductory lectures on psychoanalysis, delivered at the University of Vienna during World War I, he writes: "[T]he problem of anxiety is a nodal point at which the most various and important questions converge, a riddle whose solution would be bound to throw a flood of light on our whole mental existence" (*Standard Edition*, vol. XVI, p. 393).

These days, we seldom use Freud's first theory of anxiety. That theory, developed by young Freud in the 1880s, offers a revolutionary, even if somewhat biologistic, explanation of the somatic symptoms of anxiety. The explanation links the accu-mulation of unrealized sexual energy with the nervous system's need to reduce to a minimum stress originating in over-stimulation. That is, the source of anxiety is in drives, repressed sexuality and overflowing libido that poisons the psychic appara-tus. He reveals to his patients the physical similarity between a state of anxiety and that of sexual activity – shortness of breath, increased perspiration and heightened heart rate.

Freud listed a number of situations making sexual activity unsatisfying – absti-nence, masturbation, coitus interruptus, states of frigidity and lack of enjoyment from love-making. These situations dam the stream of sexuality, and the accumulated excess becomes anxiety in the same way, to use Freud's metaphor, that wine becomes vinegar. The toxic anxiety in Freud's early theory is libido that accumulated, and soured, in the psychic system. It is not a purely biological theory, as for Freud, the sex drive, whether fulfilled or not, is never a purely biological drive. From this point on, a distinction starts to develop, one characteristic of psychoanalytic thought, between anxiety as a psychic event with mental content and psychological meaning, to anxiety as a somatic, actual event lacking a symbolic function. The idea of anxiety – much as that of drive – is conceptualized by Freud as a link in a chain connecting the body and mind. To this day, we can place the theoreticians of anxiety on a spectrum ranging from biological, or even evolutionary, perceptions of anxiety to ones of social con-struction. The latter read the phenomenon of anxiety in contexts that are not biological or psychological-individual, but mainly social, cultural and historical.

In the same year, Freud introduced his first theory of anxiety, 1893, the Nor-wegian painter Edvard Munch created an expressionist representation of modern-man anxiety, his famous painting *The Scream*. The terror reflected in the eyes of Munch's screaming figure predicted the way the 19th century would end and the modern age would begin – a terrible war, one we now know as World War I but at the time was called simply the Great War.

The Great War was the crucible in which fundamental cultural concepts, expressing modern man's fears and anxieties, were forged. Unlike the anxieties of the pre-modern age, which were relevant only to those directly involved with the causes of danger, modern man's anxiety is mimetic. It is much more infectious than the disease itself. One does not have to be on the scene of a disaster, or in any real danger, to experience it. It is enough to see a photograph on a social network, listen to a radio broadcast or watch television to give rise to an anxiety reaction. In our times, anxiety becomes, at the blink of an eye, the share of huge publics. It is replicated in real-time, over and over, by skilled agents of anxiety who harness it to their own political and economic ends.

Freud's later theory of anxiety did not completely replace the early one, but it did place it at a different psychic location: Anxiety is not only a means of expelling soured libido or intolerable psychic materials, but it is a capsule of meaning and knowledge the subject has on itself. This knowledge travels through the psychic space, seeking an opportunity to be thought, and when it cannot be thought, it becomes a symptom, just like a dream or a compulsive symptom. That is, in the late psychoanalytic theory of anxiety, anxiety serves a dual role: To protect the *ego* from real dangers such as pain, loss or hunger, and also to blend in with emotional and cognitive development – to indicate to the ego the existence of a psychic reality outside of consciousness. The source of anxiety – and this is the point where we, as therapists, come into play – is simultaneously internal and external. This is because anxiety arises from the same drive or fantasy part experienced by the subject as foreign, as "not-me." Anxiety is similar in this regard to infantile sexuality; it is both traumatic and post-traumatic at the same time. It is traumatic because it originates in the life and death drives that act on a person's psyche since they are born and are very powerful relative to the infant or child's meager mental powers. It is post-traumatic in the sense that it "remembers" experiences and events in external reality that excited the person and were inscribed in their internal world and translates them to psychic reality even before the person has the mental or cognitive capabilities to assign meaning, interpretation and symbolic expression to them.

Becoming a psychoanalyst means looking for the particular in the universal and vice versa. It means listening to the singular plight of an individual patient as embedded within her particular unconscious-phantasmal-sexual discontent and the historical-cultural-political discontent of the group and the polity this patient inhabits.

Accordingly, it is important that dynamic therapists develop and nurture profound thinking on what is taking place in society whilst listening to their patients. Good therapy normally treats more than one person. Freud did not make up his theory of sexuality out of the ether. It was conceived and developed under particular historical and social circumstances. Analytic thought often precedes historical changes. The analyst functions as a transducer or facilitator of unthought knowledge. It is not by coincidence that Bion said that if you are not afraid to tell the patient what you are about to say, you better not say it. A worthy interpretation scares the analyst, too. It shatters his own mental equilibrium. Our social role could likewise be quite unsettling as we are required every so often to try and export some of it out to relay it to the wider public.

We should also note that our profession is becoming not only endangered but also dangerous. The image of the therapist as a privileged alien, closed-off in their room rather than "living in the real world" is now changing. Sitting in a closed room, in such proximity to people who can infect us with a disease – has become a rather dangerous affair at the moment. I have no doubt that patients and their unconscious have perceived us in very intense moments of anxiety. Some feel great kinship with us. A sense of shared fate with the therapist can advance their treatment. Other patients, such as perverse ones, will abuse this intimacy. They have "seen us in our underwear." The greatest danger is that we stop thinking. That we stop interpreting, stop inviting dreams and stop finding interest in the recesses of the mind but rest content with reassuring our patients' anxieties and containing them. The danger is that we would be tempted to only deal with outside reality and adapt to it, that we be empathic to parts that are easy to identify with. Identification, empathy and reassurances all have a place in the analytic encounter, but our expertise is to be empathic to the parts and mental regions that the patient and society at large find it difficult to own and be empathic towards. The internet and social networks thrive on projections and polarizing views. Even now, in the midst of a global pandemic, I think, the air is contaminated more with projections than viruses. And these projections would stay with us long after a vaccine will be developed, or the virus disappears and the epidemic ends. Much work awaits us, detoxifying the public sphere of projections before we feel safe to walk in it again.[1]

Note

1 This talk was held on the first week of the first Covid-19 lockdown (April 2020).

Chapter 2

Unconscious and the death drive

On the special characteristics of the unconscious system. How does analysis cure, and can feelings be unconscious? What are screen memories? Of the excitement caused by meeting the therapist outside of the treatment room, on punctuality and of a patient who refused to leave the couch at the sound of a warning siren. Thoughts on psychoanalysis and neuroscience. Recalling a nice aphorism by Nietzsche that therapists should know.

Once, as I was daydreaming in the seat of a shared-route taxi, I suddenly noticed a man not two seats from me. He looked at me and I gazed at him with a sleepy look, and we both suddenly realized – he's an analysand of mine. It was just like a scene from a dream. He took a few seconds to realize he was sitting next to his analyst; I took a few seconds to realize he was a patient I'd been meeting several times a week for a few years. Each of us apparently needed the other's recognition to validate our own. We nodded at each other, but the encounter had a completely dream-like quality, as if we continued in a crowded shared-route taxi, something of the familiar yet uncanny type of encounter we held in analysis at the time.

Imagine you enrolled in the *Introduction to Psychoanalysis* course Freud taught at the University of Vienna in the winter of 1915. You would have heard 28 fascinating lectures spread over two semesters. The lecturer would have taken you, one step at a time, through a comprehensive theory of the human psyche. The term *libido* wouldn't have come up before the 22nd lecture. By then, you would have learned of phenomena such as dreams, parapraxis and hysterical symptoms, which require only the concepts of *psychic conflict* and *unconscious* to be explained. Freud dedicated three months of this series of lectures – later published as the first *Introductory Lectures on Psychoanalysis* – to the theory of dreams. You would have heard almost nothing of libido, sexuality or transference in the entire course. In the 22nd lecture, Freud would have told you about some of the burning controversies in the field of psychoanalysis, and would suggest that you take little heed of theoretical disagreements between scientists. These are generally sterile disputes that do not lead to any breakthrough, based as they are on bits and pieces of the truth that are chosen, and savagely defended, by each of the sides. Freud

DOI: 10.4324/9781003528470-2

would have taught you a chapter in the history of the young discipline he estab-lished and the history of science in general. I, too, would like to incorporate into our talks, alongside theoretical and clinical aspects, observations on the develop-ment of psychoanalytic thought or, if you like, contemplations on the unconscious of our science.

The subject of today's talk is *The Unconscious*, the concept and the essay. With Freud, it pays to distinguish between concepts he dedicated a whole paper to and ones – such as the Oedipus complex or identification – that appear and develop rhi-zomatically in various essays, in different contexts and meanings. *The Unconscious* is one of 12 meta-psychological essays Freud wrote during a seven-week burst of writing. He published only five of them, destroying the other seven. The 12th essay, *A Phylogenetic Fantasy,* also known as *Overview of the Transference Neuroses,* was found in 1984 in the estate of Sándor Ferenczi, enclosed within a letter from Freud, asking Ferenczi for his opinion on it.

When reading *The Unconscious,* we "take a look under the hood" of psychoanalysis in its Freudian sense, which is, I believe, the main theory from which developed, during the 20th century, not only other psychoanalytic schools of thought but also other psychotherapies, including cognitive-behavioral ones (in which Freudian thought, while hidden and encoded, still exists). In the last 130 years, from the moment two people meet for a conversation, "Freudian moments" take place (Bollas, 2007). People have had heart-to-hearts even before Freud, but the Freudian moment has a unique quality, first and foremost for the special status it affords the dynamic unconscious in establishing the subject and culture. The more psychoanalytic thought develops, the harder it is for us as therapists to iden-tify its history in the clinical theory and the therapeutic hour. Even analysts don't discuss patients or the events of a session in the language of *The Unconscious*. It has a foreign tone not merely because of its out-dated language, but because it has been years since you looked under the hood of the theory you are working with. There are many reasons Freud's work retains a "foreign language" status with dynamic therapists, even when their thought and work are guided by it, and we will familiarize ourselves with some of them.

As therapists, we invite a person for a conversation on fixed days and hours. At a certain point during this conversation, a unique event begins to take shape: The patient directs an immense portion of his psychic energy at the analyst and will continue to do so for most of the therapy. We call this event *transference* as a generic term. In Freudian terms, transference is psychic/mental energy emanating from the unconscious. This energy takes various shapes and forms. Like a flowing river, it carries things with it, various trans-formations and structures. We become experts in sorting out the contents of this tributary, its function and its hidden meanings. The analyst, by their very presence, invites the unconscious and starts interpreting it. The basic rule of psychoanalysis: "Say Anything that comes to your mind," once presented to the patient, facilitates the transference as much as it gradually undermines the patient's psychic status quo.

Unconscious feelings

Freud emphasizes that a drive can be a subject for consciousness in only two ways: Attached to a representation or to an affect: "If the instinct did not attach itself to an idea or manifest itself as an affective state, we could know nothing about it" (Freud, The Unconscious, *Standard Edition*, Vol. XIV, p. 177).

Freud further wonders whether sensations, emotions and affects can even be unconscious like mental representations, whether something that is in our experience – such as anger, envy, hatred – can be unconscious at all. The intuitive answer is: Of course it can. In psychoanalysis, we constantly discuss unconscious love, hatred or guilt. The presence of the affect in consciousness is related to the degree to which it is repressed or denied, and therefore, we can discuss an unconscious feeling on a descriptive level. But on the dynamic level, there is no such thing. A feeling, as its name suggests, is something felt, and it would be a mistake to place it in the dynamic unconscious. An "affect" is an amount of energy discharged and released. That is, a mental energy attached at a certain point in time to one unconscious presentation, which can, at a later point, be released (**i.e., discharged**) and attach itself to another presentation available to consciousness. We are all familiar with it from personal experience. We suddenly tear up – we are listening to music, reading a book, seeing news and suddenly we tear up. We didn't even know we were sad, but there is a release, a catharsis. That is probably why we love art and cherish creativity, because it allows us not only thoughts but also contact with emotions – things that were once locked – with unfelt intensity, and brings tears to our eyes. What do we do when a patient tears up? If you're not thinking analytically, you're saying to yourself, satisfied, "The patient is crying; he feels something." This is far from certain. A Freudian therapist would ask the patient – "What do those tears mean?" Why do we insist? Why don't we contend ourselves with the tears? Because we are not certain that the patient knows why he became tearful. At times, it is obvious – he was talking about his losses, his pains – the pain is easily identified by the patient, who can attribute it to a mental presentation. But sometimes, a patient suddenly cries when you bill them for an hour they didn't attend. They cry for being late. They react very emotionally to a change in the room's temperature or lighting. They may burst out in tears because you understood them differently than they hoped you would. We don't know when the affect rises to such a level that we feel it.

Here is an example: A young man comes in for a psychiatric consultation following a suicide attempt. He admits that it was an impulsive act for which he was not prepared. He was fired from his work a week earlier. The day before his suicide attempt, his older brother called to offer help. The successful brother, who recently sold a company for a large profit, told the patient what he thinks he should do to improve his financial situation. The brother offered to pay for training and even employ him in his company. From the patient's point of view, these offers were aimed at controlling him and dictating how he should live. The patient says that he has hated his successful brother for many years. The moment he felt the full intensity of that hatred, he tried to kill himself. It seems, then, that the suicide attempt expressed something else than the patient's lack of will to live. It was more likely done to escape emotions such as wrath, envy and humiliation that arose in him as a response to the help offered by his "successful brother."

In *The Unconscious,* Freud has an interesting discussion about the language of a schizophrenic. Freud is interested in the patient's flowery language. It is a language whose content is often related to bodily organs. It is seemingly pre-lingual, semiotic, pre-symbolic. Freud calls it *organ-speech.* Using a process we have already seen in *The Interpretation of Dreams,* condensation, one word can represent an entire chain of thoughts, just as in a dream, where a whole world of meanings is compressed into one image that we can spend hours of analysis on, given the patient's cooperation, of course. The dream work performs a sort of compressing and encryption of the dream thoughts, and the interpretation of the dream is that action of "disentanglement" that unravels the dream's apparent narrative to uncover its hidden meaning. The same should be done with patients' words. The Freudian therapist listens not only to the "music" of what is being said but is also aware of the choice of words. Use the first hours, the intake, when you're still not familiar with the patient's language, to listen to it and sense how much weight is put on a word. Perhaps it is rather rare, and we don't often hear it. Perhaps you will notice some odd mistake in the way they speak or the way they pronounce a certain word. Our patient's words tell a story even before they are strung into sentences. You feel that some words are uttered quickly by your patient as if throwing them away, and others they are enamored with and like to roll on their tongue. Sometimes, a patient's "object relations" are revealed by the way they use words as objects in their inner world.

Talking cure

As therapists who offer "talking cure," we should have a theory, a model of cure that explains how one is cured using words. Freudian psychoanalysis has such a model that links its meta-psychological theory with therapeutic technique. It is worthwhile to know this model, as it appears in *The Unconscious.* We find there the important distinction between "thing presentation" (Dingvorstellung) and "word presentation" (Wortvorstellung). As the patient speaks, they say things that are not yet presented in their consciousness. They receive the acoustic presentation in consciousness by virtue of the patient's words. This is why we don't name the feelings a patient expresses but paraphrase what the patient told us. By that, we grant them a permanent entry to consciousness and extract them from various "false connections," as Freud and Breuer termed them in *Studies on Hysteria* and unconscious fantasies. Our silence also has importance in transferring thing presentations between the unconscious system and awareness. We are supposed to know when to be silent and let the patient do quiet work; there's a place for that. But, the process by which presentations move between mental systems, between the unconscious and the preconscious, and from it to the conscious, is a process that is greatly helped by the therapist's speech. Moreover, consider the (first) fundamental rule of psychoanalysis: The patient is asked "to say whatever comes into their mind" not only because we want to encourage them to overcome resistance to speaking of unpleasant contents – sexual, aggressive, shameful – but because we think every thought that is worded has the potential to carry something new to awareness, something the patient didn't even know existed within them. A certain word is said, and *voilà*, some unconscious thing-presentation would hop on to it and use it to transfer into consciousness.

This is transference in the most basic sense of the concept, a transmission of energy between psychic representations and words. What do we mean by saying that a person is "a prisoner of their own words"? We mean that there is not enough movement between psychic systems in their inner world, their word presentations do not serve the need to symbolize, and their words are released "under restrictive conditions." There is no gap between the words and the reality they are meant to represent. Something similar can also happen in the other extreme, when language becomes overly abstract. From a certain level of abstractness, our language becomes similar to that of the schizophrenic patient. Perhaps this is why Freud spurned philosophy. Something in the writing of philosophers reminded him of the schizophrenic's "organ speech." His letters exhibit his criticism and hostility towards philosophers.

Who really speaks in a session?

There are two people sitting and talking in the therapy room, and both are never completely cognizant of what they are saying. As a therapist, I'm not subjected to the fundamental rule of psychoanalysis, and I don't say everything that comes to my mind. But I can also never fully know what I had in mind before I open my mouth and say it. This technical issue changes between patients. I learned to avoid phrasing my interventions as a question. When you direct a question at the patient you might get an answer, but you also make it harder for them to experience, think, feel. There is something in a question mark that doesn't reach the deeper levels of the psyche. So at times I may sound certain to the patient without actually being – I'm merely examining a hypothesis without bothering to add a question mark. I would rather say "you felt shame" and discover, through the patient's reaction, that I was wrong, then ask "how did you feel" and take a considerable risk of distancing the patient from the experience. I think the unconscious needs the provocation, it needs some pushback, it reacts well to an active presence seeking it. I'm speaking in generalities now.

Two people speaking, then. But the real work begins only after they opened their mouths. What did they say, really? Work just begins when I offer my interpretation, because only after throwing a stone can I start looking for the ripples. How did the patient hear what I just said? How did I hear it? What do they do with it? The same thing happens when I listen to the patient's speech. I will often bear lack of clarity on the patient's part, or of understanding on mine. If I missed a word, I won't ask the patient to repeat it. I will take responsibility for not hearing, and check with myself what happened. I won't halt the patient's speech and ask them to fill in the gap. If I didn't hear something I didn't hear it, I won't stop them. Maybe later I will realize that while I'm not hearing a certain something they are saying, there is some erasure taking place, coming either from the patient or my self, and perhaps that would later become meaningful. Bion's concept of the *Caesura* (drawing on Freud's own use of this word) is here quite useful. Anything that disrupts the patient's mental flow, or that of the analyst, could harbor some unrecognized signification and hence can turn out to be a focal point for further development and mental growth.

I remember one patient with whom the same question would, every so often, pop into my head as I was listening to him – "what is his brother's name?" I would be slightly embarrassed of once again forgetting his brother's name, and would have to go over the whole cycle of wondering, for some reason, what was his brother's name, racking my brain over it, be embarrassed about not remembering, then finding the name. Over and over, time after time. I learned to keep silent when this repetitive riddle would appear in my head, but I had to do work with myself – why does this informative question force itself on me again, and what is the meaning of this stubborn forgetfulness on my part?

Let us discuss the unconscious system, and it's special characteristics. Freud writes of it: "There are in this system no negation, no doubt, no degrees of certainty." (Freud, The Unconscious, *Standard Edition* vol. XIV, p. 186). In the primary process there are countless options, it is reality in-potentia. The therapeutic process does not only encourage the return of the repressed and interprets it, reactivates certain segments of the unconscious – primary fantasies and psychic materials that were never in the conscious ego. Thoughts that were not yet thought and unconscious processes are subject only to the pleasure principle. That is, they do not have to take into account, for example, that you can't both be in a certain place and also not be there, that you can't be both someone's brother and also their sister, or that you can't be your father's son, and also your father's father. These logical limitations do not apply to the unconscious system. There is some great willingness in the primary process, the unconscious system, to deliver forward the libidinal investments, to deliver to other objects the energetic investment. This is what allows transference. There is someone taking care of me, and I have an inner caring object called "mother," then the carer is mother. This is why the patients finds it strange that "mother" is asking for money, and are hurt when "mother" reminds them that they still haven't paid for the treatment this month. This is the most basic meaning of transference, that a thing-presentation transfers its properties to a thing in reality, making two things that share one trait into identical or symmetrical things. A dog has four legs, and a cat has four legs, so a dog is a cat with all that entails.

As the paper progresses, Freud uses the abbreviation *Ucs.* to denote the unconscious, so as not to tempt us to think in concrete, neurological terms. It is important that we remember that we are dealing with a psychological rather than a neuro-anatomical or physiological model. We explore and treat the workings of the human psyche, not brain, and we therefore limit ourselves to psychological concepts when discussing and studying the human experience. A chemical analysis of the bonds between the carbon atoms composing the blue color used by a painter would not add anything to our understanding of the artistic experience. Measuring the levels of serotonin in the synaptic cleft when our loved one enters the room contributes nothing to our understanding of the meaning of love. Poetry enthusiasts do not need brain imaging equipment to explore the lyrical aspect of being, although bio-chemical phenomena do take place in the brain when reading or writing poetry. In other words, one shouldn't reduce human subjective experience to a physiological activity of neural networks. In a letter to Georg Groddeck, from whom he borrowed the concept of the id, Freud argues that the unconscious serves as the connection between the physical and psychological and perhaps represents some missing link in the evolution of humanity. He writes:

> To me it seems just as arbitrary to endow the whole of nature with a psyche as radically to deny that it has one at all. Let us grant to nature her infinite variety which rises from the inanimate to the organically animated, from the just physi-cally alive to the spiritual.
>
> (Letters of Sigmund Freud, p. 177)

As an analyst, I am not interested in solving the psycho-physical problem by reducing subjective experience to neural activity. Our analytic research teaches us that chronological, synchronic or biological time cannot be applied to the psychic unconscious. Unconscious events are located outside the realm of time. That is, they are not arranged on a timeline. Our consciousness, where secondary (logical) thinking presides, makes an effort to arrange things chronologically and would most often arrange the memories, the past, on the basis of emotional needs in the present. We can often see a confused chronology in patients' experiences as well, and we should not rush to correct them. A Patient might say, "I already told you that," or might even be offended that I did not remember something they are certain they have already told me. We examine why we don't remember, but sometimes, the patient did not previously say what they are saying now. They only wanted to say it and registered the experience without putting it into words and saying them in actual fact. Wishes and fantasies are often represented as actual memory traces in the mind.

Freud lists the properties of the unconscious system: "[E]xemption from mutual contradiction, primary process (mobility of cathexes), timelessness, and replace-ment of external by psychical reality – these are the characteristics which we may expect to find in processes belonging to the system Ucs." (Freud, The Unconscious, Standard Edition, Vol. XIV, p. 187).

Inner, or psychic, reality is perhaps Freud's most important discovery (and is mentioned in his writing as soon as 1895, in Project for a Scientific Psychology). The unconscious thing exists in the patient's reality and in that of our encoun-ter with them, whether we observe it and think of it, or whether we ignore its existence, whether we want to know about it or not. It exists and acts. The unconscious is always active. In an analytic situation, we make it work harder; we spur it to turn towards us. In a way, we play the role of a car mechanic, asking the client to rev up their engine during a mechanical inspection.

The Freudian unconscious and the psychoanalytic conception of memory

The path to discovering psychoanalysis had three main stops. In the first stage, Freud abandoned the dominant paradigm of 19th-century psychiatry that linked mental illness with degeneracy, heredity or physical trauma. In the second, he presented a new perception in which normal psychic activity, with the concept of *mental conflict* at its core, fills a main role in causing mental illness. In the third stage, due to his self-analysis and the discovery of the Oedipal complex, drives and infantile sexuality appear as the new cornerstones of a new psychological theory.

During his self-analysis, Freud observed a paradox presented by memory relating to childhood events: Important and significant facts and occurrences are not retained by memory, while seemingly insignificant memories are. Some of our most banal memories have extraordinary acuity and persistence, considering the lack of interest their contents hold. What do those *screen memories* cover? Screen memories are the result of a compromise between two psychic conflicts: One retains the trivial memory, and the other poses a resistance that hides the unconscious pathogenic significance. The two forces do not cancel each other but create a compromise or a condensation of two separate memories. Even if the screen memory is, from a factual perspective, entirely "false," it still has a nucleus of psychic truth. This is because it was forged from the traces of a memory the psychic mechanism had access to and retroactively weaved into the screen memory. Freud concluded the discussion of screen memories with a scandalous remark:

> It may indeed be questioned whether we have any memories at all from our childhood: memories relating to our childhood may be all that we possess. Our childhood memories show us our earliest years not as they were but as they appeared at the later periods when the memories were aroused.
>
> (Freud, Screen Memories, *Standard Edition*, Vol. III, p. 322)

Many years before writing *The Unconscious*, when he still thought of himself more as a neurologist than a psychologist, two rather revolutionary concepts appeared in Freud's writing – **mnemic traces** (Errinerungsspuren) and **afterwardness** (Nachträglichkeit), which was translated as **deferred meaning**. They presented a novel perception of memory as an occurrence registered, at one and the same time, in a number of psychic systems. Memory fragments are embedded in different areas of the psychic mechanism, where they are linked to other traces of memory. The afterwardness is an event that breaks through the linear timeline, giving a new sense to a past event. Breaking the timeline into two different moments allows it to activate, from the present, a yet unexperienced historical event/trauma. In certain cases, a childhood memory receives its full afterwardness or deferred meaning during development. In other cases, it would be a dream dreamed at a later point in time that validates a psychic occurrence in the patient's past as a "childhood memory." This happened to the patient described as Wolf Man in Freud's *On the History of Infantile Neurosis*: At the age of 5, he had a dream that gave meaning to a memory registered in his infancy – a memory of his parents having sex.

The clinical meaning of this new perception of memory is that primary thought processes and unconscious fantasies can grant the experiential validity of an auto-biographical memory even to psychic events that did not happen in reality but merely as fantasies. This controversial issue was the source of much opposition to Freudian psychoanalysis. I will not elaborate on Recovered Memories vs. False Memory Syndrome and its relation to trauma, but I will not hide my opinion from you or my patients, because our perception of the concept of trauma has far-reaching consequences, among other things, on our therapeutic technique. Freud may have said his last word on the subject in a 1933 letter to Tel Aviv-based psychoanalyst Mosche Wulff:

> To my work on the hysterical attacks I would add today that I do not insist that they should be limited to phantasies. Today I would say: fantasies, or traumatic experiences. By the way, we also know that this is not an abysmal difference, and that real experiences are often hidden behind the fantasies.
> (Freud to Wulff, March 6 1933 reproduced in: Rolnik, 2019a, p. 265)

The stratification of memory into systems allows different elements in the same memory to remain in a network of associations that have the power to "ignite" or emphasize a certain element from within memory, according to the intensity of the stimulus or the degree to which it is emotionally charged. This is how memories are surprisingly ignited in consciousness as a reaction to dreams, to answer current emotional needs or as a reaction to interpretations offered by the therapist. At times, a physical gesture I make throughout the day, at random or during physical exercise, would remind me of a similar gesture registered in my physical memory, in a dream or sometime in my past. It may even be that following the awakening of such motor memory in my body-ego, I will be reminded of a dream I had at night or suddenly flooded by a wave of memories I never knew existed in me. The appearance and disappearance of a memory in consciousness can be likened to a flickering neon sign whose light, as brief as it allows us to read another sign standing in the darkness behind it.

Another far-reaching consequence of memory traces in our unconscious is that memories can transcend our individual history and reach us through intergenerational transmission. The unconscious perceives traces of memories and enigmatic messages from the other's unconscious. This idea – which has parallels in contemporary biological concepts and studies in the field of epigenetic heredity – has significance in the psychoanalytic clinic; it corresponds with the old-established sociological concept of collective memory, coined by Maurice Halbwachs, and it also serves as an interesting interface between the psychoanalytical theory of memory and knowledge and the concept of telepathy, which garnered much interest by Freud, to the dismay of some of colleagues such as Jones and Eitingon.[1]

The concept of psychic trauma, which accompanies psychoanalysis from its first days, was influenced by the discovery of a new type of memory-less remembrance; remembrance of a psychic event that was not symbolically represented. What distinguishes the traumatic event is not necessarily its catastrophic intensity, which requires that it be repressed from consciousness, but the fact that when it emerges into consciousness it cannot be regulated or thought. It is not, therefore, memory as an event anchored in historical or autobiographical space and time, but a "rolling psychic event" that continues to distort a person's perception and chip away at their ability to accumulate new experiences and memories, and at times even completely blocks the ability to think, dream and feel; unlike a repressed memory, trauma refuses to become past. The post-traumatic person is trapped at a certain point in time. They are not reminded of the event but unwillingly live it over and over in a dreamlike state. They fall out of chronological time instead of experiencing time going through them as an ongoing event, they "live in the past" at the point where time broke.

Those sirens are nonsense; I'm not getting off the couch for them

You might have asked yourself sometimes: Why are patients preoccupied with the question of what would happen if they meet you outside of the room? Some patients are very disturbed by the question of if it was really you they thought they saw in the street. Or perhaps they have seen your partner or your child or your car parking on a street corner. Why are they so engaged by that? How do you interpret that? At times, therapists come to a supervision session agitated from seeing a patient a few rows ahead of them in the cinema. But why is it so exciting?

The patient feels like a voyeur and is excited not only because of the *primal scene* – the standard explanation for this clinical phenomenon – but also because during treatment, their unconscious is open, the engine is exposed, and they invest in the image of the therapist parts of their inner world that are not normally accessible to their conscious experience. Some patient have extended periods where they walk "with the couch on their back," even outside therapy sessions. When in therapy, we are very exposed to our unconscious, and meeting the therapist in the street is an *uncanny* experience, like meeting your own unconscious while sitting at a café. This particular state that therapy puts the patient in can have other expressions. Consider for a moment the punctual patient. Even a therapist who puts much stock in the therapeutic setting and frame can sometimes have heretical thoughts regarding a certain patient's punctuality. It may suddenly be experienced as defensive, subversive. I once called it, in my head, "vampiric punctuality." Apropos the primal scene, it can even feel as if the patient is trying to edge in on another's session. This is a fantasy, of course, because in practice, they ring the doorbell just on time. But still, their punctual arrival at your door starts to interest you, and you look for an opportunity to examine why it interests you. Your damned analytical curiosity demands that you do some work here, if not directly with the patient, then at least in countertransference. Then, one day, a punctual patient makes an angry remark, "How come there's no waiting room." You ask him to elaborate a little on that anger, and suddenly discover the effort he goes through to land himself on your doorbell five times a week, at precisely the right time, so he doesn't have to stop even for one moment. But actually, why can't he come early and wait outside for a few minutes? There's a nice, shaded avenue with benches. What happens to him when he waits for his hour? Is he ashamed? Perhaps defensive of his desire to know who else you are treating, who else sits on the same couch? The full picture is revealed: He is so punctual because he is so exposed coming in and out of analysis that he must pour himself into the clinic directly from his home – as if his body was open and his intestines were about to spill out. This is how he experiences it. Only now, years later, you learn that his punctuality was really meant to defend him from having his unconscious lit up for even five minutes without the presence of his analyst containing it. With another punctual patient, you will find a whole, completely different world, related maybe to her fear of the therapist, from what he might think of her being late to the meeting. She made you a persecutory bad-object on account of your separateness and secretly relishes it. Her punctuality is a form of defiance against the setting, a setting that does not allow her to come into therapy whenever she feels like it, and possibly came to represent both her merging fantasies and her punitive super-ego.

The sense of security given by the analytical therapy room can be disorienting if examined from the point of view of the unconscious system. During a session, a siren sounds – Tel Aviv is under a missile attack. I tell my patient we have to stop and take cover in the stairwell. He says, "Forget about it; these sirens are nothing. I'm not getting off the couch for that." I tell him that on the couch, he feels safe from various internal attacks and anxieties, but this is a rocket siren, and to keep ourselves safe, we have to go out to the stairwell. In that case, the patient needed help in distinguishing between internal and external danger and letting go for a moment of the illusion that while lying in the room, on the analytic couch, with me behind his head, he is protected from any danger.

"The more we seek to win our way to a meta-psychological view of mental life, the more we must learn to emancipate ourselves from the importance of the symptom of 'being conscious'" (Freud, The Unconscious, *Standard Edition*, Vol. XIV, p. 193).

Consciousness, Freud proudly announces, is a symptom. This whole amazing thing: Civilization, art, thinking, creating, feeling people; for him, it's all frosting on the cake. Not even frosting – it's candy sprinkled on top of the frosting on the cake. Consciousness is a symptom, and the analyst is an odd creature that is never satisfied: Whatever you tell an analyst is only the surface, as far as they are concerned. Whatever insight you share with them – they want more and are even suspicious of what you already shared. Yesterday's insight is already considered resistance to today's insight.

With all its complexity and richness, the paper on the unconscious could have used some more attention from Freud, in particular the section on the unconscious system's particular characteristics. It is neglected in that regard. Fortunately for us, psychoanalysis had theoreticians who were more systematic, such as Matte-Blanco, Bleger, Lacan, Bion, Green, Bollas and many others, who continue to explore the concept of the unconscious and its relation to the analytical technique. At this point, I also want to say something general about Freud's writing and the way his thought developed: Freud usually wrote several essays at the same time. His study was like an artist's studio – a work in progress here, another one there, while his mind – as his letters tell us – was already working on a completely different topic than the one he was writing on. For a case study, Freud would postpone writing it in full until the therapy concluded, but examples of it would appear, in bits and pieces, in other works written during it. Some texts are commissioned, others are stuck, some are easy to write and should be finished quickly to respond to some theoretic challenge by a rebellious student or some charlatan or other and there are commitments for conferences, so sometimes works overlap or are redundant. A topic at the center of one essay appears in another. Freud's thought undoubtedly changed and developed the more clinical experience he had, but if you read an early essay, such as *Psychical (or Mental) Treatment* (1890), you will find how many surprising ideas young Freud had. And if you read *Moses and Monotheism,* you will discover that old Freud had no problem going back to Lamarckian ideas to clarify certain cultural and group phenomena (Rolnik, 2022). And when reading *Leonardo da Vinci, A Memory of His Childhood*, you'd be surprised to hear that of all his writings, Freud considered it to be his best.

At times, "Early Freud" anticipates in his "unconscious" writing not only himself but also his successors:

> Ucs. is alive and capable of development and maintains a number of other relations with the Pcs., amongst them that of co-operation. In brief, it must be said that the Ucs. is continued into what are known as derivatives, that it is accessible to the impressions of life, that it constantly influences the Pcs., and is even, for its part, subjected to influences from the Pcs.
>
> (The Unconscious, p. 191)

The therapeutic process doesn't merely interpret the unconscious; it fertilizes it, encourages it to perform work, tills it. We act like gardeners wielding a cultivator, challenging the unconscious during the session, eavesdropping to what is taking place inside it and encouraging it to stay in touch with us. There is a reason your patients suddenly start dreaming intensively. They may have dreamed even before starting therapy but suddenly start to overflow, to be in dialog with the therapy, because there is someone listening. The patient's unconscious knows pretty quickly who it is dealing with inside the therapy room. If the therapist isn't interested in dreams or doesn't know what to do with them, it won't get them. Later, the patient's unconscious learns to identify the range of your radar and recognize to what extent you can listen to a dream. The unconscious also knows how intelligent you are and how much you understand it. It would even feel when you are in tune and when you are off-key or defensive in your countertransference posture when you are alert or complacent. Dreams, whether the patient's or ours, can provide something akin to supervision.

We enter here the brave world of unconscious communication between therapist and patient, slightly reduced under the heading of countertransference. Even the mystics of psychoanalysis discovered it and attached it to various new-age ideas. Thinking through countertransference is, at times, a little exaggerated and turns defensive because it comes at the expense of therapists' candid self-analysis and as an alternative to open listening to things patients say. It is undesirable that working-through the countertransference relies solely on the idea that the therapist serves the patient as a container for projections. Processing the countertransference should start with curiosity and the therapist's commitment to exploring their own inner world, whether by therapy, supervision or self-analysis. Therapists also sometimes confuse symbolic communication – in brief, saying one thing through saying something else – with unconscious communication. Let us keep in mind: If the therapist is sitting in the room, listening to the patient, and suddenly a scary image comes to their mind, somewhat surprising them, they better start quietly exploring it. Perhaps the affect they are looking for in the patient's associations is in the image of a threatening dog accompanying the therapist's attention in the last few minutes. Perhaps something has transferred into the image of the dog, perhaps that is worthwhile to examine. Perhaps the patient is scared now; perhaps they project into the therapist their fear of something. Perhaps the patient's fear is of their own sadism; they are afraid of their aggression. And perhaps the role of the dog is to warn the therapist about something related to coming close to the patient. Sometimes, an experience of fear or an unexplained exhilaration that the therapist experiences is not "transferred" or inserted into them via projective identification by the patient but arises out of their own difficulty in meeting the patient's anxieties. It is well remembered that the patient should not be regarded as the source of every blind spot, resistance or misunderstanding on our part.

In our listening, we use more than verbal association and deciphering of symbolic and semiotic communication. We do not treat the patients' speech as if it is a historical or literary text. At times, it is advisable to avoid listening to your patient's speech and instead try to "look at it," as if you were watching a silent movie, where the meaning of a scene is hidden, so to speak, in plain sight, in the actors' actions and the movement of the camera rather than in the pronounced wording. I need to try to mute my patient's speech from time to time, to pick up on a metaphor or an image – visual, tactile, acoustic, spatial and even olfactory (smells we suddenly feel) – coming from our unconscious during therapy. At times, I employ spatial and aesthetic images that come to my mind and offer themselves as the key to under-standing the patient's unconscious inner work and object relations in it. Surely, not every time I think of my daily schedule or remember a movie scene in the presence of a patient can be attributed to unconscious communication as if it was a message in a bottle transferred to me from the patient's unconscious. Things are not that simple.

It all started with Freud's assertion that:

> It is a very remarkable thing that the Ucs. of one human being can react upon that of another, without passing through the Cs. This deserves closer inves-tigation, especially with a view to finding out whether preconscious activity can be excluded as playing a part in it; but, descriptively speaking, the fact is incontestable.
>
> (The unconscious, p. 194)

These lines were "rediscovered" in the psychoanalytic conversation about 30 years ago, and ever since they are continuously quoted and used to give the psy-choanalytic encounter a mystical hue. Seemingly, this is basic to psychoanalysis. We couple the fundamental rule of psychoanalysis with evenly suspended atten-tion. We say: The patient will chatter and I won't focus my attention on anything in particular but, by degrees, absorb something. Something between the lines, something in the music, some word or held emotion would gradually stand out in the chatter, gradually punctuate my reverie, or suddenly capture my attention. I say chatter because the idea is to listen and not-listen to the contents of the speech, to fiddle with the resolution constantly. As early as the paper on technique *Recommendations to Physicians Practicing Psycho-analysis* (1912), Freud knew that was how he worked, that was how he listened, but he still had not worded it as a therapeutic tool of the first degree. Freud's close circle contained analysts who worked with free association even more than he did and adhered more closely to evenly suspended attention. Theodore Reik, for example, borrowed from Nietzsche the expression "the third ear" to characterize the analyst's attention to the patient's association. Reik was considered a "mystic" by contemporaneous analysts who had more scientific aspirations, such as Otto Fenichel or Wilhelm Reich, whose technique focused on the systematic analysis of transference and resistance (Lothan, 1981; Rolnik, 2008; Brown, 2011).

Is it not possible that the patient's unconscious would broadcast most intensely on the frequencies we are deaf to? In fields where our listening and containment capabilities are relatively weak? Some patients would locate our weaknesses and blind spots as therapists and would insist on confronting us with them for many reasons that have to do with their early object relations and their relations with dependence and knowledge. A patient who is envious of the good object is likely to draw his therapist into endless battles over fees. And, perhaps, is it the therapist that seduces patients to focus on their own neurotic areas? Either way, I think that, at any given moment, a psychotherapist's clinic will have patients that are helped by them **despite** their shortcomings as a therapist, and ones that fail to use them **specifically because** the therapist is able and willing to understand them and help them.

Death drive's finest hour

In abandoning the "seduction theory," Freud turned away from the idea that neurotic illness was invariably brought about by traumatic childhood experiences. Instead, he delved into the significance of unconscious phantasy. In a way, this move toward the internal world can be thought of as the starting point of psychoanalysis (Weiss, 2021). The psychoanalytic theory of trauma uses the familiar medical concept of trauma and imbues it with new psychological meaning. Psychoanalysis, in its Freudian or Kleinian, sense does not dismiss the role of developmental impingements or external injuries but seeks to draw the patient's attention to that unique junction between power or occurrence that originates in the internal reality to power external to the subject. Trauma, in its psychoanalytic sense, is a psychic event that the biographer or historian would find difficult to place in historical space and time. Its inception is hard to identify, and so is its termination. Trauma is an ongoing psychic event. This is also true for our – analytic therapists' – perspective of the anxiety our patients suffer.

Non-analytic psychologists often emphasize the distinction between fear and anxiety: Anxiety is irrational, and fear is rational. The virus can kill us, so we are not anxious, but afraid, of it. This distinction cannot satisfy an analytic thinking therapist. It is a distinction that does not recognize that the imaginary dimension is involved also in the seemingly rational fear or an actual life experience. Remember Freud's case study of Little Hans, a boy scared of a horse. Is the horse dangerous to Little Hans? It probably is; it can bite Little Hans. But Hans is not scared of the horse biting him, but of what the horse symbolizes: Castration. That is, Little Hans is anxious about the horse as much as he is afraid of it. And we, too, are anxious about the disease, the epidemic; good, solid reasons to fear it notwithstanding. Our work is to encourage our patients to transfer the fear of the epidemic as much as possible to their sphere of mental projections, to paradoxically "make" it into anxiety and consider its deeper subjective meaning. The more the patient dares to take responsibility for anxieties that have a grounding in reality, the better they can cope with their unconscious fears. The ability to regulate and transform anxiety that we might term "nameless" is a developmental achievement, both for the individual and on a group or cultural level. We can give anxiety distinct names such as concern, sorrow, grief, regret, shame or even curiosity, owe. Some people are enchanted by the destruction brought on by the current epidemic or by the devastation brought about by military conflicts. They may be ashamed to say so, but they sit in front of the television from dawn till dusk, excited. If we help them interpret this excitement and remove from it the general headline – anxiety – we already help them attribute meaning to what is

happening. The ability to regulate and substitute anxiety is what would determine the borders of consciousness and the ability to know others and the world.
It is, after all, our relation with the unconscious – our ability to understand and
identify in real-time the type of anxiety teeming in the world of fantasy – that
determines our relation to reality, the other and different. They will determine
the basic position from which we will encounter the unknown both inside and
out. And ultimately, even the ability to adapt to the historic reality and act as
individuals and a group toward realistic goals is derived from our relations with
unconscious anxieties and fantasies.

What do we defend against from the moment of our birth? The controversial
"birth anxiety" is probably the first burst of anxiety to wash over the *ego* at the
moment of birth. Then, there is the anxiety of separation from the object, the anxiety of the loss of the object, or more precisely, the anxiety of the loss of the object's
love. That is, the anxiety of harming the loved object.

These anxieties can be enumerated to a slightly longer list of traumatic experiences that accompany us from our birth to our death: The trauma of birth, the loss of the
mother, castration anxiety, the loss of the object's love, and most importantly –
the loss of the love of the super-ego, that is, the fear of conscience. I think that
the fear of conscience is even now clearly seen in the public discourse on the
epidemic – a sense of guilt, "we brought it upon ourselves," we sinned, we committed crimes, we polluted and we, therefore, were punished. Now, we might ask:
What about the banal, "obvious" anxiety of death? Can we understand current
events without it?

Psychoanalysis's approach to the fear of death is far from intuitive. Alongside
the passion to enjoy life and preserve it, we also harbor a drive that, from the onset
of life, acts as an alternative and a defense against life's ensuing frustrations and
mental pain. It can be summed up by the words of T.S. Eliot: "In my beginning
is my end." Humans, from a Freudian psychoanalytic perspective, deny their end
and are not afraid of the death expected of them but of the death that has already
happened. The unconscious does not believe its own demise and, at the same time,
associates dying with a myriad of unconscious fantasies. How is the death anxiety
etched in our psyche? Kleinian psychoanalysts would say that the anxiety of death
is the closest we have to an encounter with the death drive the infant experiences
in its first few days. That is, we have some proto-mental impression or even early
infantile experience with the death drive.

The death drive has varied expressions in our psyche and culture, and we would
be mistaken to only identify it with explicit behavioral expressions of aggressiveness, destructiveness or the loss of will to live. Just as there are countless expressions and instances of what we call "life," there is an immense variety of behaviors,
unconscious wishes and ways of mental functioning that express a conflict with
life, first and foremost with dependency as a fact of life. The death drive can also be
expressed in a continuing trend of mindlessness, passivity and repetitiveness. It can
be expressed in the destruction of thinking and the ability to contain thoughts. It can
create a state where the dependence on the good, true and beautiful, is annihilated

by a paralysis of the good object, expressed by an ongoing sway between life and death.

It seems that times of plague – perhaps even more so than times of war – are the death drives' "finest hour." There are patients, certainly (but not exclusively) younger ones, that are pushed by the threat to a complacent or hypomanic position. Some of them give in to a megalomaniacal bacchanalia of destruction and ruin. We hear them say, "Covid only endangers the old and weak. I'm young and healthy; I'll be fine." People turn to the death drive not because they want to die. They turn to the death drive because they put their hopes on it to protect them from the ails of life, from the increased sense of fragility, helplessness and dependence.

Virginia Woolf has beautiful descriptions of such states of mind. Before succumbing to her own death drive, she left us beautiful descriptions of the pains of living and the seductions of the death drive. In *Orlando: a Biography*, whose protagonist crosses the boundaries of historical space and time, she writes that Orlando sleeps, sleeps for long periods, sleeps for decades and centuries. Many patients react similarly. The epidemic induces a weariness and desire to sleep – whose source isn't solely anxiety. I think it is also an expression of the death drive, of the desire to silence the thinking and feeling mechanism, or an expression of an unknown fantasy to be rid of the body and, by that, be free of passions and needs the person identifies as the source of their suffering. The death drive has a way of affording various strange delights that the life and sex drive cannot. And perhaps, like Orlando, "we have to take death in small doses daily or we could not go on with the business of living" (Woolf, 1982). It is not a coincidence that people report they enjoy the feelings of weariness and even emotional numbness surrounding them in these times. I read Thomass Mann's *Magic Mountain* again, and I'm impressed that the tuberculosis sanatorium where Hans Castrop is stuck for seven years is an early 20th-century place of dreamy admiration of the death drive, or in Mann's words: "A facility of danger-ridden search for the secret of life" (Mann, 1939). Young Castrop would be cured of his tuberculosis, return to his home, and, in the last pages of the novel, would still be able to fulfill his next historical role as a German soldier trying to survive in the trenches of World War I.

Freud meets Rilke

Freud's short text *On Transience* holds lyricism, wisdom and humanity. Written at the height of World War I, as the world was truly being demolished, it is the first sketch of Freud's theory of grief and mourning, which would later grow into his renowned essay *Mourning and Melancholy*. While the people of the early 20th could not be aware of all that was happening in real time, as we can today, even in 1915, the destruction of the known world could be expected to be far more horrific than any other war. They entered the war wielding 19th-century images of time and space and emerged four years later, bloody and beaten, into modernity. On this background, Freud has a conversation with a poet – most likely Rilke, but this is questioned – over the question to what extent the loss of a love-object, its transience, damage our relationship with the world. Through the words of the melancholic poet, Freud expresses his own doubts regarding people's ability to overcome all types of loss. It is a very important clinical discussion, not an academic, philosophical one. It echoes one of the analysts' most important roles in that time: The loss is an opportunity to examine our relations with objects in external reality as well as with the inner object, and this is what Freud examines with Rilke. Rilke's relation to the inner object follows a narcissistic model; i.e., it is based more on identifying with the similar than on acknowledging the loved object's separateness and otherness. Freud "diagnoses" the melancholic poet's difficulty to accept the imperfection of the object, to accept its separateness and transience. Our relations with the internalized primary object would shape our relations with the object in reality – the loved person – and would also determine how we would react to the loss of a love object in reality, whether it is a temporary loss, such as separation, or a permanent one. The distinction Freud would offer two years later in *Mourning and Melancholy* is somewhat schematic and harsh. In his talk with Rilke, the distinction between normal grief and depression is less binary, and therefore, an air of optimism surrounds his lyric deliberation "on transience." Freud artfully draws the connection between relations with the internalized object – the degree of separation achieved from it, the level of aggression invested in it, the position we hold regarding dependence on the object in reality, as an object that is not only pleasant but also painful – and the way we experience the destruction of the object and separation from it.

The essay ends on a wonderfully optimistic note. Freud does not deny the inevitable pain of losing the love-object – be that a human being, a decaying landscape or a fatherland ruined by the brutality of war – but he believes in the mind's ability to find a substitute, mend the relations with the object that betrayed or deserted us and find solace. Solace also allows us to cope with the current crisis brought about by the epidemic, as well as with the inevitable losses we would probably need to mourn. We must, therefore, discuss the topic of mourning and blame in our work with patients in this time, even those who do not spontaneously suggest it. Mourning can be processed most intuitively through the untoward termination of therapy or the change in it – from a face-to-face encounter to a digital one. Those who find it difficult to mourn and miss risk losing the connection with the good object even during normal times, when the object hurts or merely disappoints. This is also an opportunity to examine the differences between longing and nostalgia with our patients. Nostalgia is akin to indulging in an idealized object, that is, a love that is molded after the narcissistic object choice. Such is our trade: Not even a plague hinders an analyst from questioning the unconscious determinants of his patients' musing/lamenting over the "way things used to be" before it.

Note

1 In the third edition of *The Interpretation of Dreams* published in 1910, Freud decided to add to the already-thick book a discussion on "prophetic dreams" and "telepathic dreams," something he had refrained from incorporating into the first edition. He wrote to Ernst Jones: "When anyone adduces my fall into sin, just answer him calmly that conversion to telepathy is my private affair like my Jewishness, my passion for smoking and many other things" (Freud, 1926, cited in Jones, 1957, p. 422).

Chapter 3

Technique and analytic setting

The bookcase and two identical couches. On the tension between the formal and spontaneous components of the therapeutic encounter. How interpretations are born, and why questions are better avoided. Can a patient's compatibility with dynamic therapy be predicted, and why is it hard to start therapy? Attention "without memory or desire." The deep meaning of the "time leasing principle." A patient who demands the therapist stop treating her good friend, and therapists who invite their patients to call, even on a Sunday morning. Is the unconscious photogenic?

Freud first discussed his intention to put into writing the principles of psycho-analytic technique in 1907. He planned to write one 50-page-long paper on technique. A year later, he had 36 pages. Then, as was often the case with Freud, an urgent project was given priority: The case study of the *Rat Man* (1909), which has theoretical significance alongside pearls of wisdom regarding analytical technique.

The Rat Man, Ernst Lanzer, asked Freud many questions. Freud responded that whenever someone asks questions so detailed, they surely have a prepared answer. These words by Freud can serve as an opening chord for the discussion of the nature of the analytic therapist's activity. A therapist who constantly asks questions is not a very good partner from the unconscious system's point of view. Questions lead to shallow interactions and invite, at most, a reflection from the patient. Reflection, as important as it may be to a thinking human being and a cultured person, has a rather limited influence on the analytic process. Our patients are not asked to intelligently meditate over their situation but experience something related to their situation in their transference relations with us. But, here I digress from the subject, just as the Rat Man and his questions tried to make Freud do.

In 1911, the second international psychoanalytic congress was held in Nuremberg. During it, Freud promised to compose an essay soon explaining the methodical principles of psychoanalysis. What he produced was not one overarching essay on therapeutic technique but a series of relatively short ones. These are the six *Papers on Technique*.

DOI: 10.4324/9781003528470-3

Guessing

The concept of *guessing* (Erraten in German; was translated by the *Standard Edition* as *Inferring*) takes us to the subject of analytic interpretation, which is not the focus of this talk. Guessing is, in fact, a prelude to the analytic interpretation. Why a guess rather than a hypothesis? When discussing *The Unconscious* in the previous chapter, we encountered the critical distinction between primary unconscious thought processes and secondary conscious thinking. Freud explained how the unconscious "thinks" and provided a number of fundamental principles of the unconscious process. The concept of guessing corresponds with the unconscious form of thinking, with primary thought processes. Most of the analyst's knowledge regarding their patient is not obtained through deductive, rational means. The analyst gives in to the stream of unconscious thought and, at a certain point, a certain structure is formed in their mind, an idea they suggest to the patient in the form of a guess. If you will, we can mention intuition here, but it is a rather systematic and tentative intuition. Our work is not built on one moment of brilliance but a long, sustained, disciplined, restrained and active listening. At a certain point, we feel we have something of value we should share with the patient. According to Bion, if an analyst isn't anxious before suggesting an interpretation, they are better off not expressing it at all. That is, if the therapist has something of value to say to the patient, it makes sense that they are insecure about its effect, as it has the potential to unsettle both the patient and therapist. One can't speak off-hand in an analytic situation. The patient says all that comes to their mind, not the therapist. We don't ask everything we feel like knowing; we are not there to satiate our curiosity, we are not there to amend every incorrect or mispronounced word we heard or ask to clarify words we think the patient said but not sure if we heard them right. This, by the way, is what I think is the true meaning of Bion's recommendation to listen "without memory or desire" and why it is consistent with Freud's idea of evenly-suspended attention and analytical ethics. It is worthwhile to hold back and let things clarify themselves. There are, of course, differences in therapeutic personality and working style. Some of us are taciturn, some chatty, but as a principle, we should give as much space as possible to the patient and not hear our own voice too much inside the treatment room. In the analytic encounter, we strive to leave the stage to the patient, which is to say – to their unconscious and to ours.

If I felt the need to say something in the first 15–20 minutes of the analytic hour – I would be quite suspicious of my intervention. In my subjective scale, it indicates I'm not "sitting right" in my chair. When we intervene too early, we find that our speech creates in the patient a hunger for our words. With some patients, it might even be "abused," that is, used by resistance. We suddenly find ourselves explaining to the patient what we really meant and how we got there, and a kind of "dialog" develops between us and the patient, a dialog that only disrupts the patient's, and our own, ability to be in touch with the lower levels of the psyche. I make very sweeping generalizations here that are easy to rile against. No disaster would really happen if, for one specific hour, we talked a lot and the patient found pleasure or pain in that. If the day after, she tells you that she had a dream where "an older man in a wheel chair was pleasuring himself," then you'll know how they experienced your excessive speech.

I encourage you to be interested not only in the content or timing of your intervention but also in the volume of your speech in the presence of the patient.

A surprising question

I was asked, "Why are therapy rooms so alike, and why do they always have bookcases?" – does it have to do with Freud's Judaism; does it allude to "the Jewish bookshelf"? I preferred my clinic when it was in a small room with two chairs, a couch and a handful of books. A therapy room is a place of listening, while a bookcase is a place of knowledge, reading, scholarship, absorbing. Books are, of course, part of our development as therapists and humans – for Jews and non-Jews alike – but are not part of the analytic encounter. I once visited the room of a learned analyst and found, on a bookcase next to the analytic couch, a stack of books, arranged so the patient could not see their spines. It was a rather monstrous vision, like an image from *Alice in Wonderland* or some caricature of Freud's famous recommendation to an analyst to be "opaque to his patients."

I don't put much importance on the design of the analytic therapy room. I'm a little saddened by the modern generic feel of these cute little therapy rooms with two identical chairs sitting at a 45° angle to each other and a box of tissue paper on the table next to the patient. If you will, you can learn from Freud and design your room as you see fit. After some time, the patients get used to the room, and it becomes their room as well. It would absorb their projections, and then it won't really matter if, in one corner, there is some item you didn't find a place for at home.

How does analysis cure?

Analysis combines exploration in curing. In its Freudian variety, psychoanalysis deals with exploring the patient's unconscious, and curing is a sort of (beneficial) by-product of that exploration. When we study, explore, give expression to the unconscious, interpret the transference, remove emotional obstacles and unravel developmental knots, defenses go down, splits are removed and the need for projections and projective identifications goes down. The ego can try to fill developmental gaps and continue to grow and develop. For every patient, a different part of the theory will appear to have the most curative potential, and that part will change throughout therapy. Patients feel helped by the self-knowledge they acquire during analysis as much as by the experience of being in analysis. A borderline patient once told me, "What helps me the most with this therapy is that you always end the session on time." Until she said that, I doubted whether I was helping her at all.

In his classic paper, *The Nature of the Therapeutic Action of Psychoanalysis* Strachey (1934) argues that the analysis of the super-ego is at the heart of psychoanalytic curing. The analyst positions themselves as an auxiliary super-ego for the analysand. From that position, the analyst can direct their interpretations, which is how those interpretations achieve their unique influence. Strachey explains what we mean by analytic neutrality and how it facilitates a deep interpretation, in contrast to an interpretation that just scratches the surface and does not promote mental change.

Many attempts have been made to relate technique and setting to the method's curative mechanism. Analysts are often warned from having a "desire to heal" – not because we pride ourselves on definitely not curing but, because there is a certain contradiction between the medical stance, which very sharply distinguishes the normal from the pathological, to the analytic stance, which promotes integration between various forms of mental functioning. Some analysts, in particular among the disciples of Lacan, for whom the concept of "mental health" or "normality" is maddening. I, too, have some criticism of academic psychiatry and the clinical and research mode of thought embodied by the DSM. Still, even from a classic analytical point of view, I think there is value in distinguishing healthy normality from pathological normality or abnormality in psychic life. One should not confuse normality in the psychoanalytic sense with normality in the statistical, relativist or sociological sense. For one person, their illness may be hiding in a heterosexual relationship, while another's relations with their sexuality will remain confused and painful even after they triumphantly come out of the closet or identify as non-binary.

On beginning the treatment

We often question whether a patient is suitable for intensive psychotherapy. We can test it, telling the patient we are making what used to be called a trial analysis – for a few months. I think it's not a bad idea, and for some patients, it would allow them to start therapy. We, of course, don't present it as if we are auditioning them, but if we have a doubt whether someone is suitable, or if the patient asks us questions such as "How long will it take?" or "Is there a chance?" and "Is this frequency right for me or not?" then you can say that you think you will be able to answer these questions better in two or three months.

A sharp distinction has formed in therapeutic discourse between short-term treatments and long-term psychotherapies. Dynamic therapists earned a reputation for beginning a mysterious process without telling the patient what they're going to get out of it, how long it will take, how much it will cost and when it will end. I think it is worthwhile to forego this imaginary dichotomy between a short therapy that is oriented toward symptom relief and a prolonged, meaningful, dynamic one. Analysis used to be rather short and to the point, and short-term therapies were also developed by psychoanalysts and have much theoretic depth. Some of the most successful analyses I performed started as crisis intervention or as a pharmaceutical consultation for ADD. On the other hand, a dynamic therapist who knows the value of a prolonged process and knows that processes of psychic change take a long time is still allowed to make deliberation and evaluation stops – is the method right for the patient? Then we won't find ourselves in a situation where we tell ourselves, six months later, that therapy is stuck. People speak about being at an impasse in therapy and start wandering between supervisions or admonish themselves for problems in technique when it was possible to realize, three months into the therapy, that there is some incompatibility between the patient and the method. Not every patient is suited to our method of therapy. It isn't merely a question of psychopathology and personality organization. On the contrary, some very disturbed or psychotic people are helped tremendously by analysis, and there are some sophisticated, high functioning, profoundly neurotic people for whom the invitation to use the couch is soon revealed to be a mistake, and insisting on performing an analysis with them would be superfluous.

The therapy room better be occupied by a therapist who not only likes to treat, believes in treatment and is ready to withstand difficulties but also knows when to tell themselves – and the patient – that it doesn't work. A man applies for psychotherapy and, on the first session, tells me that he's been in therapy for six years with one analyst and six more years with another. Seemingly a "homo analyticus" of the first degree. I listen to him as he lists the shortcomings of his past therapists, and an ugly thought goes through my mind: "Don't worry, there's no way you're going to last six years with me." We started meeting, and I could see he couldn't handle any of the conditions I believed were essential for treating the distresses that led him to therapy. From the first moment he insisted on e-mailing me and leaving me messages, he "bombarded" me with various concrete requests – write this, write that, this psychiatric evaluation, that medical recommendation. Something in him must have told him that he needed a therapist who wouldn't maintain a strict setting, and that same something also hoped that I would fulfill that role. I don't know what happened with his two previous therapists and if they, too, had to undergo similar tests that allowed him to stay in therapy with them. In any case, he lasted six weeks with me, and this might have been my one and only contribution to him – I very quickly agreed with him that we have fundamentally different perceptions of psychotherapy and that we're just not compatible. The fact that a patient continues to come doesn't mean that the therapist has to continue treating them. We will return to the question of therapist-patient compatibility when we discuss the internal psychoanalytic object.

Stopping an ineffective therapy or ending an unsuccessful one must be done at the right time, and finding that timing is no less complicated than orderly and diligently ending a successful therapy. It would be simpler if we agreed with the patient on a trial therapy for a few months, but if the possibility didn't arise in the first few sessions, it should be considered that the process has "exit points." Missing one might mean you would have to continue working with the patient a little more until a point where ending therapy won't hurt the patient. Lacan is rumored to have once hit a patient who announced his intention to end analysis. There is no need to justify the malignant narcissism of renowned psychoanalysts (and the history of psychoanalysis has no shortage of those) to consider the relatively common situation of a patient suddenly saying, "I want to finish therapy" while you, who might have longed to finish his therapy six months ago, have to object now because it's not good timing. You might need to continue a few more months because there is some acting out there because there is some attack on therapy and some refusal to work on the separation that might put at risk a borderline or suicidal patient. Many reasonably good therapies are ruined because of a bad ending and separation. I believe the entire subject of ending psychotherapy and separating from the patient is central. At times, the fear of ending therapy, of the separation that will one day come, will be a main obstacle to starting it. Just as in love life, some people are afraid of getting married because they are afraid of getting divorced.

The question is: Is the patient suitable for psychoanalysis? I expand the question and ask – are they suitable for dynamic psychotherapy? Not everyone that sits with you in the room comes on time and pays is really suitable for dynamic therapy of the kind you are interested in offering. If your interpretations are being stonewalled, it's better not to fake it. We hope that if we do our job well, something will also change in the patient's ability to be aided by the therapy. We believe in change, and our ability to promote it, after all. But as the years progress, you should get a feeling of when you, with your abilities, your personality and this particular patient, are actually doing work or just passing the time. It is inevitable that you will have patients like that in your clinic, but it's not advisable to have too many patients that you question whether you are even helping them. If you have too many vague patients like that, it's a bad experience that has a detrimental affect on your relations with the profession. You sometimes have to have a holistic overview of your little shop. If you have a patient that regularly makes your life difficult, that you are constantly worried might kill themselves, that you are overly preoccupied with whether they would pay or anxious that they might hit you – note that besides being "a difficult patient" they may also ruin your ability to treat others. They are not only a difficult patient. You have to remember that it is your responsibility – as it is your responsibility not to come to therapy drunk or tired or with a toothache – to make sure that your clinic won't house only patients who attack you, despise you or threaten you.

Intake is important, but it is not enough. We can't truly know whether a person is suitable for analysis before they recline on the couch. In the past, psychoanalysts in training were asked not to switch their psychotherapy patients to analysis. Patients who started analysis with a candidate in training were supposed to be new patients. There was some clinical and pedagogical sense in trainees' first analyses being with patients who did not previously know them. In practice, they found it difficult to find suitable analysis patients under that restriction. This historical detail should not prevent you from encouraging psychotherapy patients to come to higher frequency therapy or switch to analysis. However, in my experience, it's not advisable to "overcook" patients in psychotherapy and only then suggest psychoanalysis. The switch from prolonged psychotherapy to psychoanalysis is not always beneficial to the analysis, and analyses born from a prolonged prior relationship of the therapeutic dyad are revealed as the most difficult for both the therapist and the patient. Either way, the more common problem is that most dynamic therapists today work with their patients once a week, and it is difficult to maintain meaningful, dynamic therapy under these conditions.

Freud shared various things he already learned. For example, patients may ask to delay treatment. They come in, want to be accepted, want treatment, then say – I'll come next month, I'll come in September. This is usually a bad sign. It is true that professionals plan ahead, so they sometimes reserve a spot with a popular therapist, but in general, it pays to meet this procrastination with some skepticism. If you have a spot, interview someone, and if they are suitable, start with them the next day. There is no reason to procrastinate the beginning of treatment since there are resistances lurking behind every corner, and they might as well be here in the room while you're in the picture rather than the patient meeting them alone while you've been reserving hours for them the whole summer.

On Beginning the Treatment mentions other interesting issues. For example, the issue of treating relatives of patients or colleagues. These are very specific points. At times, we have no choice, and it is very hard to refuse a colleague's request that you treat their son. Perhaps there really is no one else they can turn to. It may cost your friendship with that colleague. But, try not to have flocks of patients who are too interrelated. It is a bad habit to build these "analytic molecules" where one patient was another's friend who was a third's romantic partner. Some clinics are based on this type of "extended families" that are often quasi-therapies – in practice they are revealed as patients acting out, being occupied with "peeping" at each other and their common therapist or sitting in the court of a charismatic therapist. It is rather difficult to identify such things because they sometimes take place behind the therapist's back. It's unpleasant to be sitting behind one analysis patient's head and hear her saying she's cheating on her husband with another patient's partner. Not everything is in our control, of course, but if that happens to you too often, maybe you should "change your filter" and examine what leads you to become an actor in these ensemble plays. Some perverted patients enjoy that. It is better for therapists who are inexperienced or unsure of their internal boundaries and their ability to impartially listen to associations to not yield to the temptation to treat family members or close friends simultaneously.

A woman asks to begin psychotherapy. In the first session, it is revealed that she very recently left a years-long therapy. Over the years, she was so content with the therapist that she recommended him to her friends. "I built his clinic," she says. Lately, she even recommended him to a good friend of hers. A few weeks later, after the friend had already begun treatment, she changed her mind and demanded that the therapist stop treating her. "He betrayed me. He continued treating her despite me demanding that he stops," she says, and she continued to share that her husband has also been cheating on her for years.

If possible, it's best to avoid even recommending a therapist for the patient's partner. We, of course, rely on recommendations and want to help young therapists and repay colleagues who refer patients to us and whose work we value, but it is best that we be aware of various temptations and distractions that are best examined and interpreted before giddily whipping out your phone and providing the patient with a list of recommended therapists for their friends and family.

A point that often arises at the beginning of treatments is: What do we say to patients who approach us? Patients ask whether it would help them, whether there is a chance of changing or they don't believe in that, and ask: "Do people still treat that way nowadays?" "Does anyone still work like that, lying on a couch?" I think there is no point in giving scholastic lectures. True, we want to be appealing, to convince them to try and experience, but erudite lectures on the virtues of therapy are of little value in that. Every serious therapist has their own personal experience with the benefits of therapy, but therapy is something one can't really prepare for. Especially not the kind of therapy I think ultimately becomes meaningful and helpful. I would dedicate the first one, two or three hours to the therapy contract and the conditions of the setting. This is where time and discussion are best spent rather than explaining "how therapy works." I would discuss the issue of payment, the importance of fixed days and hours and the exclusivity of the relationship that takes place only here in the room – which I willingly discuss at length with the client at the beginning of treatment. Twenty years ago, analysts held entire symposiums on whether to answer text messages from patients. Fortunately, such conferences are not in high demand any more. Patients contact their therapists in various ways. They text you, WhatsApp you, leave a message on your answering machine or send a homing pigeon. What I think you should convey to your patient is that contact outside of the hour should be minimal. There is no point in deluding the patient that you are available at any hour or that phone consultations between the hours have any value. I hear of therapists who sleep "at standby" with the phone next to them as if they were an on-call nurse in the respiratory intensive care ward. Not everything depends on us, of course, but I think there's not much point in begging patients to call you at any hour. Some therapists have made this omnipotent position a whole theory aimed at justifying the way they perceive their role as "rescuing" the patient from a catastrophe that started in their infancy and will end God knows how. There are crises in life, and at times, a patient calls at night or from abroad or tries to reach you during a vacation. It happens, but it is the exception. A therapeutic situation is not aimed at accommodating all the patients' whims and requirements. Nor is it supposed to answer all the regressive and dependent needs in the hours and days on which it occurs. There is no need be in touch outside of the hours with every patient. It comes at the expanse of work within the hours. Again, there are very difficult patients in whose lives very difficult things happened and continue to happen. Disasters happen; people die. The therapeutic setting is an extraordinarily holding environments; to function as such, your flexibility and humanity as a therapist should have real value. We have to support it rather than rush to take the place of a parent, marriage counselor or good friend in the patient's life. With a setting, patients usually don't break apart. They learn that if they want or need to – they have, a number of times a week, 50 minutes where someone will see, listen and do something with that.

Parameters

I seldom use the parameter of adding an ad hoc hour. I sometimes do so "under protests" – that is, agree to a patient's request but deliberate with myself for doing so. In rare cases, I will be the one to suggest an additional hour to a patient. At times, it would be an invitation for better work, and at times, it would be experienced by the patient or later turn out to have been experienced by him as an invitation for regression or acting out. It is a form of acting out by the patient or myself. Adding an hour doesn't necessarily serve the treatment, just like a patient missing an hour or a whole week can attest to personal development, self-recognition and emotional growth. For some patients, a long time will pass before they allow themselves to stay home with a cold and relinquish an hour. I think it could certainly be considered an achievement when such a devoted patient is able to forego an analytic hour. For some patients, it is enough that they let themselves ask you for another hour to indicate a change in their position towards therapy. The therapist's role does not end in the decision whether to accept or reject the conscious wish – we must also search for the unconscious fantasy behind it and its function at the current point in time in the life of the patient and the transference. I understand the role of a therapist as one who expresses a complex voice, saying to the patient: "It's good that you ask for an additional hour, and it's also good, precisely now, that we keep the existing setting and not allow the crisis to change it." I'm reminded of a patient, a Holocaust survivor whose childhood was taken by war, who came to his hour and proudly told me he had missed his beloved grandson's bar mitzvah to make our session. Would you see this behavior by the patient as an expression of "devotion to the therapy"? I thought there was a certain perversion of the relations with the therapeutic setting and an abuse of a certain aspect in his relations with it and with me. I told the patient that he was probably concerned that if he acted as a good grandfather and joined the family event during our hour I would no longer see him as a child but as an adult. This question can also be expanded to matters of payment.

It is not always appropriate to give a discount. For some patients, it would be reasonable to agree to their request. For others, It would even be conducive to propose it because they won't imagine there is such a possibility. For some, the right thing is not to be in therapy if they can't pay for it. Our natural inclination is to accommodate patients in the financial aspect of our relationship with them – after all, we accommodate them in so many other profound aspects. So we let them rack up debt, and by that, we sometimes ruin good therapies. I have past patients who still owe me money, and I know that the fact that we separated before they repaid it sabotaged their treatment. We expect it to sort itself out, that they won't be unemployed, that they find a solution; month after month goes by, and suddenly they owe you 10,000 dollars. And they'll pay it back when they can. I'm sure they want to pay it back when they can, but until they do, they're carrying bad therapy. I'm fairly certain that patients who still owe me money resent me for that, and they're right to. What started as a kind human gesture, experienced by the patient as an expression of generosity and containment, even nourishing and growth promoting, has become, over the years, something rather toxic and gained the potential to warp their entire therapy experience. Your rate has doubled, even tripled, and some patients still pay you the same as when you were in training and they were students waiting tables for a living. We have an inherent inclination to see "the child in the patient," which often makes us deny our own needs to better our financial situation, and the patient needs to know that they can afford to pay your full rate once their financial situation has improved.

So we give discounts, add hours and, if necessary, even cut down on frequency to save the patient expenses when they're between jobs, but not without first making an effort to understand the unconscious side of the patient's actions and ours. I wouldn't want to find out in retrospect that a patient asked to add an hour because he recently got divorced or was fired from his job, and in his fantasy, I will stop treatment soon. Accepting an unusual request too quickly would block the possibility of discovering the deeper truth at its basis. You are there to understand and be empathic to parts of the patient's inner world to which no one else can be empathic. These parts are not necessarily expressed in their conscious wish to add an hour, to call you on Saturday morning or to receive a discount. It is the setting that helps you in the difficult task of identifying the fantasy or the authentic need behind the conscious wish, even if sometimes insisting on it would make you feel rigid, petty, greedy or even cruel.

In analytical life, like in life in general, there are exceptions. But make an effort not to make your clinic exceptional by definition. Aspire to have your calendar relatively boring, with little movement, little changes. Have the number of patients you need and the ones that are right for you. I don't think it's reasonable for a relatively young therapist to work 40–50 hours a week. You have to be careful about the load you take and the type of patients you take. I don't think it's desirable to have too many difficult patients at the clinic at the same time. If you took on a difficult patient, kudos to you, but that "position" is now taken. Don't immediately take another difficult patient – to the extent that can be judged in advance. If a person tells you about suicidal attempts or various impulsive actions, if someone who has already been to numerous treatments doesn't have one good word for his past therapists – they might not be suitable for you. Don't be tempted; you don't want to "specialize" in very sick, very deranged or very ungrateful patients. It doesn't make the clinic more interesting or your work richer.

Back to *On Beginning the Treatment*. We were in the section where we didn't really answer theoretical questions. We tell a patient they will learn during the treatment and will fairly quickly see what they are getting into and what is going on here. And now we're at questions of time and money. The principle, Freud says, is leasing a definite hour. This discovery and recommendation are, in my eyes, no less than genius in terms of using the right means for desired ends in psychoanalysis. I know it is difficult to internalize and practice for both sides. It is twice as hard for a therapist who did not experience it as a patient. One should aim at a patient having a regular hour on a regular day. Regarding billing for canceled hours – I support it. I try to offer an alternative hour, although it does somewhat disrupt the deep meaning of this rule. A patient learns that the rule can be somewhat bent, that it is not really their responsibility, and you become responsible for finding them an alternative hour whenever they miss their regular one. On the other hand, we naturally don't want to receive payment for an hour we didn't work, but the rule of global billing for hours has many layers. It influences the entire clinic. At the beginning, it annoys the patient. You might lose them on the first session because they will tell you they're not willing to accept it. But, matters are even more complicated since, even if patients formally accept the rule, the first time they meet it in reality is expected to be rather biting and even traumatic. Later, the patient's unconscious system recognizes the rule as protecting the patient, not only the therapist.

Freud uses the argument of the doctor's, the therapist's, livelihood. I think that the strength of the global billing rule is a very powerful driving force for therapeutic work. It signals to the patient, the deep layers of their psyche, that therapy will happen despite the resistance, that the setting and therapist will withstand attacks and that you care about them. And they will say terrible things: That it makes no sense, that it's decadent, that it's illegal, paternalistic and an abuse of power. And you will sit there wincing, trying to justify the principle and mainly hoping that this nightmare ends. Some would even ask defiantly, "So I also have to pay for your vacations?"; "And if my dad's funeral is on the hour, you're going to bill me for that, too?" They may say it in derision, but something in there is starting to react to the rule from a slightly deeper place. This may be the budding understanding that payment for missed meetings is not an expression of the therapist's superiority and selfishness but also expresses mutual dedication and commitment to the therapy. Later, the patient will openly enjoy the billing rule and it may come to represent a benevolent "Third" in their mind. It will save them unnecessary guilt when they don't feel like coming. And no disaster took place if a patient didn't come to a session. I argue that if a patient is away for the weekend and doesn't come to a session they're paying for, it's perfectly fine and not necessarily an attack on the treatment. They're in treatment even when they are abroad. They are a patient. If they are not charged for the hours they don't attend, it's unclear whether they are in therapy at that time. Consider the important things in life we pay for even when we don't actively consume or "use," such as rent, gym memberships or university tuition. Aren't all significant relations we have in reality based on a kind of some form of "global payment"? For a certain period in the patient's life, therapy is one of those things that supersede their immediate free will. You will, of course, learn a lot about their inner world, much more than is possible in any other technique, when charging for all monthly hours. The patient and you simply learn more about the inner world. It is another level of interaction.

What we call a "Therapeutic interaction," a therapeutic encounter, a therapeutic occurrence, does not create itself. What the therapeutic encounter would look like and whether it would serve the patient for more than relieving anxiety is up to you. It is up to you more than it is up to the patient. Transference relations by themselves do not make the encounter "therapeutic," and the person holding most parameters that give content and meaning to the encounter, that makes it therapy, is the therapist. Time, money, openness, cordiality, stability, the ability to bear another's unbearable parts, neutrality, profound interpretations – all these create therapeutic relations. The therapeutic relationship doesn't stem from the fact that the patient brings their pains to the therapist. The patient has the same relations with their dentist, who certainly helps them relieve their pains. These are not therapeutic relations in the sense of self-knowledge and psychic change. The setting and our relations with the setting, as therapists, will shape the therapeutic relations. There is a certain healthy and constructive symbiosis created between the patient and the setting. A temporary symbiosis that aids maturing, not a parasitic symbiosis where the existence of one is enabled by the extinction of the other or a constant denial of their separate existence.

Does psychoanalysis not stop being analytic the more we delve into discussing technique?

There certainly is a constant tension between the spontaneous and formal components of a therapeutic encounter. I hope that my relations with technique and with the patient are at least as close and flexible as those between exploration and cure in psychoanalysis. When discussing classic analytic technique, one sometimes forgets that the papers on technique were no more than Freud's "lab notebook." Not only were they not written as holy scripture, but he was even reluctant to publish his technical recommendations. We know, for example, that he only published the important technical paper *Observations on Transference-Love* due to an influx of cases where his first students crossed sexual boundaries. There may be gaps between what experienced therapists recommend and write and the way they practice in their own clinics. At times *qoud licet iovi, non licet bovi.* We can expect to encounter discrepancies and even paradoxes between what we think and believe and how we act in practice with a certain patient in certain circumstances. At times, recommendations and positions we internalize and identify with are inconsistent with the way we apply them in reality, but this gap does not obviate the necessary existence of recommendations and positions on issues of therapeutic technique. Freud had intuitions, strokes of genius. I note in passing that even a theoretical bedrock such as *infantile sexuality* is a discovery that historically relied more on intuition than on an evidence-based examination of a scientific hypothesis. Many of Psychoanalysis' discoveries are intuitions that were corroborated during many years of clinical experience, working with a certain methodology.

We can learn much more about humans and psychoanalysis due to maintaining a certain methodological frame. After all, we're not using the analytic setting to offer a reading of a piece of art or literature. An examination or interpretation of an artistic work does not require five weekly sessions, each 50 minutes long at fixed hours. On second thought, that doesn't sound like a bad idea – sitting with a painting in certain days and hours – the way Reger, the protagonist of Thomas Bernhard's *Old*

Masters did – and seeing how the setting influences our understanding and experiencing of the work and ourselves.

The encounter with the living and breathing patient, with their beating unconscious, requires a setting and a certain array of rules. It is very broad, don't worry. No psychoanalyst would fall off their chair if you were to tell them I waived payment for a specific patient for a certain time, that I met a distressed patient on Yom Kippur Eve, or that I called an ill patient to ask her if she was feeling better. But I presume any serious analyst would like to understand what had happened there. What happened with that patient made me change my habits and stay with them for more than 50 minutes, and why did it happen then?

Years ago, I had a patient who was a poor but talented artist. At one point, he declared he was willing to pay for therapy only with paintings, not with money. I was a young therapist then, and I remember deliberating whether I should be flexible. Truth be told, it was rather tempting. He wasn't only an interesting patient, but he was also a good painter who made beautiful art that must be worth a lot of money today. The therapy ended because he wasn't willing to pay except with paintings. I thought then that it would be a mistake for him to pay me with his art. I thought it would also hurt his art if he traded it with his therapist. A different analyst, more flexible and open, might say, "You should have humored that wish of his a little further; understand it. He might have paid later. You could have interpreted it as a developmental need rather than an infantile wish or an expression of resistance, as an attempt to recreate the semiotic dyad, as a need for self-object or a pre-symbolic deficit. After some time, it would have worked itself out, and he would start paying you. Be more playful, Eran."

Freud has very little theory around technique. He had tremendous intuitions, rich clinical experience and a few insights. But, most of our clinical theory was added after Freud. Many things were lost in the analytic conversation during the 20th century – we certainly lost something of the radicality of psychoanalysis as a form of thought and a critical theory – but I think it is precisely the technique that preserves something of the radicalism and subversiveness of the analytic act since it brings us closer to an encounter with the unconscious. I don't see it as a testimony of the discipline calcifying. I believe the historical move is reversed: The more technical knowledge we gain, the richer the theory becomes. We see more nuances. We also learn to change the technique and learn to "work with parameters," as Eissler, K. R. (1953) suggested more than 60 years ago. Eissler (1974) has, for example, a paper in which he explains why it is better to ask patients to pay for therapy with cash rather than checks. And then, with all earnestness, he remarks that in the case of an analytical treatment of a woman who works as a prostitute, this recommendation is better ignored because, for her, cash is directly associated with sex.

The relationship between the technique and therapeutic setting must be in a dialectic relation with certain therapy goals, which, as we know, change during analysis. You learn what is right with a psychotic patient – for whom a 50-minute session isn't always suitable, and shorter ones are required. You learn that, at this point, it is not right to allow silence to fill the whole hour and so on. I no longer have to talk in generalities about the lack of ability for transference and say psychotic patients aren't treated on the couch. I work with psychotic patients. I think some psychotics are much more suitable for analysis than neurotics, even though the transference relations created in working with them are very brittle. But without technique, I wouldn't have arrived at all these insights. For some years, I've been asking patients not to bring their cell phones into the session and leave it in another room. When I first introduced this "rule" it was experienced by some patients, for whom cyberspace became a point of fusion with the internal object, as earth-shattering – not having their phone within reach for 50 minutes. I learned that for some patients, bringing a smartphone to an analytic hour is a little like bringing a TV set or their romantic partner. It is enough that it's there to dilute their attention and serve as an obstacle to free mental functioning, even when it is turned off. The difference between the continuous attention disorder imposed on us by technology and culture today and the free-floating attention and free association the analytic situation strives to promote is huge. Forgive my pathos, but it is the difference between enslavement and freedom.

Had I not understood, thanks to the works of James Strachey, Otto Fenichel, Susan Isaacs, Edward Glover, Joan Riviere and others (and I purposefully list writers whose 1930s papers I still read with astonishment today) what a *deep interpretations* is or how to understand a *negative therapeutic reaction*, I could not have created the discourse we have in clinical seminars regarding not just the timing in which the interpretation was offered to the patient. At times, you had the right idea but pitched it too hard – something in the phrasing, the word choice, made an intervention that was correct in content, lacking in technique and thereby less effective. Much was written on tact, playfulness and spontaneity in our literature, but before singing the praises of spontaneity, I would like to discuss technique. You, too, just like painters, bakers and many other beautiful and inspiration-filled professions, should not be ashamed of being a professional and using technique. It is a compliment to say of a painter that they mastered the technique.

On-line psychotherapy

Until recently, I was rather skeptical regarding dynamic treatment over video calls. However, the technologies surrounding us now receive their final validation, and there will be no turning back the clock. Of course, some patients hide behind the camera, but they also hide "behind the couch." Patients can hide even when we meet them daily for years. What seems like heresy from the point of view of therapists and patients of a particular generation does not seem so to a therapist (and patient) who grew up during the internet revolution. We still don't know how many variables affect a therapy encounter where the therapist and patient do not share the same physical space and are not even in the same time zone.

Let me give an example from an analysis that has been ongoing for 15 years. Every time I tried to end the treatment, believing that good therapy has to end sometimes – preferably before the death of either the patient or the therapist –

whenever I tried to lead the treatment towards an end, a major regression took place and the therapy continued. The patient and I disputed the subject. Suddenly, an epidemic breaks out and the patient, of her own initiative, offers that we switch to Zoom sessions. Suddenly, the separation I thought would never happen was conceivable. She shows me different things in her apartment, "here's this, here's that," a cat leaps onto the screen. Reality incarnate. Both she and I know – a separation has begun. Thanks to Zoom, we are at one and the same time, together and apart. By virtue of the camera, the patient would most likely do the most important therapeutic work she has been avoiding for years – separating from her therapist. I am of the opinion that there is no good therapy without separation.

Recently started therapies that would shift to Zoom sessions too early could become shallow, false ones – but not necessarily. My intuition is to avoid the camera. Telephone therapy bears more similarity to an in-person session than does on-line therapy. Something in talking to images on screens takes us to the upper echelons of the conversation, makes it harder to delve deeper, makes the encounter more difficult. During a Zoom call, most patients, perhaps also therapists, look at themselves on the screen, using the camera as a mirror – an absolute reversal of the bemused or dreamy state of mind that a therapeutic conversation promotes. The absence of the body from the therapeutic space also has, I believe, a negative influence on the quality of the meeting. It is important to me that patients whose therapy takes place over Zoom would also find a way to meet me in my clinic every so often. Using the computer camera focuses our eyes on the other person's facial expression. I don't feel comfortable looking at patient's faces for the whole hour, and looking away is often interpreted as disinterest. This prolonged close-up is too intensive for my liking.

What, then, is a good therapeutic conversation? Proper mental therapy is not a dialog but a monolog in the presence of another. The other sometimes interrupts the monolog – that's their job – but through a screen, the conversation becomes dialogic. A silence lasting long minutes is not an uncommon occurrence in a therapeutic session; it makes present something meaningful and can serve the therapist and patient in many ways. In a digital encounter, even a relatively short silence is experienced as a communication short-circuit. This is probably another reason that therapy is hard to represent on television or in cinema. "Videotaped sessions" tend to seem and sound cliche even when they are well written and acted. The camera creates an illusion that the expressed emotions or silences are what define the events taking place in therapy. As subtle, sophisticated and metaphoric as the camera is, it shows us the least important part of a therapeutic encounter – what the eye sees. Communication between therapist and patient is verbal for an external onlooker but is mostly unconscious. Vision and sight have a relatively small role in it.

I have no doubt that "the unconscious is photogenic" – which means it can be transmitted through video. I also think, by the way, that it is transmitted wonderfully in writing, in letters. Not for nothing did Freud conduct his self-analysis in writing while continuing to correspond with many others at the same time as a means of developing his analytic thought (Rolnik, 2020). Analysis can be conducted through text because the unconscious is transmitted in text, there is evenly-suspended attention and there is associative writing. Is a Zoom conversation, during which I speak freely, similar to expressing my association in seminars that took place in the clinic? I feel that talking in front of a camera has certain advantages. Most of the time, I'm not aware of talking to dozens of people, and my speech is more free than it is in a lecture hall. I'm not certain that the use a patient makes of the therapist on screen is similar to that they make of the therapist in the room. That's how things are. The Freudian tradition will seek to adopt technological advancement rather than see them as a threat. I have no doubt that had Freud lived today, he would have had a blog and a Facebook page. I also think he would not shy away from social networks.

We have to learn how to transfer as much of what we learn to the digital age. We have 130 years of psychotherapy behind us, 130 years in which we met people for "talking cure." Now, it's time to see what is relevant to on-line therapy and what isn't. Puritanism won't get us far. Our teachers had also side-eyed us when we wanted to hold, alongside five weekly sessions analyses, also ones at a "low" frequency of three times per week. It is now our turn to tell our students that "digital psychotherapy isn't serious" – and their turn to do what they must to live in the present and try to make it serious. In general, by the way, analysts are often pioneers in the field of teletherapy.

We will have to continue being analysts even when there is a virus out there or a war that prevents us from meeting our patients in the consulting room. I think it is possible, and I would rather adapt than close shop because we still have a contribution to make in this day and age.

Chapter 4

Analytic presence

Ego or self. On my relationship with Ferenczi, Winnicott and Bion. What is "the second fundamental rule" of psychoanalysis, and under what circumstances was the concept of empathy born? On tact and playfulness, on the analyst's love and negative transference.

I was asked by email:

> Following up on what you said about the analytic technique and setting, how would you consider or see the Winnicottian technique, which sees playing, the area between the inside and outside, as the central arena, rather than the unconscious? Winnicottian interpretations or non-interpretative technique often aim to promote playing, co-creation in the transitional space more than uncovering the unconscious.

In the afterword I wrote over 20 years ago for *Psychoanalytic Treatment,* a collection of Freud's technical papers, I discussed Winnicott's concept of playing. I thought this important concept was relevant to a discussion of any therapeutic technique. I wrote that reading Winnicott's writing can somewhat ease the distress of those who feel that Freud's technical writings require that they decide on the primacy of one of two psychoanalytic approaches – objectivist or subjectivist. I argued that Winnicott's writing can be used as a "transitional object" between two psychoanalytic models. Concepts such as the transitional object or transitional space – where developmental transitional phenomena occur and enable a complete separation between the object and the self, between the internal world and the external one – allow Winnicott (1953, 1968) to understand the psychological meaning of playing as an interface between the subjective and objective. Through play, we learn how to use the materials of external reality to express personal or imaginary content. Playing, then, is also a means of communication, an instrument of better understanding ourselves and the other. It is, therefore, quite fitting, as the question seems to suggest, that we liken the entire therapeutic process to a play that calls for both ritualistic and spontaneous elements.

DOI: 10.4324/9781003528470-4

Admittedly, whereas my admiration towards Winnicott the writer remained intact, my relations with Winnicott the theoretician have somewhat soured since, as I turned from an avid reader and translator of psychoanalytic literature to a "practical" psychoanalyst. In the last 20 years, my perception of analytic theories and approaches has been influenced less by the quality of writing and even creativity of analytic authors – and our discipline is blessed with many writers whose writing talent can often dazzle the reader – and more by practical analytic experience. I hope you, too, will allow your theoretical and clinical sources of inspiration and interest to change with your clinical and life experience. The internal psychoanalytic object should develop throughout our lives, and there is no reason we don't re-examine our relations with theoretical positions and ideas.

I also have some criticism on the use of Winnicott's thought in general, and the concept of playing in particular, when discussing therapeutic technique. Playing does not arise out of nowhere. Playing is serious. It includes a set of rules. A large part of our patients don't know how to play. They don't know how to play outside, and to think that we need only invite them to play and they will immediately start playing the psychoanalytic game is naive. I think what helps a person learn to play are interpretations given inside a specific setting – analytic interpretations, interpretations of unconscious fantasy, transference relations and interpretations of primitive defense mechanisms. That is, the peak of the analytic process, or the end of therapy, is when a person who can't play starts playing, a bit like with dreaming. A person arrives in therapy not using the dream space for psychic development and growth, and at the end of therapy, they already use dreaming in order to sleep, think and solve emotional problems. And by that, the therapy may have achieved its main goal. Because that's what was needed this whole time: To allow the person to start dreaming or to allow another person to be able to play.

For some reason, Winnicott is presented as an alternative to rigorous analytic technique, as if psychoanalysis in its Winnicottian form is something much more relaxed, fun, inviting and playful. From my association with analysts in the various traditions, I don't think that Winnicottian analysts, or his successors in the independent British traditions, had more spontaneous or playful elements integrated in their vision of the analytic encounter than ego psychology analysts.

Winnicott's theory is different from Freud's or Klein's, but you'll be surprised to discover the extent to which analysts – regardless of school – work similarly in terms of technique. There is a certain strain of Winnicott in Israel that I had yet to find anywhere else. If you meet Winnicott's successors in their "natural habitat" in London, you won't recognize them with the Hebrew-speaking therapists who band under a banner bearing his name. This is also true, by the way, with relation to Bion and his theory, and maybe even Kohut and Lacan, all of whom have earned unique Israeli interpretations. Bion really was multifaceted. Many Italian analysts I know have their own Bion, based on their, or their teachers', acquaintanceship with him in the many seminars he gave in Italy. On the West Coast, too, late Bion had a few representatives who were very influential over his legacy (Mason, 2000). Bion didn't make it to Israel in person, and it is somewhat difficult to understand why, in recent years, we developed a culture of interpreting Bion as an enigmatic agnostic who knows nothing and strives only to be in O with his patients. I don't even think it can be called "late" Bion, Brazilian Bion or Los Angeles's Bion. It is Israeli Bion, and some would even be disappointed to find in his writings hints of being inconsistent or a timbre too reminiscent of Klein or Freud. Of Bion's relation to Freud, of him being Freudian and non-Freudian at one and the same time, one can read in a fine paper his daughter published about 20 years ago (Bion Talamo, 1997). A London-based analyst who had the pleasure of knowing Bion told me about the way he took leave from his patients before moving to America. Bion, he said, gave his patients in London a notice of about one week before closing his clinic and moving to the States. He even remembered the justification Bion gave for this rather appalling behavior: "That could give them a sense of the unconscious." With all the carefulness ingrained in me as a historian of psychoanalysis regarding this kind of testimony, it is hard for me to read Bion without also remembering this story about him.

When reading Winnicott, Bion, Rickman, Money-Kyrle, Meltzer, Riviere, Tustin, Khan or Fairbairn and admiring, with good reason, their theoretical and technical innovations and contributions to psychoanalysis, it is best remembered that the second- and third-generation of British psychoanalysis – even those who did not undergo analysis with Freud – were serious Freud scholars before becoming innovators in their own right. They studied at the British Institute in the 30s, 40s, and 50s, where they read and researched Freud constantly, even after the *controversial discussions.* Something similar could undoubtedly be argued regarding Lacan's innovations, which are, at the same time, very faithful to the topographical model Freud but also undermine large swaths of his later thought, as if saying, "Freud is not Freudian enough once he introduced the *Ego and the Id.*" I don't think the same can be said regarding the 80s and 90s innovators in American psychoanalysis. When I read Stephen Mitchell, I thought he just didn't get Freud, neither the lyrics nor the music.

It also pays to remember that where there are stereotypes of "classic psychoanalysis," there will always form counter-stereotypes, which are just as false and do not accurately portray the technique these people use in the treatment room. Naturally, innovative and original analysts also write on extraordinary cases when presenting their work. They don't write about their daily bread, the very Oedipal interpretations they give, all the banal stuff we think is reserved only for stale analysts. Winnicott had a firm grasp of classic interpretation and even took pride in his ability to give Freudian interpretations of dreams. Even when reading Bion's Los Angeles seminars (2013), I get the impression that he relies on Freud much more than he is usually given credit for. In one seminar, he freely quotes to his American listeners Freud's letter to Lou Andreas-Salomé in order to "validate" his epistemic position.

Soon, I will know who I am

To continue the question and tie it to the question of payment, the inquirer seems to be worried that the charging rule ignores willy-nilly the psychopathology, self-object needs or other deficits of a patient who doesn't know how to play. This is certainly an important discussion related to the issue of parameters. Just as there are people we will not agree to work with three times a week, there are people whose late arrival we will not instantly interpret as an attack on the setting. But I find it difficult to accept, both theoretically and practically, the position that sees an a priori contradiction between the analytic position and the therapeutic setting to the possibility of discovering the patient's "true self." I'm not convinced that there is some moment or some stage of therapy where the patient is "ripe" to pay, "ripe" to be content with 50 minutes, "ripe" to withstand interpretations and so on. My role as a therapist is to "ripen" them. It's active work, it is done tactfully, and it is fraught with mistakes. We will never be able to tailor a bespoke treatment that fits the patient's measurement at any possible moment, and if anyone thinks that is our goal as therapists, I believe they are deluding themselves. I don't like the concept of "true self," as you can probably judge by my tone. I do not accept the binary distinction between true self and false self (Winnicott, 1960). In my eyes, there is not one "original" self, with all others false and expressing a deficit or a developmental arrest. As Borges put it, "Soon I shall know who I am." The irony of this proclamation is, to me, more analytical than the concept of "true self."

Many attempts have been made to distinguish the *ego* and the *self*. I believe this need is less urgent for those who read Freud in German or even Hebrew. When reading Freud in German, there is no special urgency felt to delimit the two clearly. In Freud's writing, the concepts of *Ich* (ego) and *Selbst* (self) are often used interchangeably, almost as synonyms (although one can see a rather consistent preference by Freud, even after presenting the structural model in 1923, to perceive the ego as the metaphoric seat of sensations, emotions and mental functions, and also the part responsible for the subjective experience). The concept of the self is perhaps more familiar and friendly, but precisely because it made significant intellectual and philosophical ripples outside the psychoanalytic conversation, it also needlessly blurs the centrality of the unconscious in psychoanalysis. The *ego* of Freudian psychoanalysis (or the *I* as some would prefer to translate Freud's original *ich*) comprises a plethora of parts that are linked in various relations, at times murky, at times harmonious. This changes throughout our lives, during crises we undergo. My perspective on the concept of "true self" is rather critical not only because it distances us from searching after the "unconscious." Who am I to know who the "true self" of a patient I only recently started seeing is? And who am I to decide that the factor that will aid the revelation of that true self is to be lenient or strict on one matter rather than another? And who can promise that the true self – and Winnicott saw the importance in the paradox of the true self's very nature as being isolated and non-communicative with the environment – is closer to the truth than what transference tells us? And mainly, I don't want to delude myself that there is some theory or technique that will fit my patients like a glove from the moment they arrive in therapy, thus saving them the frustration and pain that are shared by anyone who sets out on the analytic journey. There is no such thing.

Back to the concept of playing. Every game has a referee, and every game, if it is bent too much, can break – and at that point, players start kicking each other in the shins or pulling each other's hair, and the referee calls a foul. The therapeutic game also has a point where participants start breaking the rules, and it stops being playful and serving its goals. The same is true with analytical techniques. I don't know any analyst who has ever stopped an analysis because their payment was late, but I do expect an analyst to try and interpret it, understand it, not ignore it and give it place in the room if the patient ignores it. I take the concept of *playing* to be a wonderful concept; Freud himself describes transference as a "playground" and "an intermediate region" (*Remembering, Repeating, Working through, Standard Edition*, Vol. XII, p. 154). The therapeutic technique would also determine, to a large extent, whether the Winnicottian self could reveal itself or not.

I see Freud's papers on technique – Freud never collected them under this heading; it's a tradition that formed after his death – as a primary definition of the ground rules of the psychoanalytic game. It is the Magna Carta of modern psychotherapy. At times, however, there is no choice but to make some fundamental change to one, or a number, of the parameters in order to suit the patient or the conditions of the therapy better.

In the last few months, since the beginning of the epidemic, I kept the windows wide open when performing analyses. I changed the fundamental setting of the game as it had been played before that point. I also asked patients to allow me to open the door for them when coming in and going out. In the analytical microcosm, these changes are felt keenly because I get up first, I open the door and the way the patient and I place ourselves in the room is completely different; they can't open two doors and run out as in the past. It's a change to the setting, and indeed, many interesting things happened as a reaction to these changes. I won't rush to build a new theory of psychoanalysis on their basis, although I did learn a number of interesting things. We learned to perform analyses during the war, we sat with patients in shelters, analysts in Israel wore gas masks during the Gulf War and even in the last few weeks, we did what needed to be done to hold analyses during an epidemic. We did what needed to be done so we could continue to meet and think under fire. For some patients, I suggested we change to on-line sessions, and with some, I wouldn't dream of changing the setting like that. At times, we can't continue to meet under certain conditions. A patient wants to bring his son during quarantine. How old is he? Not a 2-year-old baby, a 7-year-old child. Let him bring the child or not? Truth be told, I don't think your final decision is the most important thing. It's much more important that you don't start telling yourself stories about the patient's "true self" being revealed only if they bring their child with them. They very well might bring, alongside the actual child, whole worlds of meanings and we will learn that it wasn't only a matter of not finding a babysitter but a wish or fantasy laden with unconscious significance. But maybe it's more important to help the patient forego the hour and stay home with the child. Maybe that's where we should focus our attention and try to understand the difficulty of accepting the rule about not bringing another person to analysis? You don't have a babysitter; you're stuck with the child; you lost an hour of analysis. I don't think it would make me a more open, flexible and sensitive analyst to bring the patient's child into the clinic and celebrate the charming moment as if it were an emancipating "spontaneous gesture."

Whether we are Winnicottians or Kohutians, relational, Freudian or Kleinian, we live in a framework of rules, traditions and methodologies, and we don't have to reinvent the therapeutic technique for every hour. Rules will surely be constantly broken by the patient and us, and we will interpret that. At times, we interpret it tactlessly, other times with undue stubbornness, and in still others, turn a blind eye because we don't have the energy for it. So the patient was five minutes late, okay. Some people are always late for their hour, so how many years are we going to spend on it? How many gems can we mine from that tardiness? I remember I was once very late for my analysis. I lay down on the couch and started sharing with my analyst, with great zeal, the resistance I felt to come to analysis that day. She laughed and said, "So what was it that enabled you to come?"

And what about empathy?

Empathy is an important topic. The concept of empathy underwent a similar process to that of playing. It became a central concept for self-psychologists, and it's somewhat difficult today to think of empathy disconnected from the theory of Kohut and his successors. Therapists quite often regard empathy as their raison d'être but forget, for some reason, that the concept of Einfühlung, which appears in Freud's writing a number of times, has a tradition in German aesthetics and philosophy that preceded not only Kohut but also Freud. Not only babies but concepts, too, have a genealogy and existence distinct from us and our theories. Empathy entered the bloodstream of historical and psychological thinking through Wilhelm Dilthey and Theodor Lipps, both of whom used it in a methodic sense as an instrument by which a researcher – whether a historian or an art critic – steps into the shoes of their research subject. The psychological conversation around the objective and subjective dimensions of psychic reality begins around the second half of the 18th century. Only then, for example, does the expression "point of view," so natural to us today, migrate from the realm of optics to the humanities and social sciences, and scholars start discussing the perspective from which they study and evaluate a human phenomenon in the past or present. In art, the appearance of perspective takes place almost 300 years earlier, but its influence on psychology and the self-perception of humans remains rather limited until Descartes's famous *cogito ergo sum*, "I think, therefore I am."

Following Winnicott, Kohut and others, we see a mother's empathy for her baby as a function that, like containment or holding, is essential for proper mental and psychic development. We even ascribe to the object's point of view of the subject as a creature with drives, a role in establishing it as a "Freudian subject." In the second half of the 19th century, when the concept of empathy entered the intellectual and aesthetic discourse, it was used by scholars, historians in particular, as a means of methodic objectivization. What must we do to understand the world, the historical or literary protagonist, or the patient? One must walk in their shoes, imagine how they felt, what they "have been going through" – i.e., how they became who they were. This is only possible if the researcher extinguishes their own self and approaches the subject of their research from a neutral position. This methodological recommendation for the historian to "extinguish the self" can be found in Leopold von Ranke, the father of modern historiography. I learned that these insights were invented not by psychoanalysts but by 19th-century positivist historians, such as Ranke and Johann Gustav Droysen, who Gadamer saw as the father of modern hermeneutics (Rolnik, 2001). Later, when we will discuss the concept of enactment, we will see that it, too, originated in historiography.

From a clinical perspective, there is something in the ideal of empathy that is at the same time very useful but also somewhat obfuscating and limiting. At any given moment, the patient's unconscious or fantasy has more than one part that stands to gain from the therapist's empathy. Being empathic to the part accessible to the patient's consciousness – the disappointment or anger they experience now in the transference – is important. It also makes working with them more pleasant, but empathy for the parts near consciousness is a form of "prejudice" that somewhat flattens the therapeutic interaction. It doesn't ensure a meaningful, authentic encounter with the patient. I am also interested in being able to show empathy to parts of existence the patient is completely unaware of or aggressively denies. Here, a brief clinical example: A patient was very upset with an interpretation I gave her. She said it was cruel of me to remind her of a chapter in her career she was not very proud of. She said: "You only mentioned this episode in my past in order to hurt me. You just want to ruin me." The next day, she reported a dream in which a shabby and dilapidated house she inhabited was being brutally demolished. As she was watching a bulldozer demolishing the house, she suddenly noticed beneath the ruins the remnants of an older building, which may have been magnificent long ago. It is as if the ugly house was built on the ruins of a beautiful Bauhaus building that could now be reconstructed and salvaged.

Had I identified only with the patient's complaint about my untactful interpretation and her perception of me as cruel, we would have missed the deeper layer of this psychic structure that her dream had brought to the fore. Recovering the good object may require us to withstand accusations of cruelty and sadism from our patients.

In Ferenczi's 1928 article, *Elasticity of Psychoanalytic Technique,* he mentions the concept of tact regarding the timing of interventions and conclusions. This is indeed an important issue – when do we interpret? What is the timing? The volume? To what extent do we insist on the interpretation? How do we phrase it? In the patient's words, or ours? Yesterday, I had a rather dramatic hour with a patient. We left quite a lot of scars on each other, and during that dramatic hour, she more or less thanked me for helping her link a very traumatic event that happened in her distant past to the way she experiences and reacts to something very similar that is now happening to her at work. Then the patient said: "But I will never forget how bluntly you said something similar four years ago. You've hurt me so much." The same interpretation she can accept, cherish and use today she apparently heard too early in the analysis. I rushed or made a wrong evaluation – we constantly evaluate how ready the patient is, to what extent they can bear a certain analysis or other and adapt the weight we put on our interpretations. We all, of course, have our own personal style; we can't be completely devoid of it – we are who we are, not another therapist. But today, four years later, as she is feeling aided, she reminds me how hurt she once was by the very same interpretation and how tactless it was on my part, how she almost left analysis then and asked how I could have said such harsh things. It's interesting that the two, the ability to accept an interpretation and use it, appear together from a position of gratitude alongside the desire to mention how that same interpretation was once difficult to process and even hurtful. She might be protesting the therapist's not being perfect and that it took four years for her to feel like the therapist helped her. It might be the voice of the envious part that wants simultaneously to recognize the benefit of analysis and deny dependence upon it as a separate good object, like a diner telling the waiter, "Today, everything was excellent. But last time I had that dish here, it was subpar."

It's hard to discuss Freud and Ferenczi as theoreticians without mentioning their relationship. Freud once wrote to Ferenczi about it: "(T)he theoretical differences between us are not more far-reaching than can be expected from two researchers who are not given the opportunity to exchange opinions and mutual influence" (Freud to Ferenczi, January 20, 1930).

A number of reasons "soured" Freud in Ferenczi's eyes, which led Ferenczi to explore new directions free from Freud's giant shadow but also to be overly contentious towards everything Freud represented for him. Some differences are of principle, and some are of personality.

This is also an opportunity to remind ourselves of the "second fundamental rule" of psychoanalysis Ferenczi mentions in the article. The first fundamental rule is free associations. The second fundamental rule – and it is very important, without it, our attention has no value – is that we ourselves underwent analysis, or at least a decent amount of psychotherapy. Without that, the patient can talk until the cows come home, and our unconscious (which, I hope you all understand, is the psychotherapist's most basic and important tool) would not know what to do with it. One of Freud's most interesting and least cited recommendations for an analytic therapist is to go back to therapy every five years. Even then, Freud considered that to be "professional maintenance" for us. Today, I don't know anyone who returns to psychoanalysis every five years. You take one-and-a-half supervision sessions, a seminar and change, present a case in a conference and consult with a friend. But in Freud's eyes, for the analytic mechanism to function as it should, every so often, it has to be calibrated, or in Freud's words, be "psychoanalytically cleansed." Alternatively, Freud suggests that the therapist continue analyzing their dreams. This can be a kind of compromise – self-analysis based on analyzing one's dreams. After all, this was the only analysis Freud himself had undergone. The thing is that only those who have undergone a good analysis at some point in their life can,

I believe, perform proper self-analysis. Otherwise, self-analyses are rather weak. There is a connection between personal analysis and self-analysis, even though some therapists proudly say that they have reached, in their self-analysis, places they never dreamed of reaching with another analyst. There is a certain exclusive club of analysts who write about it with extraordinary candor, such as Eifermann (1987; 1996) and Sedlak (2000).

In *Elasticity of Technique*, Ferenczi mentions the issue of modesty: Real modesty, rather than feigned; not a learned mannerism but an authentic expression of acknowledging the limitations of the therapist's knowledge and those of psychoanalytic science. When reading this 1928 article, one can see the extent to which technical psychoanalytic science grew in the decade since Freud wrote his papers on technique. Ferenczi touches on many points: The issue of terminating therapy is that of the analyst's mistakes. I admitted technical mistakes to patients when I realized I offered an interpretation that, even if correct, was too blunt. It might be a weak spot in my technique or character. In general, I prefer to err on that side rather than the other. I would rather make an effort to hold analyses that are somewhat challenged through interpretations, that is – work hard and keep the patient somewhat agitated and somewhat frustrated than generously butter them up in analysis and let idealizations develop, build strong transferences and let time pass, for years and months, and only then start working – when the patient is transferentially tied to me. This method is not right for me personally; I don't like idealizations. I don't take them well. Some therapists like them and have a whole theory encouraging them to foster the patient's idealization as a curative factor.

Analysis has a style, and it is developed jointly by the analytic dyad. Every therapy has its own culture of conversation. It can change, and we certainly hope that our patient's speech changes and becomes richer and more diverse. But, therapy also has a "formative period" that should not be wasted. Patients get used to your therapeutic language, your aspirations, and you should not mislead them then and fake it. I'm not advising you to overwhelm them with interpretations, but I also don't think it's wise to wait too long before getting to work. The patient may feel like someone switched their therapist. The therapist should also occasionally check whether their professional self and natural inclination haven't strayed too far from each other over the years. I sometimes meet old colleagues and see how they become almost a caricature of their analytic credo. I believe it is desirable that an analytic therapist's relation with their therapeutic theory is not too tight and harmonious. One should aspire to have profound and authentic relations with theory, and mainly with analytical praxis, rather than imitative and affectatious ones.

An analyst's love

There is always a place to ask ourselves whether the interpretation was on time, whether it was tactfully said and what it serves in a given moment. The students of Max Eitingon – who in the 20s founded the Berlin Psychoanalytic Policlinic and in the 30s the Palestine Psychoanalytic Association in Jerusalem – said that he used to berate them for "telling their patients too many things that are right, six months before they should be said." The analytic tradition has an approach that encourages us to wait patiently for the patient to be ready. Obviously, we have patients who aren't ready, but how exactly are they supposed to become ready? You wouldn't send your 10-year-old to work for a living or demand a 4-year-old to make their bed every morning. Some things certain patients just can't stand. But our patients aren't really small children, even when they have developmental arrests and even when they are terribly disturbed or suffer deep deficits and traumas. The child in the adult comes to our treatment room, and we also want to recruit the adult for the analysis. I don't think I join the patient's false-self when I see them as an adult who gets up every morning, goes to work and earns money to pay for their inner child's therapy. Our technique is aimed at both the child and the adult. We tell the child: Say whatever you like, and I will accept you as you are. And to the adult, we say: Don't throw shoes at us. Even children's therapists don't allow children to wreck their clinic. Even autistic patients are set boundaries.

Inspired by Ferenczi, we base the understanding on the fact that the issue of tact isn't a mystical one. It invites us to reflect deeply on the relationship between what we do and the inner world, as well as the deep layers of the mind. This encounter has a purpose; at times, it is very pleasant to both sides; at times, it is unpleasant to both, but this says very little about it. Ultimately, it's measured in the patient's success to take ownership of more parts of their inner world, identify them and deny less the overt and covert expressions of sexuality, aggressiveness and self-deception, or at least identify when they are disavowing a certain aspect of their inner reality. The goal is to know when and why they lie to themselves, neglecting needs and parts of their inner world. Psychotherapy, a little like raising children, is a marathon – what makes or breaks it is not details but fundamental positions, ethical principles and analytic presence.

Analytic presence

Analytic presence is much more than listening with evenly suspended attention or without memory, desire and understanding. It is a presence that always gives place to otherness in the deep sense of the word (Poland, 2018). The other in psychoanalysis is the unconscious. What is pleasant, from your point of view as a therapist, is not necessarily pleasant to your patient. What angers you may not anger them. What turns them on sexually repulses you; what seems sympathetic, accommodating and supportive in a relationship can be experienced as repulsive, rejecting and humiliating by the patient's unconscious. This is best remembered. Psychotherapists and psychoanalysts sometimes adopt a pedagogic, not to say orthopedic, position or an overly-motherly one. We are not mother. Mother is the mother inside, where there is famously more than one mother. People conclude analyses and wax lyrical on how the analyst was a mother to them – and the analyst does often love their patients very much, but it is not a mother's love. An analyst can be very sad when their patients leave, but it is a different sadness.

A patient told me this week: "I hear a voice telling me you love me." That was an interesting moment. I didn't feel my love for him at that moment. But he listened to me or connected to something inside him that must have been thus far hidden from both of us. I thought that he suddenly realized that an analyst's love is truly different than any other love. At that point in time, he somewhat stopped his attempts to seduce me and then felt loved. For years now, he's been trying to seduce me to love him, admire him and sleep with him in various ways. And now, for the first time, he told me he acknowledges the possibility that there is another type of love, the love of the one sitting behind his head, listening, trying to understand and sharing insights with him. That is an analyst's love. Recently, a patient told me: "I was helped a great deal by analysis, but I am not sure I will recommend you to my friends." Would you be offended if a patient told you that? I hope not. Surely, I wish she were able to give me more credit for the analysis, but in some cases, one must settle for less than gratitude.

In that context, Ferenczi is right to accuse Freud of "not loving him." I believe the problem was the opposite – Freud liked him too much. That is, he loved him, but not as an analyst should love their patient. This, by the way, is probably also what failed the Wolf Man's analysis – Freud admitted as much in a letter he sent to Mosche Wulff. Freud liked Ferenczi and was, therefore, content with positive transference and did not interpret for Ferenczi the negative transference. While Freud did describe the negative transference, he saw it as a form of resistance to the development of positive transference and only interpreted it in cases where it did not allow the development of positive transference. Since he didn't interpret the negative transference, Ferenczi ended up feeling unloved by him, and said so. Then Freud had to give him, this time in writing, rather nasty interpretations about Ferenczi activating his *brother complex* as a reaction to losing the election for the International Psychoanalytic Association. This interpretation may be correct – Ferenczi activating an age-old infantile complex as a reaction to a disappointment he experiences in the present – but I think Ferenczi was right in his complaint to Freud. Freud took the easy way; he gave in to idealization. He should have looked for the negative transference earlier on in the analysis.

How does one look for a subtle negative transference? With some patients, you have to carefully sift out the expressions of negative transference and demonstrate to them how they despise you or project upon you their arrogance or self-hatred. Ferenczi touches on this point in the article. He advocates encouraging the patient to acknowledge their negative thoughts and emotions towards the therapist, to help them say they think you have a bad taste in clothes, that your new haircut is bad. It's worthwhile to note when, in the patient's speech, they mention that they know, or imagine, that you are jealous of them or hate them. Patients know these things about us. They know much more about you than you imagine.

I'm reminded of the analysis of a man who intimately knew the secret intricacies of large-scale corruption scandals. I learned the hard way to turn his attention to his repeated need to fascinate me with hair-raising tales of political corruption. He undoubtedly read me and correctly identified that his stories shocked me. But he also used this to fascinate me. He imagined he was exciting me by that, absolutely titillating me, and from that moment, he could also somewhat despise me for stepping out of the neutral position. That is, the negative transference was expressed not only in discussing various wicked men who prosper – ruthless, powerful people always fascinated that patient – but in the very fact he preferred to communicate with me from that region, where he could imagine it would be difficult for me to function, where I would have a good chance of stumbling by finding some special interest in the content, being fascinated by some sensational and exciting aspect or making a remark that was more judgmental or political than analytical. It was a very intricate trap tailored for me and waiting for me. Patients learn where, despite our neutrality and impartiality, we are given to excitement and control. Control, in an unconscious sense, of activating something in our inner world that will spare them contact with their own inner world.

*

To the last of his days, Ferenczi remained very bitter towards Freud. I think that what went wrong in that historical analysis was the separation, which Freud mishandled. Good treatments often remain ill-represented in our patients' lives because we mishandle their endings. I tell my patients very early on in the treatment that I recommend they leave enough time for separation even if they decide to end the treatment prematurely. Of course, if they want to leave, they will leave, disregarding my advice, and most of them do, but it bears saying. Many times, it helps patients with a weak ego to momentarily delay the drive to react to frustration and express it in action by ending the therapy. One day, the patient says, "Right now, I feel like getting up and never coming back here, but you said you require three months for separation." Thus, the strange "rule" we mentioned at the beginning of therapy helps them to calm down and overcome a narcissistic crisis. In long analyses, I advise you to set an end day, together with the analysand, a year in advance.

What happens in separation? That is really a unique type of work. Many analysts, young and experienced alike, "lose it" when patients say they want to end treatment. A good ending is important, even if the circumstances are tragic, such as death or an unexpected relocation. Interesting things happen when separation is treated as a distinct unit of the treatment, and if done well, it can allow the patient to continue the analytic process for many years after.

Chapter 5

Desire and resistance

How does one say subjectivity *in classic psychoanalysis? On the therapist's dependence on the patient and pro-bono therapy. On the importance of the setting for unconscious communication between the patient and therapist. What is the paradox of transference? On the various sources of resistance. What is the principal difficulty in being a dynamic therapist?*

Much has been written on Freud as a theoretician, a scientist, a writer, a therapist, a friend, a father, a romantic partner, a leader of a scientific movement, a culture hero – and very little on him as a teacher or supervisor. But, when reading his letters, we find that clinical supervision and consultation took up a rather significant part of his daily agenda. In 1924, Freud wrote to a consultee of his, Edoardo Weiss:

> Dear doctor, on the 4th of February I received a long registered letter from Mr. F. G., which leaves no doubt about the diagnosis "paranoia quaerulans." I quote only one remark, that the book *The ego and the id* is based on observations of his case. Otherwise, the letter is quite impertinent, aggressive and without practical point. I think it is important to inform you about this step of your former patient, but I hope that you will not take the whole matter too seriously. Perhaps one should be warned from this experience never to publish a patient's case and never to request his cooperation before the treatment is terminated.
>
> There remains the question whether this attitude of the patient is a transitory one and is his way of separating himself from the analyst, in which case, the whole situation has not much significance. Many patients have cursed their way to health. Or you have had the bad luck to run into a latent paranoia and through the cure of his neurosis you may have freed a more serious sickness. This may happen to each of us occasionally and there is no protection against it.
>
> (Sigmund Freud as a Consultant, Edoardo Weiss, p. 50)

Freud met Edoardo Weiss, who would go on to pioneer psychoanalysis in Italy when the latter was still a medical student. There was a large age difference between the two, and Freud nurtured the young man. Their correspondence dealt with many

DOI: 10.4324/9781003528470-5

patients, with Freud providing consultation. Weiss must have proudly told a patient that "he was consulting with Freud" on his case, and the patient concluded that Freud mentioned his case in *The Ego and the Id* and everything spiraled down from there. Freud, in only a few lines, covers a wide range of topics related to diagnosis, consultation, presenting cases and terminating treatment.

For many years, there was an accepted distinction between two central schools of psychoanalytic thought. On the one hand, those who put meta-psychology and theory at the center and saw psychoanalysis as a science striving towards discovering universal truths. On the other, those who emphasized clinical theory, the analytic act and its interpretative and ontological aspects. Ferenczi's and Otto Rank's important paper, *The Development of Psychoanalysis,* published in 1924, already demonstrates how seemingly technical and practical issues – such as the length of the analysis, to what extent the therapist is active or even the distinction between therapeutic and didactic analysis – pave the way to a new reading of the psychoanalytic encounter, a reading which will later be called *hermeneutic*. In this paper, Ferenczi and Rank term psychoanalysis "the new interpretation of life." To experience psychoanalysis is to give a new interpretation of the patient's life and life in general. As a new interpretation of life, psychoanalysis would always entail more than lifting a symptom or relieving mental suffering. At the forefront of the dynamic therapist's agenda are not questions of psychopathology but ones related to the quality of the therapeutic encounter at any moment. I also think that clinical seminars, as well as good clinical writing, are meant to communicate the gentle motions that took place in that unique encounter between the specific therapist and the specific patient to those who were not in the treatment room. Those reading an analytic case study or receiving a verbatim from a session know not only the patient and the therapist's theoretical position but also the therapist and their psychoanalysis "in action."

In the paper I suggested you read for today's talk, Christopher Bollas wholeheartedly thanks the authors of an intersubjective perspective of his work but gently refutes the attempt to place him in the intersubjective school (Bollas, 2001). When an analyst identified with Freud's work hear that they are "intersubjective," they feel at somewhat of a loss – what exactly was I doing there all these hours, listening with evenly suspended attention and my "disciplined subjectivity" (Erikson, 1964) to my patients' free associations? Was it not my subjectivity making itself present while I was sitting with a patient for 50 minutes, for weeks and months, giving them my impartial attention and, every so often, an interpretation? The unconscious is subjectivity; it "comes to work with me" and takes a very active role in my listening to my patients and the way I talk to them and they hear me. In other words, if I listen freely to the patient, I generously contribute myself. Does "self disclosure" only mean sharing with patients details of my private life or my feelings towards them? I think a few of my patients know me, in certain ways, better than my wife and friends do, even though they never talked to me on the phone and don't know whether I have children. With them, I am in a mental state only they know me in, for better or worse. The therapeutic technique is meant to serve this position. We need technique to establish the analytic situation, which is the only one that makes possible analytic attention of the kind that will eventually cultivate an analytic interpretation. There is no space without technique, no field to interpret. It is not enough to have one theory suggesting an Oedipal complex and another discussing primitive mental states, an alpha function and communication through projective identification. A patient comes into the room and we assume that the Oedipal complex acts inside their mind. The fact they meet an analytic therapist still doesn't mean this would be an analytic encounter that will enable the patient to relieve his Oedipal fantasies and anxieties. This would only be the case if the patient's mind encounters the therapist's technique.

Freud was familiar with Aristotelian rhetoric. He knew the way Aristotle conceptualized technical activity. For Aristotle, technique, *techne,* is in between things that necessarily exist and those that are contingent, existing only by coincidence. Those that necessarily exist are in the realm of science, which deals with *episteme,* while technique handles those things that are contingent. That is, it acts on objects whose shapes are not the result of some necessity and are therefore also liable to change. Freud remains faithful to this Aristotelian line of thinking. He reiterates that in psychoanalysis, examination and therapy are intertwined and the technical work does not entail blind attempts but a profound examination of the way things are created.

The issue of technique entered the psychoanalytic conversation for the first time in 1890, in one of Freud's early papers, *Psychical (or Mental) Treatment,* even before *Studies on Hysteria.* As early as that – even before the concept of "psychoanalysis" was born – Freud first noticed that treatment by hypnosis was strange and unpredictable. In the same breath, he also indicates for the first time the possibility of making a curative use of words. He even criticizes physicians who would rather limit the scope of their interest to the physical, leaving the field of mental study to philosophers. In 1890, Freud still expected physicians to show more interest in the mental aspects of diseases. Fifteen years later, in 1905, he would speak before a medical forum for the last time – asking doctors to withdraw from their clumsy attempts at psychoanalyzing patients.

This reversal of position reflects an understanding Freud reached in the intervening years – that psychic treatment requires specialized training, which physicians lack. He will develop this argument further in *The Question of Lay Analysis* (1938). Unlike hypnosis or hydrotherapy, psychotherapy is not a branch of medicine but a separate science. One should also note the way Freud and Breuer divided their work on *Studies on Hysteria* – Breuer writing the theory and Freud the technique.

After *Studies on Hysteria,* Freud's patients were no longer under hypnosis. They were up and unruly and were required to perform psychic work which caused them a considerable amount of resistance. And it's not only the patient that resists therapy: Resistances arise also in the therapist. Assuming you're not a sadist, it isn't easy to put your patients through mental pain, and one would assume that the therapist would also go to some lengths to bypass the patient's pain regions – and their own. There is something in the image of the surgeon – seemingly contrasted with that of the mental health professional – that portrays, alongside a neutral and objective position, also immunity, commitment and determination regarding how things should be done. After all, as early as the first encounter, the patient tells you: "What do you mean? I'll come to see you a number of times a week, always on the same days, same hours? Can't I call and change the hour if it doesn't work for me?" and you say, "No, you can't. You can't because I can't do my work under any other conditions," and the patient asks, "And what if I have something unexpected at work? What happens if I'm in a car crash? What happens if my son . . . if I can't get a babysitter?"

A sort of negotiation begins to unfold not only between you and your patient but also between the therapist and his theory or his internal analytic object. Do I feel strict when insisting that we meet on the same day and the same hour? Or do I feel like a steadfast professional? Moreover, for us to be able to think freely and offer the patient our attention, we have to, for example, ensure our own livelihood and be free of constant anxiety that patients may cancel sessions and we won't make a living. If we don't feel like we can make a living from this work, it would be very hard for us to do it. There is something forced in telling a strange person who only now entered your clinic for the first time that you care about them. You might not even yet. You may in the future, but you don't quite yet. We have a unique therapeutic profession. It makes us take an interest in people and want to experience a profound relationship with them out of an emotional partnership. At first, this is what we offer the person who walks through our door before we form a real personal connection, before we feel committed to them. You will still treat them even if you don't love them. And often, the patients whose treatment suffers are the ones you really love because it's harder to perform unpleasant work with them. You recoil from maintaining the setting when they undermine it and hesitate to offer them interpretations that may cloud the good relationship you have. While with patients you don't love as much, or even not at all, you can be at your best. Notwithstanding the merits of gratitude to mental growth, it is far from certain that you did more good for a patient who hugs you when they leave than for those who leave in anger, slamming the door behind their back. To truly explore these nuances, you have to have good relations with theory, ones of curiosity, skepticism and honesty.

Occasionally I am being asked by students: "Isn't the fact that therapists are financially dependent on their patients an internal contradiction in the work itself? Doesn't a state where the therapist is paid by the government or an HMO allow for a fundamentally different treatment?"

I don't think there's an inherent contradiction between our dependence on the patients on one level and the dependence patients develop on us on another level. There is a direct relation between the level of dependence a living organism has on its primal object and its potential for growth and individuation. Dependence is a fact of life, and it establishes the human subject's relation with drive and with the object. Even if our patient is "the emperor of China" with limitless money and power, psychotherapy is expected to express the patient's conflict with dependence as a fact of life. We might be able to interpret a patient who doesn't pay us or delays therapy, their refusal to acknowledge our being flesh and blood with needs and anxieties.

This is definitely an important and useful intervention at a relatively late stage of the therapy. I would not demand a patient to acknowledge me as a person with dependence needs early in the therapy. At that stage, I would interpret it for them slightly differently: As an attack on their own dependence needs, which they project on me.

I believe good free therapy is possible, but performing it has to be learned. Not only is it possible, but psychoanalysts were pioneers in this field of pro-bono intensive psychotherapy and even psychoanalysis as part of a public clinic. The first psychoanalytic public clinic was founded in Berlin in 1920, after the First World War. Hundreds of analyses were performed during the 13 years it was active. Some of the treatments were free – even when performed in the analysts' private clinics – and some were covered by health maintenance organizations. This model was also replicated at the Palestine Psychoanalytic Association, where it was practiced for several decades. With time, psychoanalytic therapy in Israel became associated with a relatively high socio-economic status. This is not the case everywhere. In Germany, an analytic treatment is a service offered by most HMOs. Most German analysts don't know any other way of making a living. Their clinics are filled with patients who do not directly pay them. The HMO gives them an hour bank for each patient, depending on their mental condition and the type of treatment they want to offer them, and if they want more hours, they write a periodic report describing the need for continued therapy for more hours. They have to justify it and learn to do so.

Do we use the method to tempt the patient to start therapy rather than the therapeutic relationship?

There's a slogan in Hebrew, "I came for the price and stayed for the service." With us, it's often the other way around: The patient comes "for the service" and stays despite the price. At first, they might be somewhat apprehensive at the weird therapeutic contract you present them with, but in most cases, they relatively quickly learn to enjoy it and find benefit in the unusual relationship therapy offers them. They learn that even when they are angry at you or the setting, they can use you. In doing our job, we are certainly more dependent on the patient than a surgeon is, and it is, of course, much more pleasant to work with a patient who wants the therapy. But, we often struggle with large parts of the patient's inner world. They fight against us, trick our ability to understand the patient and their inner world and search for opportunities to devalue our interpretations. In some psychotherapies, the therapist's central experience, for long periods of time, is that they are the only one who cares about the patient and the therapy. As mentioned, I don't think we should hide from the patient the conditions we need to work with them. For some reason, many therapists prefer to gradually reveal that they prefer, for example, high-frequency psychotherapy or the importance they set on fixed days and hours. If we, based on our experience and theoretical perspective, reached the conclusion that these are the optimal conditions for the psychic work of exploring the inner world, I think it's best to be open on issues of the setting's conditions. It is very difficult to help a patient that only comes once a month.

The fixed setting is the essential prerequisite of exploratory and transformative psychotherapy. Sometimes it's the setting that does most of the work, even more so than the therapist's brilliant transference interpretations. The setting treats the patient. Why is that so? Because the unconscious system is sensitive to permanence just as much as it is sensitive to diversity and otherness. We want to come to a point where a deep, I would say direct, communication is formed with the patient's unconscious. This channel of communication would not open without permanence and stability. I sometimes think of the unconscious-to-unconscious communication in biological terms: The patient's "unconscious matter" has to be in the "therapist's blood" at a certain level. This allows the "receptors" that absorb and process it to develop and function properly. It may also be true vice-versa: That is, the patient's ability to use our unconscious would not develop without a stable setting to allow the analyst's presence to be absorbed by the patient's psyche.

Without a fixed, stable setting, there may be an intelligent chat, at times accompanied by psychic release and emotional discharge, but not a deep conversation between one unconscious and another. In dynamic psychotherapy, certainly Freudian psychoanalysis, this is the central theory that explains change and psychic growth. It is what allows interpretations to be effective. Dynamic psychotherapy is not a normal "heart-to-heart." As an analyst and an educated person with life experience, a therapist can sometimes make rather intelligent observations to a person standing beside them in line at the post office. But, their words are not expected to have a lasting effect on the person's mental functioning and self-perception. A therapist's words have value when they are said inside a setting where the patient's unconscious is directed towards the therapist and ready to receive their interventions. They will be concrete, measured interventions given tactfully and repetitively. They will be stated over and over and over, so the patient experiences their influence on them. But a fundamental prerequisite for the meaningful encounter between these two people's unconscious systems is that they meet on fixed days and hours, and another host of rituals that aid the therapeutic space and the analyst to gradually fill a transformative function in the patient's inner world. There were even analysts who believed it would be best if the therapist wore the same clothes when working with certain patients. Permanency allows the setting to absorb the patient's deepest parts. There are certainly changes, cancellations and disruptions in the setting. But, they are identified as such and discussed, and when they are interpreted, this interpretation echoes into the patient's inner world. The goal is not to "condition" the patient to get used to the setting but to allow the setting to take part in the therapeutic process.

Do you argue that the setting creates the transference?

The setting aids the development of transference as a certain function in the patient's psychic life. Once the transference becomes functional, it can be used to promote psychic change and growth. Transference is a universal human phenomenon that can be understood from various angles. Our mind functions through transferences from the moment we are born. They allow the baby a kind of primary orientation in the strange and foreign world they are born into through identifying points of similarity between various objects. This is why we also have transferences towards the bus driver or car mechanic or our children. But these transferences aren't useful from a therapeutic perspective. The transference we want to produce is one that the patient, aided by the therapist, can use for psychic work in certain regions of their inner world. We don't want just any transference relations with the patient. We use the transference towards us and even intensify it in various ways. The way to produce functional transference is through the setting and the analytic attitude in its wide sense; otherwise, it is a mundane transference: A transference our patient has to their favorite author, their most hated politician, an admired tennis player or a brilliant movie star.

Dynamic therapy relies on the paradox of transference. The patient knows little about the therapist but feels very close to them. They meet a stranger who allows them to be close to themselves. Who else in the patient's life is at once both so foreign and so close to them? Their unconscious. The relationship with the therapist becomes, during the treatment, the closest thing the patient has to their unconscious world. The patient's transference to the therapist makes their relationship *uncanny* (unheimlich). This is why your patients "talk to you" in their mind, even between sessions and during the weekend, and why they are so excited when they meet their therapist in the street. For this to happen, the therapist cannot interrupt the patient from freely transferring large parts of their unconscious world to her. We don't interpret all aspects of transference. We don't rush to correct the "reality testing" of a patient who is angry at us for having to wait outside for two minutes before we open the door for them. We won't ask them, "What's the big deal about waiting outside for a couple more minutes than usual? Are you a baby?" We will encourage them to test the relevant aspects of transference that would allow them to be in touch with the particular part of their psychic reality, their fantasy, that ignites as a result of waiting more than usual before we open the door for them. The therapist also doesn't interpret for the patient their wish to be loved whenever they arrive at therapy on time. But, the therapist can certainly think that it's better to suggest a transference interpretation to the fact that the patient exhibits anxiety and great distress from being slightly late for their hour.

As dynamic therapists, we give our consent to being with a person for a prolonged period in a mental state of open and impartial attention. In psychotherapy, two people put themselves, for a protracted period of time, in a special condition that has no parallel "in real life." We will allow the patient to transfer into speech and project upon us large parts of their internal world: Archaic wishes for merging, sexuality, aggressiveness, senseless compulsive thoughts, fantasies of revenge and masochism. The patients were never allowed that by anybody, not even their mother and father, excellent parents though they may have been. They never received something like that. Their mothers demanded that they be good children and love them. Their fathers sent them to bed. Even if they were wonderful parents, they constantly demanded something. We don't demand anything.

Even if they stay silent for the entire hour, we don't punish them. We interpret. And if you do your job faithfully, it's a difficult job. It is not very pleasant to be in this type of relationship with people. The major difficulty in being a dynamic therapist is not "listening to people's troubles and suffering all day." The major difficulty is to respond to the other's pain or be in the presence of the patient's dependent or sadistic parts in a way that is different from the way normal people react to communication and strong emotional demands the other makes of them. Responding analytically to the other's pain or their aggression or seductiveness does not come easy to anyone. Dynamic therapists absorb and rub against people's unconscious in tremendous amounts. In order to withstand that, they undergo a long training, but it still requires immense effort, self-discipline and self-maintenance on their part. A terrible amount of restraint is needed. You won't hit your patients; you will not sexually abuse them, even though the temptation would sometimes be very formidable. The levels of dependence on you they will develop would be staggering, and you will not use that to your advantage. Even when the patient denies the nature of their relationship with you, perhaps enticing you in various ways to enter into a romantic or social relationship with them. You will remember the goals of the therapeutic encounter and will not yield to these temptations. This is what you are paid for; this is your reward. And if you start working gratis, or if you expect the patient to love you in return for treating them, there is room for concern for the patient.

The therapeutic situation invites fantasies of dedication to another and annihilation of the self in both the patient and therapist. One hears of therapists providing gratis treatment for various reasons that are sometimes hard to follow. The therapist's own masochism and omnipotence are often involved in such acts of kindness. Payment, whether high or low, doesn't only keep both sides' contact with reality in a potentially regressive situation; it also protects the patients from abuse and the therapists from the illusion they do not have dependence needs themselves. Still, in a therapeutic relationship, we also take into account particularly difficult life circumstances and sometimes encourage a patient to also receive some concrete help from us in addition to containment and interpretation.

When working with children and youth, one can often see that just when the therapy starts to pick up and good work is being done, the child arrives at a session without payment. It is painful to see how parents, unconsciously, interrupt treatment by not ensuring payment, causing the child to be late, taking vacations or cancelling the child's hours with you, even when the child cares about arriving to sessions on time. You would not stop a child's therapy too quickly, even if their parents attack it somewhat, delaying payment for it.

Since the dawn of life, the inner world has held dialectical relations: Between experience with meaningful objects in reality, to the unconscious fantasies and the relationships that develop with fantasies, internal objects and drives. The human mind, like the respiratory and digestive systems, is a dynamic and open system of projections and internalizations. Even the relations between an adult patient's material reality – their financial situation, for example – and their fantasy world are dialectical. Freud and Klein knew that a century ago and incorporated it into their technique. In her beautiful paper *Love, Guilt and Reparation*, Melanie Klein reaches the conclusion that losing a source of livelihood is just like losing a mother's love and that material or psychological help is experienced in the unconscious as proof of the existence of loving parents (Klein, 1937, p. 337). But for the concrete help of a dynamic therapist to be experienced as mother's love in the patient's inner world and for it to survive the attacks of the bad object or the anti-libidinal object, the therapist has to be identified by the unconscious system as a significant and robust good object. When a therapist feeds a psychotic patient or an anorexic one – I find it easier to support such interventions in a psychiatric ward – it may seem like "concrete help" from the outside. In certain cases, an act of feeding or monetary help to a patient from their therapist would be more useful and nourishing than help from social services or an incidental philanthropist. And the story of Freud feeding the Rat Man may also come to mind. The "caloric value" of such help will be determined by the unconscious fantasy that would take part in shaping the feeding experience. If the patient experiences the therapy I gave them for free as an attempt at sexual seduction or a way of dominating their mind, as me insisting on showing them that I am a good person or even as a proof that they deserve compensation from me for a wrong they suffered as a child, then it may have been better to avoid giving concrete help and content ourselves with interpretations concerning the wish for concrete feeding.

Resistance

We meet resistance practically from the first moment of therapy. Appropriately, it was recognized as one of the fundamental phenomena of any therapeutic encounter not only by Freud but also by the theoreticians of hypnosis and suggestion therapy who preceded him. Resistance is not only a characteristic of meaningful therapeutic encounters but also part of the psychic mechanism and the way the mind works – even without being challenged in a therapeutic encounter. You recall that I argued something similar regarding transference as well.

Resistance and defense were once key concepts that were dealt with extensively in analytic literature. Now, we seek more subtle nuances than the historical concept of resistance. We are used to looking for *attacks on linking, enactment, negative therapeutic response, acting out* and similar sub-species of resistance. But here, too, it is slightly easier to make heads and tails of, as well as verbally describe, the events taking place in the clinic if we know the history of key concepts in psychoanalysis. We owe the development of psychoanalytic techniques to resistance. Even the psychotherapies that preceded the "talking cure" were familiar with, and discussed, resistance. Freud filled existing observations with new content and a psychological explanation – the "psychic conflict." The earliest name he gave to his group of neurotic patients was "defense neuroses," that is, neuroses created by the psychopathological mechanism of the ego resisting the pressure applied to it from the inside, resulting in a mental conflict and the development of a symptom as the product of a compromise.

As a starting point for my short discussion of resistance, I selected two rather early key points in Freud's thought. We will start with a paragraph from *Psychical (or Mental) Treatment* (1890), a pre-psychoanalytic paper whose importance cannot be overstated:

> If we put a healthy person into deep hypnosis and then tell him to take a bite out of a potato under the impression that it is a pear, or if we tell him that he is meeting one of his acquaintances and must greet him as such, he is likely to prove completely tractable, because the hypnotized subject has no serious reason for resisting the suggestion. But in the case of other instructions – if, for instance, we ask a naturally modest girl to uncover herself or if we ask an honest man to steal some valuable object – we may already find the subject putting up a resistance, which may even go to the length of his refusing to obey the suggestion. This teaches us that even in the best hypnosis suggestion does not exercise unlimited power but only power of a definite strength. The hypnotic subject will make small sacrifices, but, just as though he were awake, he hesitates before making great ones. If, then, we are dealing with a patient, and urge him by suggestion to give up his illness, we perceive that this means a great sacrifice to him and not a small one. Here the power of suggestion is contending against the force which created the symptoms and maintains them, and experience shows that that force is of quite a different order of strength from hypnotic influence. The same patient who is perfectly tractable in putting himself into any dream-situation one may suggest to him (if it is not actually objectionable) may remain completely recalcitrant towards a suggestion which denies the reality of, let us say, an imaginary paralysis. Here is the further fact, moreover, that precisely neurotic patients are for the most part bad hypnotic subjects, so that the struggle against the powerful forces by which the illness is rooted in the patient's mind has to be waged not by a complete hypnotic influence but only by a fragment of it.
>
> (Freud, Psychical (or mental) treatment,
> *Standard Edition*, vol. VII, pp. 300–301)

Freud dedicates a large part of the paper to describing the disappointment awaiting those who seek to find a lasting influence on psychical processes through hypnosis. This is how he ends it:

> On the other hand, it is not surprising that physicians, to whom hypnotic mental treatment promised so much more than it could give, are indefatigable in their search for other procedures, which would make possible a deeper, or at least a less unpredictable, influence on a patient's mind. It may safely be anticipated that systematic modern mental treatment, which is a quite recent revival of ancient therapeutic methods, will provide physicians with far more powerful weapons for the fight against illness. A deeper insight into the processes of mental life, the beginnings of which are based precisely on hypnotic experience, will point out the ways and means to this end.
>
> (Ibid. p. 302)

The last sentence summarizes, I believe, our main field of interest as dynamic therapists to this day: To identify and remove, or at least lessen, through psychological means, the internal causes of resistance to psychic change. The patient seeking a cure does not know they will invoke resistances to it. They also do not know that their disease, the very thing they suffer from, is itself an expression of resistance. That is, the resistance took part in creating the disease, and we should, therefore, expect that it will not remain dispassionate when faced with our attempts to cure the patient. Freud uses very aggressive images, and resistance is indeed a concept that unequivocally communicates the intensities and forces that take part in creating mental suffering, the various symptoms and the relations with the analytical situation and the therapist.

This next quote from Freud is taken from the postscript of *Fragments of an Analysis of a Case of Hysteria* (Dora's case study). Freud deliberates on the reasons the treatment of Dora ended prematurely:

> No one who, like me, conjures up the most evil of those half-tamed demons that inhabit the human breast, and seeks to wrestle with them, can expect to come through the struggle unscathed. Might I perhaps have kept the girl under my treatment if I myself had acted a part, if I had exaggerated the importance to me of her staying on, and had shown a warm personal interest in her – a course which, even after allowing for my position as her physician would have been tantamount to providing her with a substitute for the affection she longed for? I do not know. Since in every case a portion of the factors that are encountered under the form of resistance remains unknown, I have always avoided acting a part, and have contented myself with practicing the humbler arts of psychology. In spite of every theoretical interest and of every endeavor to be of assistance as a physician, I keep the fact in mind that there must be some limits set to the extent to which psychological influence may be used, and I respect as one of these limits the patient's own will and understanding.
>
> (Freud, Fragments of an analysis of a case of hysteria,
> *Standard Edition*, vol. VII, p. 108)

On the one hand, we say that without transference, there is no treatment. On the other hand, transference is undoubtedly also weaponized by resistance. While treating Dora, Freud realized that in "talking cure," just as in hypnosis, resistance limits the psychological influence. Once we ask the patient to say anything that comes to their mind, we expose them to fierce internal resistances. Freud still doesn't know how to use transference to understand the source of Dora's resistance and, therefore, has to contend with a rather feeble apologia of "the patient's right to resist the physician's influence." A few years later, Freud would know that reviving resistance is an inseparable part of curing. It is not only an obstacle that can be surpassed, as he still considered doing in Dora's case, by presenting a warm and loving facade to the patient.

We should not entice our patients to love us out of an illusion that by that, we would avoid resistance. Even if we could do so for a while, that temporary gain would ultimately be detrimental. They would not be exposed to the truth expressed by resistance. That is, resistance presents difficulty but also a large potential for self-knowledge. The patient's insight on resistance is often partial. It would always be our role to illuminate some aspect of resistance that the patient did not consider. Resistance and transference are similar. They both prevent repressed content from rising to the surface of the psyche and also recreate something of the unconscious fantasy tied to that repressed, disavowed or split-off content. Emotional pains, unconscious wishes, denial of psychic reality – these are all expressed through resistances that seemingly do not betray their origins. Transference itself, that special relation of a patient to the therapist, is an expression of resistance. We are, therefore, faced with a serious challenge. Transference is, at times, more a weapon of resistance than therapy. The patient who fell head-over-heels in love with you displays resistance no less than one who acts hostile. They not only long to come closer to and unite with the therapist. The same part of their infatuation that is now in the service of denying separateness also prevents them from accepting you as you are and using you to familiarize themselves with their own psyche. The therapeutic alliance, the "unobjectionable positive transference," to use Freud's own words, can lure both patient and therapist into a complacent state of mind.

Freud makes ample use of the concepts of resistantial transference and transferential resistance in his papers on technique. This transposition is worth noting in the original German. At times, the expression of transference seems to encompass resistance and should concern us and, at times, what superficially seems as resistance is actually resistance to the transference. Consider, for example, a patient that remains silent. Often, a prolonged silence is an attempt by the patient to push off thoughts related to the transference. Thoughts, it doesn't matter whether good or bad, they have about the therapist. Resistance is employed in transference but does not establish it. There are other reasons for transference. And, as mentioned, from a technique standpoint, it is important that we be interested in the question of when transference – positive or negative – starts acting as resistance and when it aids the analytic work. We welcome the patients seeing us as allies, confidants, even loving us. We don't correct their reality testing; we accept the transference. But, where it aids resistance to treatment or limits the amplitude of therapeutic relations, we will attempt to suggest an interpretation.

Resistance accompanies every step, not only in therapy but in life in general. It accompanies our psychic lives and mental functioning. Resistance is not only an expression of the tension between the pleasure principle and the reality principle but is one of the fundamental expressions of the conflict between the life drive and the death drive. In a clinic, it's best to discern the source of the resistance – is it in the ego? That is, an increased anxiety from a certain source? Or is it coming from the id? That is, representing some drive derivative. The drives are conservative; they love maintaining their course rather than changing. When we are libidinally invested in an object, for better or worse, it is difficult to convince us, the id, to invest differently, to let it go. This is one of the reasons dynamic therapies are long. The process by which a drive changes direction and foregoes a masochistic investment in favor of an investment in a love object is a long process. The drive isn't easily convinced, and until it is, it produces resistances. We, too, for our part, make life difficult for the drives. Our technique and ethics continuously frustrate it.

The super-ego is another important source of resistance. This resistance is more difficult for patients and therapies to identify because it is unconscious and silent. The super-ego, unlike its more graceful depiction in popular culture, is a structure deeply rooted in the id and phylogeny. "I am a perfectionist," "I aspire to excel," "I love it when things match my expectations" – all these partial insights people have on themselves are a tiny part of their super-ego. The super-ego is located deep in the unconscious and can be brutal and sophisticated in its forms of resistance to life in general and therapy in particular.

For example, the patient, a senior executive and entrepreneur, seemingly knew that he was competitive, ambitious and perfectionistic. When a quarter ended, it was revealed that the patient did not meet his business goals. As long as he was very successful in business, the dark side of his competitiveness and ambition remained dormant. Now, when achievement eluded him, his super-ego really came into play. Now it was its turn to make it clear that the key to the patient's happiness, even sanity, is not necessarily financial success, but to be perceived, always and in any situation, as a "child prodigy" – avoiding dependence, weakness or uncertainty in any way. In accordance with that, the patient made a number of successive rushed and irresponsible investments to "show his partners who's the boss," even creating false reports for investors to justify the last fundraising. Obviously, the company's real "bosses" are now the narcissistic and psychopathic parts of the CEO's super-ego. The narcissist patient's super-ego does not forgive and does not show compassion, not to their owners and not to their environment.

In this context, I once again mention Strachey's paper on the nature of the therapeutic action of psychoanalysis. Analysis of the super-ego fills an important role in that paper, but decades more had passed before we understood in detail to what extent resistances are related to the structure of the super-ego and to what extent they can produce infinite analyses where everything seemingly works just fine: Interpretations are given, and the patient cooperates with the treatment, but some status quo is formed and does not allow for a change. To use a generality, therapists relatively quickly learn to identify and remove resistances that originate in the ego and id through containment capabilities and transference interpretations. Resistances that originate in the super-ego, however, pose a challenge even to experienced therapists. This is why it is often better to bring up in a consultation session or a clinical seminar not the new, turbulent patient, but the old, mild-mannered one, the one who found themselves some new status quo inside treatment without developing a negative therapeutic response.

We said that resistance is structural and embedded in the functioning of the psychic mechanism. Take, for example, the dream. Why is a dream so encrypted? Because resistance is active in dreaming. Waking cognitive processes are also interrupted by resistance. A significant part of the ADHD we meet in both children and adults in the clinic arises from an emotional-psychological source. That is, there is some continuous disturbance to their ability to think. If the mind has to defend against drives, wishes or destructive or anxiety-causing fantasies, if it is overwhelmed by raw sense impressions of emotional experience that are not mentalized through the alpha function, it has no recourse but to turn off or sever some of its activity intermittently. In the clinic, we see how a patient suddenly becomes "confused" or feels "dull" as a response to an encounter with painful psychic content made through an interpretation we offered.

Resistance, says Lacan, expresses the incompatibility between desire and speech. From there, he also derived the conclusion, which I accept, that resistance should be viewed not only as an obstacle to analysis but also as an achievement of the patient who resists the suggestion. The analytic procedure has seemingly strayed very far from hypnotic suggestion, but it is always there to a certain extent, and it is very possible that the patient's resistance regulates the suggestion made by the therapist.

As far back as 1926, Edward Glover argued that even the interest the patient takes in psychoanalysis is an expression of resistance. A contemporary dynamic therapist won't see anything particularly strange or original in this idea, but a century ago, therapists still needed it pointed out to them. David Eder – a pioneer of psychoanalysis in Britain and Palestine – suggested seeing the dream as an expression of resistance to analysis. Freud, too, had already realized that recounting a dream during the analytic hour can be seen as an expression of resistance. A dynamic therapist's clinic would always have its share of "Scheherazades" who can weave tales of fantastic dreams from the first minute of an hour to its last. There is nothing that cannot be used by the mind as resistance to performing mental work that requires effort or pain. The significant importance we ascribe to identifying various manifestations of resistance can also lead to absurdities. For example, in a clinical seminar, a therapist says she interpreted, to a patient who recently started the analysis, the speed with which he walked towards the couch as resistance. I guess something in the patient's behavior seemed to the therapist to be a *reaction formation* or indicating a *counterphobic* position. But perhaps the opposite is true. Perhaps it is the therapist who was somewhat alarmed by the new patient's willingness to recline. Perhaps the interpretation was meant to relieve her anxiety, and she preferred to continue to "talk it out" with the patient instead of just fulfilling their respective parts of the therapeutic contract: One reclines on the couch and speaks, and the other listens and every so often says what she hears.

Every person who undergoes analysis or psychotherapy has, at any given moment, resistance to therapy. I won't interpret their arrival to therapy as resistance to therapy, even if they don't look me in the eyes at the door and instead rush to the couch. Perhaps later, I will find out that they drive at insane speeds to get to the session on time, and they might one day tell me about terrible arguments they have with their spouse in order to come on time – i.e., that by the very fact they did get to therapy in time, they are already in the masochistic position of a martyr.

We also don't automatically consider it an expression of resistance whenever a patient doesn't share everything that goes through their mind. "They're allowed" to recline silently and just be for a while without babbling constantly. And what about a whispering patient? Or a mumbling one? Are they, too, under the influence of resistance? Could be. But, you can also try asking the patient to raise their voice rather than being quick to understand their whispering as a resistance or an expression of an attack on the therapist. In the same way, if a patient has a habit of bringing up what they really care about in the last two minutes of the session, you can bring that to their attention.

Chapter 6

Listening and containment

When to break a patient's silence? The difference between being silent and listening. Expanding on the topic of containment and its relation to theory and interpretation. Praises for eulogies written by psychoanalysts.

Not too long ago, I was asked to take a peek at the homepage of a New York-based therapist by someone who considered approaching that therapist for analysis. I wasn't familiar with the analyst, but I did see he had a frequently asked questions section. One of the questions he posed to himself was, "As a psychoanalyst, do you believe Freud and all that sex stuff of his?" to which he answered, "Psychoanalysis is first and foremost a technique of listening. Most modern analysts no longer hold Freud's view that humans are motivated solely by their sexuality, and Freud himself changed his position in light of his clinical experiences."

There's something interesting in the way a contemporary analyst uses this question and answer to "seduce" patients. The impression created is that our American colleague focuses on listening but also takes care to "shake off" the Freudian stereotype of an analyst interested in their patients' sexuality. To alleviate not only his patients' anxiety but also his own, he claims that Freud, too, changed his mind on the centrality of sexuality. I assume that the question and answer were meant, first and foremost, to calm a hypothetical patient who is deterred from seeking mental help due to their sexual secrets. It is as if the therapist says to that patient, "I am **not** the kind of psychoanalyst who has sexuality on their mind when listening to you." Would you expect such "self disclosure" from a psychoanalyst who says, and I think correctly, that psychoanalysis is, first and foremost, a technique of free attention to the patient?

What makes the therapeutic encounter unique, different from any other human interaction, is the therapist's attention. It is a particular form of attention that is the responsibility of the therapist, and for it to develop and accompany the process, certain conditions have to exist in the mind of the therapist and in the therapeutic setting. It was a foundational moment in the history of psychotherapy when a patient silenced Freud and made him sit quietly and listen to her. I don't consider listening as solely a mental or emotional position from which it is easier to understand the patient and interpret the events of the therapeutic situation,

DOI: 10.4324/9781003528470-6

but something even more fundamental. The attentive therapist allows the patient to talk and more meaningfully broadcast their unconscious world. Our ability and commitment to listen will determine, to a large extent, the patient's ability and commitment to speak. It is active listening, even when the room is silent. We will soon discuss the difference between being silent and listening. It is an important distinction, and our patients learn to feel the difference between a therapist who is merely silent and one who listens. Sensitive patients do not miss the therapist's voice and are not bothered by their prolonged quiet listening. They do suffer from the kind of silence, which they identify with some disruption to the listening. Therefore, one of the first questions we are engaged with when meeting the patient, even early on, is whether this particular patient allows us to listen to them. "Allows" is a rather broad definition, and as mentioned, listening is our responsibility, even if the patient makes it difficult for us in various ways. Listening can be disrupted in ways that are often evasive and hidden. That is, ostensibly, the patient does not interrupt us from sitting and listening, but we can gradually feel that we are constantly activated towards some direction by the content of the patient's speech, by the affect, the projections, a direction meant to sever our attention, to invite a different kind of presence, more proactive, overly amused or even overly intellectual and interpreting. Therefore, while they are listening, the therapist asks themselves every so often if there is something hindering them from listening freely and if something is preventing them from paying attention to what they are paying attention to.

Therapist are supposed to know when they are listening comfortably and when their listening is strained. For me, a reliable indicator of comfortable listening is that I am able while listening to also contemplate psychoanalytic theory somewhat. I will take an interest in this thing the patient and I are doing here and now and be interested in the therapeutic act from an ontological and historical point of view. I would like to develop this idea of the presence of theory in the therapist's mind. It is not a scholastic matter; quite the contrary. There are situations when I feel that the patient tries to reduce my attention to them, that they know how to create, using their familiarity with me and with their own needs, a sort of incline, a magnet that pulls my attention in a specific direction. Grab my attention, as the expression goes. The theoreticians I'm interested in are those who have an interest in listening to listening and who don't operate only within the theory they follow and promote. It's not that they don't have a theoretic preference – a preferred theory of mind and clinical perspective that match it is a good, even important thing for a therapist to have. But they are also able to observe the presence of the theory in their mind and be somewhat distanced from it.

Silence has a role in the analytic technique. We keep silent so the patient would be freer to transfer to us, to project upon us their inner world. We speak where we believe our silence no longer serves the analytic purpose, and the patient has to be shown, in the good old words of Paula Heimann (1956), "Why is the patient now doing what to whom?" From a perspective that emphasizes silence as a means of encouraging transference, it is very understandable why analysts would advise a supervisee that they are too silent. From this perspective, the prolonged silence stops fulfilling its enabling role and instead blocks the patient's ability to look inward and understand the transference they make or the form of mental functioning that dominates them as they do. When I consider not how much the analyst speaks but what is happening within them, their attention, when I consider listening as an active stance rather than a passive one, then I encourage a continued mental movement by the patient, which would not be possible in any other situation in their life. This space between monologue and dialog, the intermediate area we aspire to create in the analytic hour, where the patient is slightly aware and slightly unaware of the presence of another person, that at one moment I am completely separate from that other and in another inside them and mixed with them. This movement, so unique to the analytic encounter, is supported by the therapist's attention. Analytic attention is like a medium, like water for a swimmer. The patient needs our attention to swim, to be treated by analysis. They can't do without it. I think listening can even be contrasted with silence. Silence does not function as a medium. Silence can be likened to a buoy, somewhat limiting the motion of the swimmer. The patient has to swim around the analyst's silence. They try to penetrate it, break it, bypass it. They try various techniques aimed at breaking the analyst's silence. Attention, on the other hand, should not disturb the patient but support their speech. They may not even notice the therapist's silence if it broadcasts presence and vivacity. The difference between listening and silence in the analytic situation is easily demonstrated: Sometimes the therapist examines, behind the patient's head, something in their diary or notebook or else their mind wanders outside the analytic situation. Some patients would immediately react to that by halting their speech. Somewhat like babies that cannot be calmed sitting down but only when carried, their entire weight resting on the parent's hands, patients are also very sensitive to the therapist's mental state and their level of attention. There are also patients who are seemingly "easily held" who wouldn't notice it even if the therapist falls asleep or loses consciousness.

I'm not seeking to argue that the therapeutic interaction is comprised only of the therapist listening to the patient's words. Additional actions are needed. But, the more experienced we are, the more advanced our analyses are and the more developed use our patients can make of the analytic encounter, there is less need for interpretations and less need for intervention, and attention fills most roles. Listening allows the patient to realize their projections and capture them in mid-air, even before we intervene and interpret them.

I learned that I need the presence of a patient in order to think about psychoanalysis properly. Thinking about psychoanalysis is, for me, thinking about the human experience from a certain point of view – one that is also useful for the patient. Once someone is willing to "turn on the faucet" of their unconscious, filling the room and me with their free associations, I understand something about life and psychoanalysis, which I might have previously known but did not really think and feel. I believe some patients are aided by our relationship with psychoanalysis just as much as by our relationship with them.

Containment also has a third

Containment, a central concept in psychoanalytic thought, is in a dialectic relation with listening and interpretation. In his latest book, Robert Caper describes how Wilfred Bion's experiences as a tank commander and a combatant in World War I's field of battle made containment such a central concept of psychoanalysis (Caper, 2020). In a sense, Bion continues Freud through the concept of containment. Freud, too, makes ample use of military and political metaphors when describing the inner world and therapeutic encounter. Bion's WWI Distinguished Service Order was awarded to him for his ability to contain and function in a state of anxiety. We meet primary anxieties in various situations, whether when sleeping, under pressure or in a time of crisis, and we must contain them. Sleeping is difficult in times of crises because we project into our internal objects a particularly large amount of anxiety, and they are ruined by the projections. The same happens in depression. But containment is more than bearing the anxieties; it is the unbearable psychic matter the patient transfers to us. Containment isn't only the fact we don't shout at the patient or hit them and we stay in the room even when they insult us. We neutralize the projections and make psychic materials that are unthinkable and impossible to process mentally into thoughts that can be thought. Bion calls it the alpha function. This neutralization also allows us to continue to listen. In the clinic, what sounds like an interpretation is, at times, not an interpretation at all, but the therapist's reaction to something they couldn't contain. Instead, they hid the pressure they felt to cleanse themselves from psychic content that is difficult to think and process in the form of an interpretative intervention, curious intervention or a need to verbalize something.

The dyadic, motherly model of containment explains how it comes to be that the patient or baby projects anxieties from their mind into that of the mother or therapist, who, for their part, maintain an open, thinking and understanding position – maintain reverie. Little by little, the baby, or patient, internalizes the container that can think and calm, and when we create an interpretation, it already encompasses the containing position. The patient's mind cannot create an interpretation, connection or meaning if the therapist does not help them contain the difficult mental matter inside them.

Containment and interpretation complement each other. It is important to make the unconscious conscious, but containment capabilities allow the formation of meaningful interpretations in the therapist's mind, and of course, also their ability to bear the discomfort or anxiety this interpretation breeds in them. At times, processing the raw unconscious, or unmentalized sense impressions, requires that we first cohabitate with them for a considerable time. Only then can it be interpreted and receive its place in awareness. As mentioned, however, these are dialectic relations. If you can contain difficult and unpleasant things, if your faith in the analytic process can withstand partial knowledge and accommodate misunderstanding, there is a good chance that, at some point, you will also be able to preform integrative mental and analytic-interpretative work. Fantasies and perversions can be brought up in your presence, their negative transference to you can be freely discussed, you can stand criticism and disappointment from the therapy can be expressed to you. For some psychotherapies, their main contribution to the patient would stay in the realm of improving their ability to contain themselves more than improving their ability to understand themselves. This is deeply affected by the analytic worldview, ethics, technique and their inter-relations.

The challenge is to try and be accountable to ourselves, whether our interpretations were born out of containment and connection we made, or did it *sublate* the containing position? I use here a term from Hegel – sublation (aufhebung) – that could have found a place in psychoanalytic thought. We can also discuss what Bion called, following Keats, *negative capabilities*. That is, my interpretation has shorted out the communicative process my patient tries to realize with me. Ostensibly, we offered a connection and understanding, but the very fact of intervening at a certain point, the point where we chose to "cut" the patient's speech, is an expression of the inability to contain a gap in knowledge, an expression, even, of impatience and mental evacuation.

For example, a patient is angry after you tell them you can't give them an alternative hour to one they canceled. You can say: "You are angry at me because you are concerned that my refusal means I don't love you for some reason." But for us to produce such an interpretation, we have to withstand their anger, the attack, and despite their anger still think of them and what they are going through. That is, whether the interpretation you suggested is correct or not, the very fact of being able to produce an interpretation and suggest it expresses your containment capability – a function the patient lacks. They couldn't contain the frustration and responded to it from a schizo-paranoid position. And you, relatively calmly, suggest to them an interpretation that includes this containment function. And again, the interpretation can be incorrect because that was not the reason for their anger and not the leading unconscious fantasy, but still – the therapist's intervention has value because it wasn't out of identification with the patient's anxiety and anger but from a listening and containing position.

An example of the opposite situation: A patient is very angry about some aspect of the setting and starts yelling. The therapist says: "Let's keep things civil here." They place a boundary. They say, "Don't talk to me like that." They communicate that they can't contain the patient's anger. They can't contain the attack and even "issued a warning." That is, not only did they not suggest an interpretation for the patient's anger, but they also deflected the attack and did not give the patient the opportunity to internalize the ability to contain anger and frustration.

Bion developed his container-contained theory while trying to understand how he is able to use analytic interpretations to help psychotic patients. Almost coincidentally, he discovered that even patients with a thought disorder can make links if they internalize the therapist's containment function. The container-contained theory offers a breakthrough not for the discovery that psychotics can be treated using the analytic technique, even lacking a strong transference, but for the discovery that the psychoanalytic curative mechanism includes not only making unconscious matter conscious but something much more basic and fundamental. In *On Dreams* (1901), Freud explicitly discusses patients who don't allow the therapist to "quietly listen to them." I believe Freud intuitively understood that a patient has a significant impact on the analyst's ability to listen to them. In practice, Freud lost many patients because he was unable to contain their attacks on him. Freud knew to consider what patients say as transferences and not to take personally the sexual wishes they expressed towards him. But when patients attacked him – and in particular when they attacked psychoanalysis – he often "retaliated." He could understand dreams; he could understand things we can only aspire to; he had a phenomenal capability for reading unconscious grammar. But, his containment capabilities and the understanding that containment has value in and of itself in the development of the mind and therapy – that knowledge was created in psychoanalytic theory later.

We can also ask whether we can position, alongside the maternal container-contained model, another one: Can containment have the capacity to neutralize toxic un-mentalized materials and also a function that aids the patient in identifying the attacks they make on the container, that is, on the mind? Caper discusses a "paternal containment model," i.e., every container has a Third. The mother can bear the baby because she has a father in her mind. It can be her father; it can be the baby's father. And I add that the therapist can bear the patient's attacks because they have theory in their mind. That is the third. It protects my container.

If I feel attacked, stupid or incompetent as a therapist, I rely on the theory as something that relieves my anxiety. That serves me as a container, which is created and maintained thanks to a relationship I have with someone else besides the patient. I can, at one and the same instant, hate the patient but love the theory; I love psychoanalysis as a human achievement. This allows me to withstand the patient's attacks without attacking them back or without diplomatically deflecting them.

Can severing our listening capability by the patient be considered an attack on linking?

It can, but attacks on listening capabilities are more elusive than overt attacks on linking. An attack on linking would usually be an attack on the interpretation, the meaning, dependence, giving. We will see that attack on linking in a patient's reaction to our interpretations – deflection, contempt and various strategies of undoing linking. I recently suggested an interpretation to a patient. He listened quietly and then nonchalantly leaned towards the tissue box, took one, loudly blew his nose, waved the used tissue at me and asked, "Do you have a trash can?" This is an example of a loud attack on linking. In contrast, attacks on listening are done in a way that neither we nor the patient are immediately aware of. It won't be announced by fanfare. But when we feel it, we have to take responsibility for it and act so we can listen again. A practiced pianist doesn't lose their balance because someone sneezed in the auditorium while they were playing. One sneeze also doesn't unnerve a theater actor. The same is true for us – not everything is an attack on linking. A large part of attacks are made by the therapist themselves on their own listening capabilities. It is we who "step on our own shoelaces" rather than the patient. It was we who didn't find peace and quiet. In this sense, I'm not a great proponent of countertransference virtuosity, which sees the patient as responsible for everything that takes place within the therapist. Much of the things that happen in the analyst's mind are part of the patient's unconscious or their projections into us, but in a large part of the cases, I myself am responsible for finding in me the attack on listening. I don't recommend that anyone makes an "It's not me that's tired, the patient must have deposited in me . . ." festival out of a sleepy hour in the clinic. The patient may be partly responsible for the boredom or tiredness you feel, but until you can verify that, it is important to find ways to stay awake.

Going back to the example I read before, from the American analyst's webpage, I can imagine how difficult it could be for such a therapist, if they did come across a "Freudian" patient who insists on focusing on infantile sexuality, to listen to a patient so focused on sexuality. I assume this analyst would find it more difficult to listen to this type of communication and may even make some moves to block it.

Doesn't a therapist detach from the patient when they consider theory?

It may seem that we disengage from the living, pulsating other who is with us in the room and give in to meditating on theory, which is, for all intents and purposes, a libidinal object of the therapist. But I don't see the very fact that theory is outside the patient or that it is a certain object of desire for me as an obstacle to coming closer to the patient and making emotional contact with them. Loving analysis is, in a certain sense, "the high road" to loving the patient. There are many extra-theoretical parameters that take part in the therapeutic encounter, and theory is part of my unconscious, my presence in the room. You often heard senior analysts advise, "Forget all the theory you know." This maxim is only valid if you see theory as a prosthetic or a scalpel rather than a living presence in the mind of the analytical therapist. Asking a dynamic therapist to forget their analytic object is just like asking a pianist to forget the notes. Of course, they think of music rather than reading the score as they play. But to me, it seems absurd to argue that the ability to make music is disconnected from the notes.

What happens to the therapist's listening when the patient is silent?

One of Dorothy Parker's short stories contains the phrase, "When the phone didn't ring, I knew it was you." Many things happen to us when the patient is silent. I had an hour like that this week, where I took an interest in a patient's unfamiliar silence. A long-time patient who normally likes talking in analysis was silent for a long time. Whenever I listen to that patient's silence, I'm not entirely sure it is him. Truth be told, it was somewhat refreshing to hear him being silent. I know he's slightly depressed; he had a big life crisis and is not accustomed to talking about it. He normally speaks about things that thrill and excite him, less so about the emotional movements that take place in his life, but are cumbersome and hard to articulate. So I'm sitting behind my patient's head and reveling a little too much in his silence for the last few days. Today, I had the idea to check whether there was anything in particular I should be listening to in that silence. I am willing to let him be, and that's fine, but I wanted to make sure that when I'm listening and he's silent, we would be, more or less, "on the same page."

Walking the dog without a leash

I think about my attention to a patient during the hour a little like walking a dog without a leash. Yes, I want the dog to be able to run around and be happy, but I don't want to completely lose sight of it, to not know where it went. It's important for me to make sure, every so often, that I'm not just wandering about with my evenly-suspended-attention – that I know where I am and where the dog is. I don't think it's right to let too much time pass without making a sound. Some analysts tell of these sorts of ghost analyses they held for years with patients who didn't make a sound. It is, of course, very interesting, and there is a large canvas to paint various thoughts and theories on mental psychic retreats and primitive mental states on the basis of these massive silences that sometimes develop in the analytic field. But I'm interested in the question of what the therapists did in that time. Faced with the patient's silent presence, what had to develop was a therapist's silent presence. One doesn't have to fabricate interpretations to prevent it. Even a quiet "Umm" can often help the patient. Silent patients often have to be reminded that they are silent. When you tell a patient, "You're being quiet" or "I'm listening," they often "plug in the speaker" and share with you what has been going through their mind in the last few minutes. They would hum some song that was playing in their head or verbalize a visual or tactile hallucination they had a moment ago and didn't think you'd be interested in. At times, I even employ an active technique, suggesting to a silent patient that they discuss a specific topic or recount what took place in the hours before the session. I wouldn't mix this active technique with forced fantasies of the type Ferenczi used for a while or other behavioral techniques such as guided imagery. But again, there are cases where interpretations alone could not extract a patient who is stuck in a fantasy leading to muteness, or some psychic retreat, for a prolonged period, unable to communicate with us. In analysis, switching from reclining to sitting is not guaranteed to loosen the patient's tongue, and I don't favor that strategy.

Freud thought that the patient's silence indicated that a homosexual position had made its way to the forefront of awareness. This insight is perhaps supported by his idea that a homosexual position is a complex concept. It includes both a yearning for merger and anxiety from otherness, and I think it also includes what Melanie Klein would later term *envy*.

Do the therapist's facial expressions signal to the patient that they are actively listening?

Psychoanalysis somewhat challenges the ethos of observing an object in general and of looking someone "in the eyes" in particular. Our culture considers the eyes to be "the window to the soul," and looking someone in the eyes is associated with searching for the truth. And suddenly, the analytical technique prefers listening to the patient's words over looking at them and completely forgoes looking them in the eyes for the benefit of internal exploration. In analysis, facial expressions do not have much communicative significance because we don't see each other's faces. I also hope that when a patient is facing you on a chair, you don't make too much use of facial expressions on the one hand or reading the patient's expression on the other. To me, it even seems too invasive to comment on the facial expressions or body movements of the person sitting in front of me or reclining on the analytic couch next to me, even if the goal of the encounter is to understand them or be in emotional contact with them. I remain relatively faithful to an analytic tradition where the patient's body language is not interpreted, except for particular cases. I even try not to look towards the patient when they are on the couch so as not to fill gaps in listening and understanding with visual impressions. When that happens and I find myself interested in the patient's clothes, how they smell, the way they walk or the disappearance of a familiar ring from their finger, I would try and "file" this impression somewhere and won't rush to interpret it. I would ask myself whether my glancing towards the patient, or them towards me, has a scopophilic quality or one of anxiety. I will wait for it to resonate with something in the patient's speech, with an additional signal from the unconscious. One patient gives a quick glance towards my lower regions whenever she leaves. Should I ascribe this compulsive symptom that I noticed developing sometime in her second year of analysis to her repeated complaints that every man who passes her in the street stares at her breast? Some psychotherapy patients are sensitive to the therapist averting their eyes. Some patients don't like the therapist's gaze, and some therapists (such as Freud) don't like to be looked at. It appears as if, over the years, more analysts positioned their chairs so they would be able to see the face of the reclining patient. I guess that in an age that gives such preeminence to vision and visual imagery, even analysts find it hard to forego it. Who knows, maybe someday soon, we will feel the need to add emojis to our interventions.

Does the relationship with theory produce envy in the patient?

Some patients' envy is hardly noticeable, but there are signs that in their fantasy, the therapist takes the role of a *big Other* with a large tome that allows them to understand anything about the patient and their world. It is a rather classic situation, the patient being suddenly preoccupied with the books on your shelf or by your couch. At that moment, the patient imagines that if they had the knowledge themselves, they wouldn't have needed the analyst. There is envy of the theory as a response to the experience of dependence on the other's creative mind. But, relations with the analyst's knowledge can fill several lectures, and I won't rush to interpret a patient's interest in a book they imagine I'm reading right now as either jealousy or envy. At times, the exact opposite is true: The patient might have noticed a book lying by the therapist's couch, but the book they discuss in their associations marks the partnership created between them and the analyst. They write it together, and there is no reason why a patient who knows that their therapist writes would not see themselves as a partner in some way in their therapist's creative work. Our patients are fully within their rights to see themselves as partners in our journey or even as our teachers.

Knowledge of theory enriches the internal analytic object and the clinical repertoire. The ability to identify, while listening, elements from theories makes the therapist's theory of listening richer and more open. But, we should also know the slightly neurotic nature that characterizes our relations with a certain theory. Sometimes, a theory will take over our attention and make it difficult for us to distinguish between "selected fact" and "overvalued idea" (a distinction offered, following Bion, by Britton and Steiner, 1994). Sometimes, our favorite theory functions as a "prejudice" and narrows the range of our attention to the matter brought up by the patient.

Any psychoanalytic theory offers a "package deal." Alongside the theory, we receive not only a developmental schema, a model of the mind and a curative mechanism, but also a stereotyping of other theories. We don't have to accept every component of the deal offered by producers of psychoanalytic theories, who often hide various neurotic and idiosyncratic sides to this deal. They would mainly take care to hide from you where their theories overlap and agree with others. I suggest you learn to know the papers in which theoreticians present their relationship with, or departure from, other theoreticians who were their therapists or supervisors. As a historian, I had the chance to read a fair number of obituaries written by analysts for their colleagues and therapists and noticed that this genre, the necrology, has absorbed a not insignificant part of the unconscious of the development of psychoanalytic thought. See Winnicot's eulogy of Strachey or his paper on Klein, Guntrip's paper on the analyses he had with Fairbairn and Bowlby and Mr. Kohut's two analyses. These papers show us how a theoretician, a person who later created a theory, met another theoretician and was treated with a different theory. This is also an interesting lens through which controversial discussions can be read. Freudian Edward Glover chastises young Paula Heimann, who "plays with Freud's theories as a kitten plays with a ball of wool" (Glover, quoted in King and Steiner, 1991, pp. 559–560). Putting aside for one minute Glover's patronizing tone and his (non-Freudian, in my eyes) underestimation of the importance of "playing with ideas," from his point of view, Heimann represented Melanie Klein's position in the controversial discussions out of a "misunderstanding" of the Freudian position. We are also somewhere on this spectrum. We understood Freud or Klein or Laplanche as we did. Perhaps, like the American analyst we met at the start of this session, you too think that "Freud himself eschewed that whole sexuality business"? A therapist's understanding and consideration of a theoretical model or a technical recommendation can serve a function of neurotic "compromise formation" for all intents and purposes.

I want to quote a poem on reverie, written long before psychoanalysis discovered the word and redefined it to suit its needs. I think an analytic therapist's relationship with theory can be rather similar to the relations between reality and reverie described here by Emily Dickinson (Dickinson, 2016). We learn a large number of theories so that, when the need arises, we can dream them up as we listen to our patients.

To make a prairie (1896)/Emily Dickinson
To make a prairie it takes a clover
and one bee,
One clover and a bee.
and reverie.
The reverie alone will do,
If bees are few.

Chapter 7

Transference, enactment and countertransference

Containing strong transference for months and years, or being empathic towards the patient? On the importance of symbiosis between the therapeutic setting and the patient's inner world and the forgotten concept of "transference neuroses." A patient asks to leave their phone on during the hour. Is it true that anything the patient does that annoys the therapist is acting out, and everything else is enactment?

We discussed the way our listening is related to containment. The setting serves both listening and containment – it supports the fundamental rule of psychoanalysis on the one hand and increases the patient's receptivity to the analyst's interventions and interpretations. It seems to me that patients and therapists who grew up in the digital age find it more difficult to accept the classic analytic setting on account of its relatively clear divide between presence and absence. Have you noticed that younger patients sometimes seem unable to ring the doorbell or use the building's intercom? They would rather send a text, "I'm here," and wait for the door to open. Millennials often leave the room at the end of the hour as if they were an internet user changing a tab or a ghost fading away rather than a person parting from another with whom they have been talking for the last hour. Eyes instantly change focus from the therapist to their mobile device, and the patient walks through the door without saying goodbye or closing the door behind them. Still, I wouldn't be too quick to reinvent the analytic technique to adapt it to the age of screens. In the words of Downtown Abbey's butler: "I'd rather be convinced than defeated."

What might have been somewhat absent from our discussion until now is that piece of theory that explores the way the therapeutic setting absorbs the patient's unconscious. The analytic hour and the inner world are gradually fused into the setting, which the patient internalizes as a psychoanalytic object. I implore you to read José Bleger's paper, where he discusses the analytic setting as a "social institution" that serves a role in absorbing the psychotic and autistic parts of the patient (Bleger, 1967). Bleger argues that a healthy symbiosis is formed between the setting and the analysand, which enables the exploration of early narcissistic object relations that find refuge inside the setting. Bleger's brilliant analysis of the analytic setting aids us in understanding not only many clinical experiences but also socio-cultural

DOI: 10.4324/9781003528470-7

phenomena, such as religious rituals and festivals, which superficially may seem almost insane but function as a lightning rod for the psychosis of individuals and groups.

People who have undergone analysis remember, for years after it ended, the days and hours of their sessions. This symbiosis between the setting and the patient is expressed in many ways, even during analysis. Acquiescing to the convention to offer an alternative hour to one the therapist or patient canceled often proves to be either pointless or even harmful. Some patients would routinely fail to arrive at the alternative hour you found for them, but even when they do arrive (because they are disturbed by having paid and not receiving anything in return, or for another reason), the encounter is more "for the record" than for analysis. On the other hand, we would see how analysis takes place, symbolically, in the patient's mind and dreams, even when sick or on vacation. This doesn't happen spontaneously, but it is the benefit of a setting that continues to function in the patient's mind and allows a better degree of separateness from the inner object. The tension between the analytic hour's fixed timeframe and the fluid time experienced by the unconscious and the unitary dyad with the primary object continues to exist in patients for many years after the end of therapy. The analytic setting improves patients' relationship with time. There is also a large similarity between the mental state arrived at by those who regularly practice meditation and the mental state that patients and therapists reach in good analytic hours. You help the patient to "practice psychoanalysis," literally. It is a state of being and a mental state that will be available for them to return to even after ending therapy. This is one of the goals of working on vacations and separations during dynamic treatment: To allow the patient to learn to use the analytic object after the end of therapy.

I sometimes encourage patients to perform a symbolic act of maintaining the analytic setting while they, or I, are on vacation. Patients, at least some of them, use the fixed hours not only as a transitional space but also as a transitional object. Either way, the familiar hours, already recognized by the patient as their point of contact with the inner object, are practically irreplaceable from the perspective of the unconscious system, and patients will surprise a therapist and arrive at "their" hour even when they are expected not to, such as, during holidays. Naturally, the therapist breaking the setting would produce more powerful shockwaves than the patient doing so. I remember a patient who, for years, was convinced that the only reason for my summer holiday was to gradually "wean" him from being dependent on therapy. He didn't even imagine that I really wasn't at my clinic on those dates. I informed him that we can't meet. In one instance, he admitted to arriving at his hour during my vacation and being rather surprised that I didn't answer when he rang the doorbell.

Transference neuroses

In the summer of 1888, Freud wrote to his Berlin-based friend, Wilhelm Fliess, asking for a recommendation on where a patient, at the time in Freud's care, should spend her summer holiday. The patient was previously treated by Fliess and wanted him to decide on which sanatorium she should visit. Freud writes:

> [S]end me a card by return mail on which you have jotted down the name of one place, and rest assured that this will be the place where Mrs. A. will spend the summer. But please spare me from having to make the decision; this would in no way satisfy her, for the power over the spirits that belongs to you cannot be **transferred**.
>
> (The complete letters of Sigmund Freud to
> Wilhelm Fliess, p. 21. Emphasis added)

This is the first instance of the term "transference" in Freud's writing. Freud acknowledges the power of suggestion but also understands when a therapist of his kind should not place himself as an object of transference. Today, we would most likely interpret for the patient her wish that we tell her where to spend the summer.

The Interpretation of Dreams already contains a schematic description of transference: transferring a certain amount of energy from the unconscious into a thought or image found in the pre-conscious. Transference is, in fact, inherent in the way we think. We transfer mental energy between different mental systems, giving words and conscious thoughts the weight of unconscious thing-presentations and thoughts. A year later, during Dora's analysis, Freud was much clearer on what exactly is the unconscious content we tend to transfer between the unconscious and conscious systems. He links, therefore, two insights he reached separately: The first insight relates to the repressed sexual content at the basis of hysteria – an insight he reached as early as 1887, and the second insight relates to the unconscious content transferred to consciousness during analytic therapy. This is how he concludes that the unconscious contents transferred to him from Dora are of a repressed sexual nature.

In the postscript to *Fragments of an Analysis of a Case of Hysteria* (Dora's case study), Freud asks, and answers, the question of what transferences are:

> What are transferences? They are new editions or facsimiles of the impulses and phantasies which are aroused and made conscious during the progress of the analysis; but they have this peculiarity, which is characteristic for their species, that they replace some earlier person by the person of the physician. To put it another way: a whole series of psychological experiences are revived, not as belonging to the past, but as applying to the person of the physician at the present moment. Some of these transferences have a content which differs from that of their model in no respect whatever except for the substitution. These then – to keep to the same metaphor – are merely new impressions or reprints. Others are more ingeniously constructed; their content has been subjected to a moderating influence – to sublimation, as I call it – and they may even become conscious, by cleverly taking advantage of some real peculiarity in the physician's person or circumstances and attaching themselves to that.
>
> (Freud, *Standard Edition*, vol. VII, p. 116)

The theory of transference was further developed by Freud (in Vienna), Karl Abraham (in Berlin) and Sándor Ferenczi (in Budapest). Gradually – mainly due to the work of Abraham and Ferenczi – criteria developed, tying modes of transference to degrees of object relations or patients' psychopathology. Abraham suggested the ability to remove the libido from the ego and transfer it to the figure of the therapist as a basis for distinguishing between hysterical transferences, characteristics of hysteria patients and transferences characteristic of psychotic patients. This is the source of the belief that psychotic patients are unable to create transference and, therefore, unsuitable for psychoanalysis. Freud held this view, although, in practice, he certainly did treat psychotics. The theory, on the other hand, continued to nurture the distinction between neurotic transferences and the narcissistic-libidinal hold characteristic of the psychotic structure, which does not allow the creation of transference and, therefore, does not allow for a deep and sustainable influence. Between these two types of transferences – neurotic and psychotic – Freud placed the transferences characteristic of melancholic and hypochondriacs.

In his important paper *Introjection and Transference* (1909), Ferenczi argued that first love and first hate result from transferring pleasant and unpleasant auto-erotic sensations towards objects that elicit these sensations. He concludes this idea by saying that transference is a special case of addiction to displacing unconscious drives in neurotics who seek to evade unconscious complexes and pains. In fact, Ferenczi says the greater the propensity to transference, the greater the neurosis. The patient who exhibits exaggerated interest or invests large parts of their libido in figures in the external world is acting out of internal frustration. A neurotic's transference is the negative image of the psychotic's. The psychotic is "self sufficient." They invest their entire psychic energy in their auto-erotic self and remove their interest from the object.

Neurotic patients are commonly fond of transferences. Christopher Bollas (2000) used the fitting expression "transference addicts" to describe certain patients, and I think the same is true for therapists, too. Therapists can also develop an addiction to being objects of transference. It's sometimes difficult for us, too, to do the work that will somewhat soften, somewhat unravel the enchantment.

The theory relating sexuality, early object relations and modes of transference gave much weight to the distinction between types of transferences as a diagnostic tool. Compulsive and hysterical transferences in the psycho-neuroses group were termed *transference neuroses*. This somewhat forgotten concept is interesting – more than a psychopathologic diagnosis, it is a "temporary disease" that develops in the analytic situation and is used to promote treatment and curing. The physicians among you may remember Gram staining: For bacteria to be visible under an optical microscope, they have to be stained. In the microbiological lab, Gram's staining method allows for an initial distinction between groups of bacteria – ones that are stained by it and ones that aren't. In the same way that in the microbiological lab, some bacteria are Gram-positive and some are Gram-negative, in the psychoanalytic lab, some patients develop transference neuroses and some do not.

What, then, are "transference neuroses"? They are new versions and adaptations of unconscious self/object relations that develop in the patient's relationship with the analyst. These transferences warped a certain aspect of the realistic object's here and now. Classic analysts were once experts at producing transference neuroses. It had both diagnostic value and therapeutic function. Suggesting an interpretation to a patient in a transference neurosis enhances the chance that the interpretation would lead to a structural change in their inner world. Thanks to transference, the patient is in somewhat of a "time capsule," and the therapist's intervention, which seemingly takes place in the present – we can use the concept of *caesura* here, if we wish, to feel more current – is able to produce a change in the historical psychic structure. Transference neurosis is unique to the analytic situation. The patient doesn't start therapy with transference neuroses, but to the extent that they develop during it, the patient becomes more accessible to the therapist's intervention. This gives the therapist an opportunity to work "by the furnace" and strike the iron while it's hot. Such a patient has a very strong and vital experience. It is an antiquated, somewhat tautological concept (after all, transference is, by definition, a kind of neurosis), but I find it sometimes useful clinically, especially in those cases where I try to word, to myself, the function of a certain transference by the patient has. As mentioned, I see a patient's ability to give in to the dream-like and enigmatic nature of their relationship with the therapist as evidence of their ability to use the analytic situation and a good therapeutic technique by the therapist. I believe that the development of transference neuroses is a better indicator of the development of therapy than the development of dependence on the therapist, for example. Regression to dependency in no way ensures that the patient is opening up to the influence of therapy, and some patients would develop a malignant dependence on the therapist as protection from contact with psychic pain and a substitute for growth and development.

Enactment and communication potential

The second kind of patients don't develop transference neuroses. They are – to stick to the biological metaphor – Gram-negative. At times, we would have to surmise that they belong to another group of psycho-neuroses – that of "narcissistic neuroses." Here, we are dealing with reprints of auto-erotic drives projected onto the figure of the physician, what would later be termed *transference psychosis*. The clinical picture doesn't have to be particularly dramatic, and many psychotic transferences take place "under our radar" for prolonged periods. But at a certain moment, these patients' transference is revealed to be missing mainly the dream-like and playful nature known from transference neuroses. The patient no longer "feels you don't love them," but more or less informs you that you "hate them," "deliberately mistreat them" or are "envious of them" for some reason. These psychotic transferences sometimes have a delusional quality and require a slightly different technique. Perhaps the patient that Eduardo Weiss consulted Freud about was one such patient, "acting" neurotic until reaching the moment in therapy where he needed to air his psychosis into the transference also. Freud, as his letter to his Italian supervisee shows, was not concerned with psychosis breaking into the analysis in this manner. These parts are difficult to identify during intake or weekly psychotherapy, and you will meet the patient's psychosis mainly in intensive psychotherapy or analysis. In my experience, it mostly happens after a prolonged separation, as a reaction to a significant loss in the patient's life or to a distress that suddenly fractures something in the transference. In this context, I'm reminded of a patient who very early lost their mind when they suddenly heard my voice on the radio or a patient who "waited" for her partner to die because she fantasized that, in that case, her therapist would come to the wake to console her. Disappointment from that half-conscious scenario not materializing leads to the psychosis breaking into the transference.

In his *Papers on Techniques,* Freud began systematically conceptualizing transference and basing the analysis of transference as the central pillar of the psychoanalytic curative technique. As early as then, he marks the two main axes along which discourse on transference runs to this day: Is transference a real relationship, happening at the moment, with two actors (patient and therapist), which has the power to afford the patient an emotional experience that will fill the place of the earlier lacks that shaped their "conditions of love," *Liebesbedingungen*? Or does the therapist have to remind themselves, at every moment of therapy, that everything that takes place in transference is merely a revised edition of unconscious fantasies and wishes, meant merely to liven and regressively recreate the patient's early object relations? Out of these two positions of understanding transference, we derive the various perceptions of the role of the analytic therapist. Are they an opaque screen, an absent presence, whose entire role is to translate the various transference phenomena for the patient while indicating their infantile origins? Or are they an active partner in an ongoing, mutual relationship, which is not essentially different from other relationships the patient establishes in their life?

I presented these two positions in a rather dichotomous manner. In fact, Freud doesn't present to his readers such a dichotomy between transference as fiction and transference as something realistic. A case in point, the paper on transference-love ends in a rather radical resolution: That any love is, in a way, transference-love, and that any transference-love also has realistic components. In any case, the analysis of transference quickly takes up the central place in the Freudian clinic, replacing the interpretation of free association and dreams. But if we are occupied mainly with identifying transferences and interpreting them, we are less free to listen to our patients.

Let us discuss countertransference and enactment. First, I want to present a short clinical tale that we can use in the discussion. A patient comes in and says: "I have to keep my phone on today. Social Security promised to call me back, and I can't miss that call. I've been trying to reach them all day to work some things out for my mother. It's driving me mad." The patient reclines on the couch with the phone by her side. The analyst doesn't say anything. Every so often, the phone rings or beeps, and at the end of the hour, the awaited call from Social Security did not come in. At one point, the analyst says: "We couldn't separate you from your mother today." The patient answers, "I knew you wouldn't like me being on the couch with the phone on." Later in the hour, she snaps at the analyst: "You never could stand me!"

Let us consider the transitions between enactment and acting out. These can be subtle, and it is no coincidence that analysts are divided on the question of whether the concept of enactment is even necessary.

Enactment has a communicative potential. Identifying it allows us to understand the unconscious processes that the patient and therapist take part in. Joseph Sandler's (1976) time- honored concept of *role responsiveness* includes many things that seemingly involve the therapist going "out of bounds" of the setting but are still almost a form of interpretation. They express the therapist's attunement to a certain part of the patient in the hope of being in touch with it, to "bring it into the conversation" in action rather than words. There is a difference between acting out and enactments that are anti-analytic or undermine the possibility of understanding, such as crossing sexual boundaries, and acting out and reenactments that don't fall under verbal communication, but do serve as a kind of participation by the therapist's unconscious in the therapeutic communication, which can advance the analytic process.

In his paper *Remembering, Repeating, Working Through* (1914), Freud focused on a new type of memory: *Acted out* memory. Some patients are unable to remember their past and verbally communicate their experiences, but their seemingly forgotten memories appear as behaviors and are reproduced, or repeated, in relation to the analyst. It may be that a patient who was abandoned in their childhood would not remember that or discuss it, but in their adult life, they would develop all sorts of somatic symptoms when traveling. They may be quick to dismiss romantic relationships or professional opportunities rather than be abandoned by them. The situation of abandonment repeats the same pattern, but the patient is unaware that they are acting something in the present instead of remembering it, experiencing it or identifying in it the traces of some unconscious fantasy. Many years have passed before analysts acknowledged that not only the patient but also the therapist acts out certain things in the hour. From that point onwards, we started thinking of the therapeutic occurrence not only through established concepts such as repetition compulsion or acting out but also through the concept of enactment.

The historical fate of the concept of enactment bears some resemblance to that of the concept of empathy. Both have migrated to our discussion from another discipline and, at one point, became identified with a certain analytical position or school. Renowned British historian Collingwood argues that in order to understand a historical figure, the historian re-enacts, in their imagination, the figure's deliberations and actions. The path to a complete historical representation is through the historian re-enacting the state of mind, considerations, forces and deliberations of past characters (Collingwood, 1994 [1946], pp. 282–302). Some link enactment with relational thinking, mainly in the context of early unrepresented trauma. I believe this is a mistake – both historically and theoretically. Analytic Schools tend to appropriate concepts, which then somewhat lose their communicative value. Enactment had numerous synonyms in psychoanalysis even before the rise of the relational paradigm: Symbolic interaction, role responsiveness, projective counter-identification and others.

I once heard a veteran analyst saying, tongue-in-cheek, "acting out is anything the patient does that annoys the therapist. Enactment is everything else." I think it was Ted Jacobs who said that, the same Ted Jacobs who coined, almost 40 years ago, the concept of countertransference enactment (Jacobs, 1986). He said that when he first presented that concept to his New York colleagues, they believed he was either an exhibitionist or a narcissist. "They were wrong," he said in a recent interview: "I'm both an exhibitionist and a narcissist." (Jacobs, 2018). I would somewhat disagree with Jacobs on this point. I believe the places we should take an interest in are exactly those where something that may have "annoyed us" in past encounters with the patient, for some reason, completely lost interest to us. If I'm completely undisturbed by a patient being repeatedly late, if their attacks on me or habit of angrily storming out of the room at the end of the hour have completely stopped unnerving me – then informative enactment has probably long since become regressive acting out.

Going back to my earlier example of a patient who waited, while on the couch, for a phone call from Social Security. We should examine the analyst's decision to allow the patient to recline on the analytic couch with her phone on. What may seem at first blush as rather reasonable flexibility in response to the needs of an outside reality was found to be an invitation for an attack by the inner mother, or a sadistic super-ego, on analysis. In any treatment, there is a vast amount of communication not only through the patient's words or dreams but also through some kind of enactment inside transference and countertransference. By "enactment," I don't mean only the thoughts, fantasies and associations that go through the therapist's mind during the hour, but also actions, positions and a certain climate that gradually start to characterize our form of listening and presence alongside the patient.

From a Kleinian perspective, enactment is regarded more critically. Some even see it as the "acting out version" of projective identification. A Kleinian therapist would see critically any expression of action implying that they have been activated by the patient's projections instead of containing and interpreting them (Steiner, 2011). In contrast, among contemporary Freudian and relational therapists, some would see enactment as a positive intersubjective phenomenon that combines intrapsychic aspects of the patient and therapist. From this perspective, enactment is not only an expression of a failure of containment but a source of knowledge regarding the patient that is not accessible to the analyst in any other way. I believe every psychoanalytic theory today uses some version of the concept of enactment in its clinical conversation, which is evidence enough for its importance in the clinic, even if no agreement has yet been reached regarding its precise theoretical definition.

The patient's unconscious world sometimes detects the therapist's unconscious position even before the therapist themselves knows that they are in some countertransference enactment. The therapist had not yet accounted to themselves for emotionally distancing themselves from the patient – because the patient rejects them, entices them, threatens them or frustrates them – but the patient has already somehow noticed that distancing, perhaps even verbalized it to themselves. In our example, it is not a coincidence that it was this session in which the patient said she had been feeling her therapist couldn't stand her. She really thought, and projected onto the therapist, that what she shared during the analysis made the therapist dislike her and think she was a bad person. That is not very different from what she secretly thought of herself and what led her to seek therapy. This is why she didn't respond to the analyst's acquiescence and flexibility as a good, enabling behavior but responded to it and the interpretation as proof that the therapist dislikes, perhaps even fears, her in the same way her mother did. For this reason, it is possible that had the therapist positioned himself more on the "rigid" side, refusing to change the setting (perhaps offering an interpretation along the lines of: "You bring mother to me so that I can protect/repair her for you"), the patient might have been angry on a conscious level, but in a deeper level would experience the analyst as a stable figure, unafraid of her anger and willing to protect analysis from the inner mother's omnipotence or greed, and from the attacks of the bad object. In other words, what seems like reasonable or helpful enactment in the first 30 minutes of the hour can be revealed as acting out in the second half.

As early as Freud's 1914 paper *Remembering, Repeating, Working Through*, it is clear that the analytic situation, by its very nature, encourages repetition. In treatment, one always repeats something, not only through speech. The re-enacted drama is not limited to the patient remembering events and emotions from their past or their free associations. It is always also unconsciously communicated to the therapist's inner world, thereby producing diverse mental or concrete acts. If the patient was a rejected and neglected child – that would be reproduced in the room even if they don't smear mud all over your carpet or forget to flush. The therapist can be suddenly impatient without knowing why. They may feel disdain towards the therapy without being able to put their finger on what in the patient's behavior is troubling them. With some patients, you would gladly and without reservations accept a small gift for the holidays, and with some, you will feel the need to ascertain to yourself – and, despite the tactlessness of it, to them too – that it is not flattery or a "bribe." There are patients whose greetings at the start of an hour I perceive as authentic and pleasant and others whose same greeting I would perceive as purely defensive, desperate or demanding.

One patient asks, at the beginning of almost every hour, "Is everything okay with you?" That question usually has an unpleasant, even alarming quality, as if I have a duty to inform her in advance if something in me can disturb her continued mode of object-relation to me as a "subjective object." I believe that through projective identification, this patient – a past victim of a "Munchhausen syndrome by proxy" who suffered from severe dissociative episodes – was turning me into a mad and dangerous Mother who could lose her mind at any moment. A few years ago, I had an unforgettable dissociative experience in the company of that patient: I felt it was time to finish the analytic hour, glanced at my watch and couldn't understand what the hands showed. It was a few horrifying seconds before I could give meaning to the numbers the hands pointed to and understand what time it was (Rolnik, 2009).

Another patient greets me at the start of the hour with a childish, sugary tone, like the voice of some cartoon character. For a long while, I looked for a way to turn his attention to the unconscious fantasy behind this way of address. Little by little, I identified enactment in the patient's infantile tone at those moments and in the response it elicited in me. I realized he was not only tempting me with his eroticized cordiality but also sending me a "friendly warning" at the start of every hour not to come close to "less-than-cute" regions, which will taint our good relations and may elicit his anger or aggression.

Let us assume that the analyst from the previous example, the one with the phone, is aware that the patient thinks he is hostile towards her and wants to "prove" otherwise. He, therefore, relinquishes a part of the setting, letting her feel special. This is done from a defensive, inauthentic position. Our perception of countertransference is derived from our perception of transference as taking part not only in what the patient tells us but also in the emotional climate the patient induces in us. Even when the therapist "can't stand" a certain aspect of the patient's behavior or character, they have to decipher it inside the relationship, inside the particular transferential space where that aversion appears. Do they feel, alongside the aversion, also shame? Or, to the contrary, is it accompanied by a strange joy or erotic thrill that can imply a sadomasochistic wish or fantasy projected into them? The therapist has to understand that they are an extraordinary figure in the patient's world since the patient funnels into them parts of their inner world they don't funnel to anyone else. The patient brings us rather unpleasant, disavowed parts of themselves without being aware of doing that. That is what they are in therapy for. Other people might not know them as objectionable. This is also the reason, ultimately, that the patient would feel loved by the therapist – not because the therapist was empathic to attacks on them or because they infinitely contained them or saw things "from their point of view," but because the therapist helped them, through interpretations, to be in touch with difficult or unbearable parts of their inner world, without denying them as part of who they are. An analytic therapist doesn't say to the patient, "You stink, but I don't mind." One day, they might gather the courage to say, "I thought the reason you don't shower is to keep me away from you" or, otherwise, "You imagine penetrating and merging with me through your body odor, the way your mother imposed her enemas on you." Such interpretations are not easy to hear (or speak), and it is certainly an intervention that might somewhat sour the atmosphere in the room, but it is not the same as when her classmates told her, "Go away, Stinky!"

I sometimes experience the patients' transferences – even those that make it very difficult for me to be in their company – as a type of gift. Through these challenging transferences, they allow me an emotional partnership in their world that has no equivalent, even in my relations with people very close to me. When we are willing to accept strong transferences for months and years, the question of whether we succeeded at every moment to be empathic to what the patient experienced becomes less critical in my eyes. It is somewhat like improvisational theater in the sense that the therapist's commitment to "step into the scene" and act in a play written for them by the patient's unconscious is more important than the quality of the acting they exhibit while doing so (Lubrani Rolnik, 2009).

This is how patients receive the analyst's love, a unique kind of love. The therapist's love is embodied in their commitment to accept and be in the presence of parts of the patient's world to which no one gave meaning and interpretation. In truth, therapists endure things that even good mothers won't. The therapist's ability to bear the transferences and projections is derived from their willingness to examine various transferential phenomena, hidden and overt, as they are also expressed in countertransference. Why does the therapist continue to think of a certain patient, rather than another, after the hour? Why, with some patient, do I not mind their phone remaining on, while with another, I would be uncomfortable? Transference fulfills a certain function for the patient inside the treatment at a certain time, and countertransference has a function, too.

Despite everything said and written in the praises of enactment and working-through the countertransference, I believe it is a mistake to see countertransference, and it alone, as the "highroad" to the patient's unconscious. I mostly listen to what patients say. Every so often, I examine with myself something more fundamental in the way I listen to a certain patient – what they invoke in me, what is taking place in this analysis lately and what is unduly absent from it. There would be certain circumstances where our unconscious communication and its influence on countertransference would interest me more than symbolic communication. But, the very fact we identified enactment within the hour is not evidence of our failure to contain or understand the patient. If there is a persistent attack on the setting, we would consider it differently than enactment. Acting out necessitates a different approach, not only because it can have far-reaching ramifications for the patient's life but because it is an overly regressive mode of communication that blocks both the patient's and therapists' ability to be in touch with their inner world. If the patient is in love with the therapist and refuses to leave the clinic at the end of the hour or lurks by the therapist's car or if a patient of yours suddenly appears naked before you in a swimming pool's changing room – then the therapy is in trouble. Such acts have to stop if therapy is to continue.

Chapter 8

From listening to interpretation

The intellectual roots of psychoanalytic interpretation. On interpretative presence and the limits of the patient's understanding. When should we offer an interpretation, and what is a "silent interpretation"? The 9 o'clock patient vs. the 10 o'clock one. What is behind the hand that takes one's own life?

You might remember that *The Unconscious*, the pinnacle of Freud's meta-psychological papers and perhaps the most important theoretical paper in the whole of psychoanalytic literature, contains the following lines:

> Furthermore, experience shows that we understand very well how to interpret in other people (that is, how to fit into their chain of mental events) the same acts which we refuse to acknowledge as being mental in ourselves. Here some special hindrance evidently deflects our investigations from our own self and prevents our obtaining a true knowledge of it.
>
> (*Standard Edition*, Vol. 14, pp. 169–170)

Freud mentions humans' inherent resistance to knowing their own minds. He also gives a general definition of psychoanalytic interpretation that is both concise and precise. To interpret is to fit a chain of events into a mental context. Just as a historian requires skill and method to fit political and social events into their historical context, the analyst's role is to find the mental context.

No other concept is more identified with psychoanalytic therapy or the psychoanalytic attitude than *interpretation*. Interpretation is an inseparable part of the therapist's technique, and the history of thought regarding it is very much congruent with the history of the analytic technique and, of course, also the history of meta-psychology. The concept of interpretation can never remain unaffected by developments in technique or meta-psychology. It would, therefore, serve us well whenever we have a new model or some new conceptualization related to the analytic curative technique to examine how the status of interpretation reflects them.

The birth of the concept was in the interpretation of dreams, more precisely, in Freud's self-analysis, which relied, to a large extent, on interpreting his dreams.

DOI: 10.4324/9781003528470-8

This was the first appearance of a very specific sense of interpretation, which is still with us to this day but has absorbed other meanings along the way. The quintessential analytic interpretation is an intervention by the therapist in the speech of the patient, with the aim of enabling the filling of gaps in the patient's memory. Freud realizes that ascribing meaning to things the patient just told him doesn't only allow the patient to resume their speech, if it was stopped for some reason, but brings new matter to their memory. In psychoanalysis's early curative model, remembering is important for its own sake, even though by *remembering,* Freud means not only objective life events in the patient's past but also additional mental contents the patient lost contact with.

Through interpretations, the patient's unconscious communicates with the therapist's unconscious

Psychoanalytic thought is founded on the premise that mental events and psychic phenomena, in sleep and while awake, are meaningful. When Freud was concerned with extracting repressed memories and integrating them into the patient's speech, interpretation was revealed to work magic. The therapist speaks – links what they have heard or guessed in what the patient said or didn't say, and "voilà," a whole new world of memories bubbles into the surface of speech. Very quickly, the fate of interpretation starts to overlap with that of the theory of dreams – our first interpretative theory – in another sense: Freud stops seeing the interpretation of dreams as an art in itself but rather as one of many tools in the journey to discover the psychic truth. Accordingly, the use of interpretation also changes. Around 1909–1910, the analytic interpretation stopped being an explorative act and was instead considered an act of communication between the therapist's mind and the patient's. Through interpretations, the therapist's unconscious communicates with that of the patient. Even the analyst's silence has a positive meaning. We learn to be silent or hum in the right places to encourage patients to perform mental work. But the analyst's speech, mainly their interpretations, have a very central place in the therapeutic encounter, and it is this role that sets this encounter apart from any other human interaction.

The psychoanalytic interpretation draws on, and is still in dialogue with, a number of intellectual traditions. First and foremost, the **Aristotelian** sees interpretation as an act of exposing hidden but predetermined actions and meanings. Another interpretative tradition is the **phenomenological** one. It develops in geographic proximity to Freud, and its representatives see the act of interpretation as one that "peels" context and social and normative strata from reality, exposing the thing-in-itself in its essential, or pure, form. An **existential dialogic** tradition is also relevant to psychoanalysis, seeing interpretation as an interpersonal interaction, which would later be termed *relational.* This exists in the Jewish tradition (Martin Buber), the Christian mystical one (Meister Eckhart) as well as in Buddhism and other philosophers. Another tradition, the hermeneutic tradition, would later be identified with the inter-subjective approach to psychoanalysis.

Psychoanalysis adopted inter-subjectivity from philosophers such as Heidegger, Husserl and Gadamer, who see the act of interpretation as a form of being. Gadamer discusses a *fusion of horizons* between the interpreter and the interpreted object, an act that not only extracts meanings from the psychic or historical text but contains within it a transformation of the interpreted content of the interpreted object. We can recognize each of these four interpretative traditions in psychoanalytic thought on interpretation. Each of these traditions would influence our position and technique.

Analytic interpretation

For many years, Otto Fenichel's book on psychoanalytic technique, published in 1945, was considered the comprehensive psychoanalytical encyclopedia. Fenichel defines the act of interpretation as helping the patient to become conscious of something unconscious by naming it the moment it makes its way toward consciousness. This definition already expresses a trend of expanding the concept of interpretation: Naming something that makes its way toward consciousness. Fenichel incorporates the dimension of timing into the definition of interpretation. Freud, too, identified the timing in which the interpretation was given as critical for its influence. He believed that the best interpretation is given to the analysand just before we believe they can make it themselves. This, of course, is an illusion since the analysand requires the therapist's presence and words even in order to think and experience something they already knew. But, an analytic interpretation is never only its content. An interpretation is a whole world of relations between content and form, composed of rhythmical, tonal, temporal and repetitious aspects. A psychoanalytic interpretation will be voiced again and again during therapy. It will be amended, nuances will be added to it from its transferential contexts and it will change in dialogue with the patient. To give a somewhat sweeping generality, one might say that in every therapy, we give a rather limited number of interpretations and repeat each of them countless times – in different variations, at different time points, with different emphases. This is interpretative work. It is repetitive. Repetition is a characteristic not only of the repressed but also of the therapeutic encounter.

The art of interpretation lies in the ability to use various combinations of words and intonations to produce a mental motion, a motion forward of insight, self-recognition and even a love of self-knowledge. The art is to create this alloy in which the interpretation – even if not crystal clear, due to not being phrased definitively or even completely intelligibly to the patient (or the therapist) – would have a "caloric value" for the patient's mind. From the moment it is aired into the world, the interpretation makes its way to the patient's inner world in unforeseeable ways. At this point, a new kind of psychic work starts. To remember and speak, the patient had to work against internal resistance. Now they have to do work of another kind: Use something we said. We listen well to the way the patient heard us. We can't say anything definitive about an interpretation without receiving the patient's feedback. At times, we would learn that an intervention that was said offhandedly just before the end of the hour echoed in the patient's head for years, and they repeat it to us only when the treatment is terminated. It became a seminal moment for them, without giving us an opportunity to examine, or even learn, how it influenced them. I have this rule of thumb: When I want to sample a therapeutic hour in consultation or a clinical seminar, I look for the therapist's interpretations and what the patient said following the interpretation they were just offered. Try to take your session notes and see for yourself how representative this small fragment is of what happened during the entire hour.

Beginning circa 1923, the dominant approach in the analytic clinic became that of seeing an interpretation as a continuous process rather than a confined event. There will always be therapists whose interpretations would have a more precise content, seeking the leading unconscious fantasy in the patient's associations and transference, and others who would not be so meticulous about the content and the structure of the interpretation but more concerned with the music, the color and the temperature with which it is given. I think that all of these aspects are important, but in some analyses and hours, we can practically see how we tend to neglect a specific aspect of the interpretative act. That is, with a certain patient, we tend to emphasize the content of the interpretation more and are less attuned to, or less accommodating of, the patient's sensitivity to how we say it or the timing in which it is said. At times, it would take us too long to understand that we gave a good interpretation but perhaps waited too long before suggesting it to the patient – that we "sat on it" for too long. Some patients need to hear our thoughts relatively early in the hour because from the moment they left us after the previous hour and to the moment they re-entered the room to see us again, we were already "spoiled" inside them. Our interpretation can't be given after only 20 minutes of passive listening. Some patients need to hear the analyst's mind, the analyst speaking first. Perhaps the analyst didn't have to produce interpretations; perhaps they could have made do with some grunt, signaling they are still alive, that they are not angry, but listening and trying to understand whether they are enjoying themselves or not. This is knowledge accumulated in each analysis – when is it right to make a sound and how long of an intervention is suitable and bearable for the patient. When are we just giving them a "word bath" that is not right for them when they require interpretations that are rapid, topical or enigmatic?

At times, the patient needs us to interrupt their speech more than interpret it. An interference, more than an intervention or interpretation. The obsessive patient requires you to interfere with their speech even if you don't have anything really substantial to say because, otherwise, they won't allow themselves to perform a mental action, except for an obsessive repetition that shatters any meaningful connection that comes to their mind. For such a patient, clearing your throat, chuckling or sighing can bear significance on par with an interpretation in terms of the influence it has on the patient's mental functioning during the hour. A cough or a chuckle can bring about a transformation in certain patients whose speech is "stuck on overdrive." I recently listened to a patient and asked, "Now, are you speaking or blabbing?" He was a little offended, but it paid off. His associations began sounding more alive and communicative.

As mentioned, the days are long past when interpretation was perceived purely as an act of methodic objectification, by which we transfer some thought or truth from our mind to that of the patient. But still, many therapists are anxious about using the word "interpretation." To their ears, it rings hard, cold, all knowing and patronizing even. I want to preserve the use of this word. True, one can look for, and find, synonyms that might be more pleasant to the post-modern ear. We can use "intervention," "speech" or "suggestion"; we can butter it and make it more palatable to ourselves and our patients. I believe we would be amiss to forego the concept of interpretation. If change is required, and our interpretative technique always bears change and development, it is not by using the word the noun. It has long been a verb, as we know. An interpretation is an always changing work-in-progress.

One cannot detach the discussion of the concept of interpretation from metapsychology, a more holistic perception of the psychic mechanism and the structure of the human mind. Interpretations are a therapist's "trademarks," her idiom. Once we open our mouths, we are revealed. We are revealed to the patient, and we are revealed to ourselves. This is why students of psychotherapy, as well as psychoanalytic candidates, sometimes find it harder to repeat in consultation what they told the patient during the hour. While remembering and reconstructing hours of psychotic speech by the patient is not an easy feat, this is not a lapse of memory. The difficulty arises, I believe, from anxiety brought about by the need to repeat to another person, a third, what we said to the patient during the hour. It is a kind of self-disclosure very similar to that required of the patient during the hour. This is true on the sociological level, where we share with our professional community (in a clinical seminar or a paper) but also when alone in the room with a patient. When we open our mouths, we, in fact, start breaking down transference. Perhaps we also give it new fuel, but a silent analyst is protected. Their silence has a function, of course. It has great significance in the therapeutic encounter, but can also be used as a retreat. Consultees or colleagues sometimes find it difficult to reveal to us what they do in that room with patients. Then, in consultations or supervision, the therapist says, "The patient said this; the patient said that . . ." contrasted with detailed verbatims of patients, the therapist's intervention is described in a rather broken and vague manner. The therapist is unsure when exactly they said what they said. In my usual habit of exaggeration, I would say, to the ears of an experienced therapist, patients sound very similar, but each therapist's speech sounds very different from any other's. What I mean is that once the therapist makes their voice heard, we know better what happened in the room. We know whether we are listening to the unconscious fantasy and whether hearing it is justified. The interpretation says where the therapist was listening, what they heard and where they are aiming. Once a therapist speaks, a whole new world is revealed. A patient can speak for the whole hour, and we will find it difficult to know where they are and what they are really going through. It is the patient's privilege to use speech as camouflage. Ten experienced analysts can spend two days in a clinical seminar, debating the way they understand two and a half phrases uttered by a patient. But when the therapist speaks, most of the mystery goes away. If they do their work properly and really make an effort to produce an intervention, then their interpretation would make it clear how **they** heard the matter and how **they** perceive what is taking place in the transference. Even more importantly, I would say, is that the patient's unconscious really starts transmitting to the therapist's mind once they hear them speak, once they hear how their mind works.

So, if there's anything I would like you to take away regarding interpretation, it is this: First, do not be timid about using the word "interpretation," not with yourself or colleagues and not when you're with your patients. Don't be anxious about the word, use interpretation. Second, be wary of seeing interpretation through the aura of a top-tier intervention reserved only to grand-masters. An analytic interpretation of a therapeutic event is often menial work consisting of shoveling tons of dirt during the therapeutic hour. While we don't tend to talk much, interpret we must. This is the only way by which the patient's unconscious or inner world is tuned to us and directed towards us. When dealing with various elements of technique, I said that the fixed hour, or hours, conditions of payment and time, the analytic position and the frame are what draw the patient to speak out of the depths of their psyche. We also deal quite a bit with the importance of listening and containment and the relations between them. But, all of these are not enough to establish an analytic situation with a transformative potential. Matters of time and money have immense importance for the degree of depth, meaning or triviality of the interaction, but no less important is *interpretative presence*. Interpretative presence is not an all-knowing presence but a presence that wishes to know, that is not afraid of knowledge and, in particular, a presence that is not afraid of lack of knowledge and error.

I should emphasize that by "lack of knowledge," I don't imply a nihilistic, new-age, relativist or merely affectatious philosophical stance. "Not knowing" is a clinical fact of life, and hiding it from ourselves or the patient, serves no purpose. That is, as long as I keep my mouth shut, the patient may mistakenly believe that I understand everything they are saying. I sometimes have to say something for them to understand that I don't understand. Even if they apply pressures of a merger on me or drown me in idealization, I have a duty to, every so often, make a verbal motion to remind them, and myself, that I don't understand, that I don't know, that I want to know. That is why, in the analytic game, we sometimes "take the shot" even when we're not in an ideal position to score. We don't aspire to make a clean, "nothing but net" point.

An analytic interpretation is also a matter of tact, of style; we can't keep throwing "from the same spot": The same interpretation with the same assurance, the same tone – if we don't get any feedback that we are doing work. It would be foolish, even violent, and any therapeutic situation carries a potential for suggestion and indoctrination of the patient. But these risks are greater when we don't interpret than when we do.

Is every speech an interpretation?

On the one hand, there's a part of me that wants to maintain the classic definition of interpretation as an attempt by the therapist to link something unconscious with something conscious. A classic interpretation uses the conjunction "because": "You are quiet because you are afraid that when you talk, you will come up with something aggressive about me." That classic interpretation links defense with an unconscious drive, wish or fantasy. Creating a link of causality between a primary and secondary process – or between a certain form of mental functioning and an affective state – contributes much to the patient's familiarity with their internal reality. But not all of our interpretations follow this classic format. Today, it is rather difficult to say "because." This has to do with the status of our knowledge, and knowledge in general, in our times. On the other hand, I already mentioned my recommendation that we all lose the question marks. Don't act coy. Even if you're not sure – everyone knows you're not an all-knowing genius and are unsure – don't worry about that. If the patient feels that they are in the presence of someone who thinks anything they say is pure gold, then that's what they think about you. They may be wrong or they may be right, but mannerisms, feigned stuttering and dropping question marks on every step would not change that. What might change that is the interpretation you would offer the patient or yourself. Do you really think you know? There's no shame, I think, in daring to think I know something and learning I was wrong. I won't suggest flourishing an interpretative intervention with a question mark.

In dynamic therapy, therefore, I don't think one should communicate with the patient through questions more than is necessary. Questions get answers. Questions do not address the deeper layers of the psyche but recruit the conscious part and the upper levels of mental and cognitive development. Our patients answer questions throughout their lives. They don't come to us to think and ponder logically. Of course, they also think and ponder during the hour, but that is not what brings about psychic change. Most therapeutic happenings operate without the patient understanding cognitively how it does and what happens to them during it. A patient tries to tell me what comes into their mind and someone tries to guess what they said, interprets, says or offers an intervention. This causes them to experience something and affects a change in them if the interpretation is made inside the transference, at the right time, the right tone and at a certain intensity. This allows the psychic structure to change gradually; this is how internal relation to anxiety or an unconscious fantasy changes; this is how denial of aggression, sexuality, guilt, confusion or sorrow gradually lessens – not through intelligent musings. Many wise and sensitive people – philosophers, theologians, writers, painters and poets – walked the earth before Freud, asking profound questions about themselves and the world. "Introspection" did not require the invention of psychoanalysis. Questions belong to a different discourse than the one I want to offer my patients. Philosophy and the sciences stress the significance of how to phrase a question in order to find the truth. In the psychoanalytic clinic, we seek a truth written in a language and grammar different from those legible to consciousness. It is a truth that has to be experienced to gain the status of reality. There might be a place to distinguish psychotherapy from psychoanalysis in the context of using questions. Psychoanalysis is a journey to the unknown, and questions directed at the patient tend to reduce this journey, making it a guided tour in the "suburbs" of the patient's consciousness.

Of course, The discourse between the patient and therapist takes place on many levels. The life therapists share with their patients includes various levels of relations and forms of communication. They ask questions related to their life story, to their symptoms, and are interested in whether they are healthy, vaccinated or suffered through traffic. Still, when we interpret, it is better to omit the question mark. Even a simple interpretation, such as, "Were you ashamed?" would be more meaningful and evocative if we dare to say simply, "You were ashamed."

Do not be afraid to make mistakes. It sometimes seems that therapists tend to "over-cook" interpretations for too-long periods and then sit on them. They are afraid that the interpretation would break the patient apart, so they phrase it as ending with a question mark. They are afraid that the interpretation would sever something in the patient's experience, reducing at once the infinite variety of possibilities by which the patient can be understood. They are mainly anxious about their own interpretation breaking them apart. This is true, to a degree, because when we interpret, we place ourselves against the energy of the patient's id. It's scary; it has to be. If you perceive that the patient invites you, in their fantasy, to penetrate them anally, it is very natural to feel some resistance to phrasing and sounding this notion. But that is how things are; that is what you have been hearing for several hours in your patient's speech – the wish for anal merger with the therapist. You might delay this interpretation for a day, two days, a week, two weeks, but once you start to word your own thoughts using the concepts of anal penetration, my suggestion to you is: Tell the patient that. You might be wrong, and the patient would ask you if you went totally mad, but only through the interpretative severance of the patient's speech would you come closer to something meaningful and true that allows both continuity and the formation of something new.

Interpretation as an expression of the therapist's love

Stifling your wilder thoughts and making the lion's share of your work sorting and filtering interpretations would make your work not only tiresome but also fruitless. Our work requires abundant restraint, but what we restrain is acting out. We are not supposed to restrain our interpretations. Sexual, aggressive, avaricious, abusive drives – those we should control and restrain. This, however, allows thoughts to come to our minds more freely and intensely than outside of the room. After all, there is a certain function to our restraint or abstinence. I remind you again: The analyst foregoes usual expressions of love and, in return, allows themselves unusual ones. One of the most distinct expressions of the therapist's love is interpretation. That is the privilege of this form of encounter: While the patient is allowed the very difficult, almost impossible act of saying all that comes to their mind – we are not supposed to say everything that comes to our mind but are certainly required to do something with what the patient said. Interpretation is our only way of rewarding the patient for their willingness to share their most private feelings and emotions with us. Empathy, compassion, acceptance, containment or holding – as important as these are to a meaningful analytic encounter – they are not a sufficient reward for what the patient needs and what they expect from us.

Interpretations come in various types. They don't have to be the last word, as if such a thing existed. Yes, we sometimes feel we suggested a wonderful interpretation that the patient didn't pay enough attention to, one that did not "receive the respect it deserves," it wasn't listened to, wasn't understood and nothing was done with it. That is where our work starts. But if you don't attempt to have the patient's mind encounter the products of your own mind, no work would be done. Obviously, the position from which the therapist can suggest an interpretation has to do with more than their own understanding and the patient's mental state. The therapist has to learn to recognize when they themselves are in a state where they can suggest the interpretation. At times, the interpretation can be correct, and the patient is in a position to use it, but the therapist is not in an optimal emotional position to suggest it. Even when you believe you understand what is taking place in the transference or your patient's fantasy, it is very hard to suggest a good interpretation the patient can receive from you while you yourself are soaked in persecutory or sadistic parts the patient deposited with you. It could be a matter of minutes or days before an opportunity presents itself where both you and your patient can once again receive something from each other.

I will say again that if we are well situated in our role, we invite the currents and parts of the patient's inner world that they can't direct at anyone else. Those are parts that limit the patient's ability to adjust to reality and fulfill their career and love-life potential, but I don't think it is right to term them "sick parts" or "insane parts." This terminology presupposes that a person's happiness depends on them abandoning their madness or an idealization of it. Our clinics have people, who Bollas (1989) terms *normotics*, for whom it would have been better to have freer access to the insane parts of their inner world. But we also meet a fair few number of patients who cherish, in a rather childish and defensive manner, the right to indulge in their psychopathic and perverse drives. That is why during analysis, I prefer to discuss parts and forms of thought the patient is not in touch with or whose existence they turn a blind eye to – and these can be not only omnipotent and aggressive but also soft, sane and striving for intimacy, reliance and yielding.

We do not judge the patient; we do not make an astounded face when they tell us about their perversion; we do not mock them. That is also what makes our interventions, which may sound rather simple to an external listener or the reader, into expressions of love. We demand almost nothing from the patient. Remember that. They have nothing like that in their life. We do not want them to grow up, get married, get divorced, finish their master's thesis or make sense. We want nothing of all the things their id, super-ego or environment demand of them. You might say – we ask for payment. Yes, we want money, and in a timely manner, but this is (in part) to preserve the analytic situation so we can meet. Why do you think Otto Kernberg, in one of his case studies, reacted to a borderline patient's threat of suicide by saying, "If you commit suicide, we will not be able to meet tomorrow"? My understanding is that he did it not only so as to shift the patient from modes of impulsive action according to the "pleasure principle" towards modes of secondary thinking which are considered the "reality principle." He acted deliberately, emphasizing the analytic setting as a condition for their next encounter because he knows that a therapist's "passion to heal," whether through empathy, containment or kindness, does not improve the chance of extracting borderline impulsive patients from the talons of their death drive. In these patients, the life and death drives are fused to such an extent that it is precisely when they feel a dependence on the good object and the therapist's love, precisely when they feel life's pain, that they are in the greatest danger. I believe that this is also a central reason why patients sometimes try to commit suicide only when they start recovering from a depressive crisis rather than at the height of the depressive episode. The psychiatric explanation for this recorded phenomenon argues that even the will to commit suicide requires mental strength, which the deeply depressed patient is unable to summon up. This explanation cannot satisfy anyone who understands the dynamics of object relations in depression and the interrelations between death and life drives in analytic concepts. At times, what is behind the hand taking one's life is not the wish to die but rather the fantasy that the good object can only be preserved by forever distancing it from the bad object and its destructiveness.

In consultations, I sometimes find that therapists expect too soon not only mutuality in their relations with patients but also that patients would "see them as people." Seeing the therapist as a person is a state achieved at the end of therapy, not its beginning. If we are lucky, the patient will one day see us as people. A rather significant treatment could also end without the patient getting to the point of seeing you as a person. A patient can make a considerable developmental way in their self-knowledge and their object relations and part with the therapist while still leaving them a slightly strange place in their inner world. The patient might never see the therapist as a person, even though they made significant headway in that regard with their spouse, children and friends, and see others as "whole objects" or "objective objects" that can be relied on and used.

I don't correct a narcissistic or hysteric patient's inability to see me as a complete object or as a subject. The analytic situation increases any patient's tendency to see the therapist as a subjective object or selfobject. The transference-neurosis that develops in a meaningful therapy recreates primal object relations and narcissistic and omnipotent forms of mental functioning. It is only natural that it also recreates archaic fantasies of merging. There is a moment where I explore and interpret the patient's abusive relation towards me, but not because they abuse me or heart my feelings – it is my responsibility to guarantee I don't feel abused, and maintaining the setting is enough to aid with that – but because I have something to say regarding their unconscious "love conditions," their cruelty or abusiveness as a defense against an experience of intimacy, dependence on the good, acknowledging separateness or an attempt to bypass envy.

Are some interpretations dangerous?

Let's unpack this question: Is the anamnesis we took at the start of treatment meant to warn us that our patient is sensitive to a certain kind of interpretation and that we may be repeating a childhood trauma by applying a certain technique with this patient? Does early sexual trauma always lead to intolerance of certain interpretations? What if the patient does not even remember being a victim of massive trauma, and the issue did not come up during intake or the beginning of therapy? Would we avoid using interpretations until we are certain, beyond a shadow of a doubt, that there is no background trauma? We can't always know for certain what is our patient's personality structure, let alone their emotional temperature. How much can they hear, how much can they understand, where we would trigger defenses too early in the treatment, and where we would trigger ones that should be summoned – so we can mitigate and perform analytic work against them? You may have noticed that humor can have a similar effect on your patient: One day, the person would be terribly offended by an ironic remark. The day before, your irony helped them come closer to something meaningful, and you shared a laugh. Today, they're not in a depressive position, so your humor doesn't speak to them. Rather, their suspiciousness makes them very sensitive to irony and double meanings. The same holds true for our interpretations. There is no way of knowing the unknown, i.e., doing our job, except for speaking with the patient. To speak to them means to offer interpretations of the things they say and the thoughts and feelings they elicit in us.

True, any interpretation has a certain potential for violence. It contracts and, at the same time, expands the interpreted object's range of experience. So the question arises again – do we say it in one tone or another, a soft loving tone or a neutral tone, a normal voice or an extraordinary one? It's a matter of experience and style and obviously changes from patient to patient. You don't use the same tone to talk to the 9 o'clock patient as you do with the 10 o'clock one. Even Hanna Segal and Bion did not use the same interpretation with the same tone and the same exact phrasing with all their patients, although their theory did not change very much between patients. For authentic "analytic conversational norms," with all they entail, to form, we must speak to the patient candidly and in a way that reaches them. We have to aspire for emotional contact. An understanding nod and a sympathizing look do not create contact. To be even more radical: An interpretation can be empathic even when it evokes much resistance on the part of the patient, and even if it turns out to be inaccurate. Good mothers have a speaking presence. Mothers constantly speak to their children and provide meaning to the baby's sense impressions and utterances. Are you too hot, too cold, are you hungry? Look – a dog, good dog. Later, we'll wear a coat, sweetie, and go see grandma, and I hope there won't be problems with the car, like there were last week and so on. The analyst, even when talking more than usual, is rather taciturn due to the asymmetry of the roles. Analysts give more place to the patient's speech than to their own.

I believe that in the first five decades of psychoanalysis, therapists had to be taught to stay silent sometimes – that is how I imagine the historical development – and in the last five decades, we have to be taught to speak up again. Some therapists are talkative. Some analysts embark on a rather winding argument when they start an interpretation.

And what if it's not time yet? And what if the interpretation is perceived by the patient as "coming on too strong"? There's also the concern that our speech would harm the patient; that is – there's danger. Therapy can harm the patient, but the fact that you missed one interpretation that you gave a senseless babble is not where the danger is. If your presence in the room is suggestive, verbose and domineering, that can harm a weak, injured and pliable patient. But it's not necessarily the interpretation that does that, and we can assume that therapy has other symptoms of oppressiveness or indoctrination. A seductive, flattering therapist who only echoes the patient's narcissistic needs back to them is no less oppressive, from the unconscious system's point of view, than a therapist who positions themselves as the authoritative, all-knowing "big other." If we interpret, we, too, are more vulnerable. Patients see precisely what we understand; they see exactly what we listen to. I would even say that the patient who is trying to "catch us" can see "what we've got" through our interpretation. If they seek to disparage us, to undo their dependence on us, they are waiting to hear us speak. Then we can hear the part that's laughing – "Hahaha, is that all you have to say? You listened for so long, and that's all you have to say?" You should hear that this is how they hear it. You should show them that you heard something inside them mocking the interpretation you just suggested and blowing it off. It could be a clever, authentic part, unwilling to give the therapist unlimited credit and accept any interpretation they offer, but it can also be revealed to be a suspicious, undermining part that blocks the patient's ability to recognize psychic reality or accept something from the outside.

Winnicott argues that part of the aim of interpretation is to show the patient the limits of our understanding. Anna Freud, who is seldom cited nowadays, also thought so. If we see a therapeutic encounter as an expression of the love for truth, why hide that truth? People don't automatically know what they think and feel, not internally and not towards others. The therapeutic encounter is a wonderful opportunity to see the limits of understanding and how my understanding of myself and others can be deepened. Remember: Analytic relationships are based on sincerity. The therapist doesn't tell the patient everything they think and feel, but when they speak, it should be candidly. In order to set this as an ideal in therapeutic relations, I personally do not need a special analytic theory to encourage me to make gestures of "self-disclosure." This position is embodied, as I understand it, inside psychoanalysis in its original Freudian sense. The therapist's presence exposes them even when they are neutral or don't offer tea or coffee during the hour. It exposes them mainly through their interpretations. To the patient, it exposes that part that is important to the patient – the therapist's mind. We don't expose our sexual passions, our physical pains, and, for the most part, not even our musical preferences or political views to our patients. But we do expose to them, and we should do so generously, that part of us that received their psychic energy, the symbolic and unconscious semiotic communication.

The never-ending debate over the importance of *neutrality, anonymity* and *abstinence* often misses its mark, as it mostly lacks the same aspect of analytic relationships that tie means with ends. The analytic position, in its classic sense, is very generous. One can sit for an entire hour, rack their brain, search for something to say, and end the hour with a cutting remark – "Look, I've been listening to you for the whole hour, searching my mind for something to tell you. Unfortunately, there is nothing I can say today. Do you have any thoughts about that?" For a patient whose fundamental experience is that no one wants to understand them, just saying I tried and couldn't understand them serves as an interpretation. It exposes something of the enactment that took place within the hour. Moreover, in certain conditions, such a banal statement can expose that "selected fact" that was shimmering in the air of a given hour without us being able to note its existence. Such an intervention can "release" to the patient's speech new unconscious matter, or one it denied even if it was conscious – thereby fulfilling the criterion of an interpretation. Interpretation becomes an interpretation only after we examine its impact. Not all interpretations are born in our minds as interpretations.

*

Freud's beautiful 1926 paper *The Question of Lay Analysis* has a subheading: Conversations with an impartial person. Freud seems to have had such a conversation with a senior Austrian official who wanted to understand what was taking place in the treatment room of an analyst who was not a medical doctor – whose legal status was not regulated – following a complaint made by a patient of Theodor Reik. Freud uses this conversation with an impartial person not only to emphasize the difference between a medical action and an analytic one, to hone his position on the subject of psychoanalytic training, but also to discuss various issues of analytic technique. At one point in the conversation, the impartial person "loses it" and says: " 'Interpret!' A nasty word! I dislike the sound of it; it robs me of all certainty. If everything depends on my interpretation who can guarantee that I interpret right? So after all everything is left to my caprice" (Freud, *Standard Edition*, vol. 20, p. 219). Freud is aware that the word implies tentativeness, the fact that the procedure is one of trial and error. In the deepest analytic action, even that which operates in light of the principle of making unconscious matter conscious, there is a process that ultimately aids the patient in somehow using the knowledge they had beforehand. That is what takes place in therapy. We don't only make the unconscious conscious but remove the obstacle – anxiety, omnipotence, guilt, foregoing excitement – that prevents the patient from using their mind, what they know of themselves and the world. When you give a good interpretation, the patient often responds by saying, "I knew that but hadn't thought about it." Christopher Bollas (1987) borrowed from Freud the title and subtitle for his first book, *The Shadow of the*

Object, at roughly the same time as Bion found in Freud the idea of the caesura, which he also took in new directions.

This is then the experience of accepting an interpretation. I would say that an interpretation that doesn't produce a sense of old-yet-new, familiar-yet-strange, "I knew that but hadn't thought about it" – is an interpretation that was either said prematurely or that something in the way it was worded did not allow the patient to link it with something more they know about themselves. At times, a word or two, a pause or a certain intonation is what makes all the difference between an interpretation that is crystal clear in terms of the content but would not touch the patient in a way that brings about an experience of expanding understanding.

Why does it have to be said? Keeping quiet would have the same meaning

Keeping quiet would not have the same meaning. The patient requires the therapist's words for them to know something else about what they said while they were talking. Even if the therapist's interpretation adds nothing to what the patient said, the patient needs to hear what they said in order to experience it. "To have heard something and to have experienced something are in their psychological nature two quite different things, even though the content of both is the same," to quote *The Unconscious* (Freud, *Standard Edition*, vol. 14, p. 176). Winnicott once told that in one of the early sessions of his analysis with Strachey, he said, "I talked for the whole hour, and you didn't say anything," to which Strachey replied – "Neither did you." I believe this is an intervention equivalent to an interpretation. What Strachey told Winnicott is that the fact one is silent while the other talks still doesn't mean that one said a lot and the other said less. Strachey didn't deny not speaking in that hour, but he gave Winnicott the opportunity to experience something of his listening to him. He thought Winnicott did not say much, even though he spoke at length.

My role is not to be "performatively" silent so as to show that I have nothing to say or to send the patient the message that they are rambling. The therapist's silence can be interpreted by the patient in countless ways. I might want them to be left in the dark; I might think there is some value in dismissing them from this hour without receiving even one word from the therapist. When you speak, you may find out that everything the patient said in the last few minutes was guided by their fantasy that you are silent in today's session because you are angry about something they told you in the previous one and want to punish them.

We should make an effort to account to ourselves whether we performed the hour well. Like a musical composition, an analytic hour can be performed in many ways, but it can also be completely misunderstood and performed badly. We have to consider that possibility, too, as part of our self-critique. We have to know that we sat there in the room and it didn't work well. It's not the end of the world; there are many hours like that. We should examine why it happened, when, with what patient and so on. I'm uncomfortable with a culture that praises the psychotherapist's silence and mystifies it as a form of communication with the patient. It is usually psychotherapists who have never held an analytic hour in their life who tend to be smitten by silence and see prolonged silence as evidence that they are in O with the patient. We are part of a "talking cure" tradition, and in the journey towards the O the therapist's speech is no less important than the patient's. Our patient's words, and our own, reveal at times, and at times they cover. But, a meaningful psychodynamic therapy would not form out of either of our "collected silences." If all I do is nap in my chair, cradling in the countertransference and thinking about what my wonderful analyst would have said here, what my wise supervisor would think of this dream or what Bion or Meltzer would do in this hour, fantasizing the infinite wealth of possibilities by which I could have understood, or not, what is taking place in the hour – then I most likely have a problem and aren't "putting in work."

I may find it difficult; perhaps I'm sleepy or bored; then, I would make an effort to form something of that into words that I can offer the patient. A patient says, "I think I terribly bored you today." Naturally, you wouldn't answer, "You did terribly bore me," but something of that observation by the patient, whether it is a massive projection or an accurate reading of what you had been going through during the hour, would become an interpretation you would put to them before they leave. Winnicott (1965) tells of a 10-year-old girl who once told him, "It doesn't matter if some of the things you say are not true because I know which are and which aren't." Think of that girl when you find yourself over-deliberating whether to tell your patient something. They will accept you even if you guessed wrong and "didn't score."

Two caricatures analysts

One is the silent therapist: A veritable indrawn Zen monk whose inner work is supposed to perform some transformation in the patient magically. The other is of the analyst as a sniper, lying in ambush for days and months until the interpretation comes to them, and they "squeeze the trigger" and hit the unconscious's bull's-eye. We have these two caricatures in our minds. Bion, who is often hailed as epitomizing the first, was far from being that silent. He gave interpretations that, at times, were reminiscent of the early days of psychoanalysis, textbook Oedipal interpretations. These two caricatures or stereotypes can paralyze the therapist at certain hours and even encourage an idealization of silence. So, at times, I just have to overcome some internal resistance and force myself to say something aloud just to know what I think and feel at a certain hour or because I learned that in order not to drown in the countertransference or get lost inside my head, I need the patient, as a consumer of my thoughts and words. They need me in order to know I was listening to them at this moment, and I need them to escape the grasp of the death drive that often assumes the guise of emptiness and complete lack of knowledge.

But here I have an example of the opposite situation, where, over and over, a patient made me regret intervening in his speech. I once worked with a new immigrant, a sharp, intelligent man who knew several languages and wanted his analysis to be held in Hebrew. I was completely fine with that. There was something refreshing in listening to a man who has a limited Hebrew vocabulary. The unconscious likes not to be wrapped in linguistic fineries, and it would certainly benefit someone of my rhetoric inclination to practice simple sentences for a bit. It took me time to realize I shouldn't make an effort to find words or phrasings that would be easier for the patient to understand. He's an immigrant, not a child. I learned that where he seemed to be asking me for a dictionary definition, interpretations melted away. Where he understood – he understood. Where he didn't – we carry on because his defense would "home in" on the linguistic side and make any interpretation I offered a short Hebrew lesson. That made me think twice before I opened my mouth.

It is true that performing an analysis in a foreign language may have its advantages. The analyst, too, can gain something from learning to speak plainly. I hypothesized that this classical ideal of the silent analyst developed partly as a response to psychoanalysis immigrating from central Europe with the rise of Nazism (Rolnik, 2007, 2012, 2025). The senior analysts in Berlin and Vienna immigrated to the United States, Britain and other countries from 1933–1939. Only a small percentage – non-Jews – were left in German-speaking countries. Some of these immigrants, or refugees, had rather basic English because they grew up in a world where German was the more eminent language of science. Now, they have to hold analyses in New York, Manchester, Copenhagen and Jerusalem but their speech takes a smaller share of the hour. They certainly don't understand everything the English-speaking patients say, perhaps are embarrassed to use their broken English and lose something of their authority and status. Perhaps they felt guilty for saving themselves and leaving their mother tongue behind. Perhaps the classic ethos of the silent analyst was born then out of these particular historical circumstances?

Chapter 9

Still from listening to interpretation

What can we learn from iconoclasts, and what sense can we make of Kleinian and Lacanian analysts' disregard for ego psychology? On wallowing in countertransference and the almost obsessive inclination to identify trauma born of external reality as the origin. Is dissociation a contraindication for using interpretations? A case of a patient falling into the "symbolic equation" as a response to the therapist sneezing and the difficulty of leaving the couch at the end of the session.

Today, I'm conspiring to encourage you to interpret to your patient what you understand is happening in the therapeutic situation. A therapist should get an urge to interpret, at least once or twice, during a therapeutic hour, and they shouldn't spare efforts in helping the patient develop a taste for that form of intervention we call "an interpretation." It is a broad concept, as often happens in both psychoanalytic language and other fields of science: While we don't want our concepts to be too rigid, we also don't want them to lose their meaning entirely, or else they could not serve a communicative function between us professionals. If we called anything the patient says during a therapeutic hour "defense" or "resistance," then these concepts would have lost meaning. If we describe anything that happens during the hour as "enactment," and anything the patient does outside the hour would be considered (or, more properly, denounced as) "acting out," then we would not have the language to describe the idea of expression through action, as distinct from expression through speech or remembering.

Psychotherapists can have a repertoire of choice interpretations they remember, just as jazz players play standards and chefs prepare certain classic dishes – a beef bourguignon, for example, or an omelet. It's part of their professional repertoire – even if they sometimes overuse it. Any professional has a number of techniques they master, and, over the years, we should acquire familiarity with some interpretations, know when to use them, when to hear them in the hour and when to suggest them. There is such a thing as a classic psychoanalytic interpretation, a sort of "psychoanalytic beef bourguignon." You will read them in Freud and in many other analysts as you expand your familiarity with clinical literature – in Bion and Masud Khan and Haydée Faimberg, in Michael Parsons and Irma Brenman Pick and Christopher Bollas or Thomas Ogden. You will find them used by the greatest

DOI: 10.4324/9781003528470-9

innovators of psychoanalytic thought. We often have a tendency to learn from the iconoclasts, and we forget that they, too, once studied under someone. The most classical Freudian to have worked in Chicago for a number of decades was Heinz Kohut. So today, I want us to think about the existence of a classic analytic interpretation alongside various variations of interpretations, including those that don't fall under the classical category but should still be considered under the category of an interpretative intervention.

During their first session, a patient asks his therapist: "How can I trust you if you see me during a pandemic, despite the risk of infecting one another?" To which the therapist answers, "I wonder how you would have made me feel guilty if there wasn't a pandemic?" I would call that an interpretation, even if it does ring somewhat sarcastic. The therapist wants to help the patient see what he is trying to do at that moment and tells him that what he actually wants to do is deposit some of his anxiety and aggression with her. What makes it an interpretation is that the therapist's words can help the patient, if not right now, then sometime in the future, learn something he denies about himself but still exists in his fantasy. Something about the relationship between feelings of guilt and aggression. We can call this interpretation a "trial interpretation." These were once used to test whether a patient was a "good fit" for analysis. During intake, the therapist would offer the patient an interpretation and examine how they reacted to it. Did they fall apart? Get mad? Stop and think at all? Do they understand that there is someone here trying to give them something they can't give themselves? How do they manage their first encounter with that language? Therapists believed they could predict suitability for analysis this way. It was a great theoretic saga – how to choose analysis patients. I believe a trial interpretation is not enough: The only way to tell whether a patient is suitable for analysis or psychotherapy is trial analysis. But staying here, in this little verbatim, a classic trial interpretation might have been more detailed: In the immediate transferential context, our patient complains that the therapist agrees to meet him for therapy during an epidemic. The therapist could perhaps have offered an interpretation relating to his guilt, that he blames her as a defense against his own anxiety about being in therapy. She could have said, for example: "What you're saying is that coming to therapy isn't easy for you because you carry inside you something that might hurt me." Ultimately, the patient accepted the therapist's offer to start analysis. What she did must have been somehow related to him agreeing to come the next day and the day after that, and so on. Something must have worked. Through the interpretation, the therapist enticed the patient to start analysis.

Silent interpretations

The concept of a *silent interpretation* was suggested in 1969 by New York-based analyst Hyman Spotnitz. It refers to an interpretation the therapist silently verbalizes to themselves during the hour without sharing it with the patient. As tedious as it might be, I find it difficult to present a concept without also recommending that you familiarize yourselves with its genealogy and the historical context in which it "entered the bloodstream" of theoretical and clinical discourse. Spotnitz (1969) suggested the concept in a time of a growing stream of theoretical and clinical works based on analyzing schizophrenic patients. In those years, much work has been done in the Washington Chestnut Lodge Hospital, by Harold Searles and Frieda Fromm-Reichmann, among others. West Coast analysts of the time were also searching for ways to reach psychotic patients. This is, by the way, why they invited Bion to give a series of seminars. I myself was never a fan of the American psychoanalytic culture, but still, there is something completely undecipherable to me in the condescending attitude Lacan, Klein, Green and their successors take towards American psychoanalysis, in particular ego psychology.

In any case, perhaps more than the UK, it was conservative America, then dominated by ego psychology, that was a place of pioneering analytic work inside the framework of psychiatric institutions, even with chronic schizophrenic patients. That was the context in which Spotnitz discussed "silent interpretation" as a means of aiding the therapist to regulate regression when treating severe patients and containing massive projections of the kind that occurs when analyzing schizophrenic patients. The silent interpretation can include components originating in the therapist's countertransference, which they do not wish to share with the patient. This idea of a silent, or silenced, interpretation has been appearing in the work of many writers ever since. We have even become accustomed to hearing it mentioned as an excuse when therapists are questioned about avoiding speaking their minds to a patient. In consultations, a consultant would often say: "That's a very interesting hour. Do you think you could have told the patient something of what you're telling me now?" And you would answer: "Yeah, I didn't think it was the time; I had it on my mind, just not properly worded; I thought I'd wait some more, think it over again."

I believe that even when we interpret wordlessly, as we very often do, it is worthwhile to stop and consider "turning on our monitor" every once in a while and consider letting the patient hear some of what comes to our mind. I'm reminded of a conversation I had with an experienced analyst, who told me: "Isn't it great, the job we chose? You get to sit behind the patient's head, remember being seven and going to the movies with your mom and they pay you to do that." And it's true, we do sit in the chair and remember going to the movies with our mother. But we also have to do something with that memory. We're not there to endlessly wallow in the countertransference or use the patient to continue our self-analysis. We often interpret silently, we make use of the countertransference, but then we say something to the patient. As I argued here more than once, The most effective and fruitful interpretation you gave on a certain week can be revealed as the one you first blurted hesitantly. The very fact we overcome our resistances and speak, the very fact we overcame some hurdle – of anxiety, of complacency, of drowsiness, laziness, narcissism, idiocy – puts us at a new vantage point, it brings us closer to the truth of that hour. Painters, too, sometimes find out that a blotch of paint mistakenly splashed onto the piece or an unintended brush-stroke is retroactively identified as a turning point in their journey to discovering the finished work.

Language closing and disclosing

In The Interpretation of Dream, Freud writes: "There is at least one spot in every dream at which it is unplumbable – a navel, as it were, that is its point of contact with the unknown" (Freud, *Standard Edition*, vol. 4, p. 111). In analysis, as in sane life in general, no solution is ever final. A good interpretation would always leave some "change," a remainder. It is a question not only of the limits of our understanding of the other but an even more fundamental one: To what extent can words cover reality or enclose it, particularly when it is the reality of the drive and the unconscious? And yet "The recesses of feeling, the darker, blinder strata of character, are the only places in the world in which we catch a real fact in the making," wrote William James (1929). Our words attempt to encompass some mystery, some enigma concerning psychic truth and mental facts. You might be familiar with C.N. Bialik's beautiful essay Language Closing and Disclosing.[1] Even when we offer an interpretation we had put much thought into, one that is good and beautiful and finely worded, there comes a moment where, if we overdo the interpretative pretense, it will all break down. Just like making a meringue – the shiny, stable peaks we have at one moment break down in the next. The patient has already taken part in our verbosity and understanding to reach another level. They may applaud us, but it won't truly reach them. We are required here to practice a form of artistry and skill, to hold the tension between a touching and accurate interpretation to minimalism, concession and waiting for the next thing to come up. Freud demonstrates this well, not only in his clinical writing. In his research on Leonardo da Vinci and Moses, we can see him expounding brave, fantastic interpretations while repeatedly cautioning himself against decisiveness and judgment; he skips forward and back on the border between certainty and doubt, knowledge and lack of it.

Whenever I hear the phrase "fine tune," I experience a mild allergic reaction. It has become very popular nowadays – no doubt through the influence of the world of algorithms and optimizations – but in the context of analysis and communication between therapists, I still find it grating. I don't see a patient to "fine tune" them. I see them to encourage them to be in touch with parts of their inner world they've lost or avoid contact with. I use analytic attention and interpretations to do that. These would sometimes touch them and sometimes not. They would be clear at times and vague at others. What we do in a therapeutic hour is search for psychic truth. And experience shows that the more the analyst can bear confusion, vagueness and lack of knowledge, the greater our chance of coming closer to that truth. Whenever we are tempted to discuss precision with the patient, we also play along with the part interested in denying psychic reality.

For a mental health therapist, for therapists who seek the patient's truth, the wish to "fine tune" encompasses the fantasy of an ultimate solution, a final goal, a single answer to the mystery called "man." I don't believe such a thing exists. This may be a too-personal distaste, evidence only of my own limitation as a non-fine-tuning therapist. A good interpretation is not one that hits the bull's-eye and collapses the patient's entire internal organization. An interpretation "ruffles the patient's hair" and allows them to be in touch with something new but also still recognize themselves. In some patients, we can look for expressions of envy as an affirmation that our interpretation is a good one. Envy arises not only in response to good interpretations but whenever acceptance and dependence rise outside of the patient's full control. Envy is derived from infantile omnipotence and the death drive. The all too zealous lookout for the ultimate interpretation is akin to theoretical fundamentalism and is in itself a manifestation of the death drive.

Freud, while having more far-reaching positivist aspirations than any other analyst of his time, was free of the need to find closure and know everything. In a letter to Jung, he wrote:

> I can see from the difficulties I encounter [in this work] that I was not cut out for inductive investigation, that my whole make-up is intuitive, and that in setting out to establish the purely empirical science of ΨA I subjected myself to an extraordinary discipline. This and all sorts of random influences have quite prevented me from working this week; all I can do is wait for better days.
>
> (Freud to Jung, 17 December 1911)

More than a decade later, in a letter to Siegfried Bernfeld, he wrote:

> I do not believe in the relativism, as it is called, of our knowledge. I believe in the possibility of absolute truths, that is in the existence of real facts, even if our positions require that we ceaselessly correct and improve them. On this point I remain as "unmodern" as can be."
>
> (Freud to Bernfeld, 22 May 1932 in: *Letters of Sigmund Freud*, p. 258)

I think these two quotations demonstrate how Freud was capable of hovering between two complementary epistemic positions of explaining and understanding.

A good interpretation is, in the most general sense, one that aids the mental mechanism, the mind, to overcome the pain involved in meeting a psychic reality. When we offer one, the patient feels relieved or surprised. The interpretation might be accompanied by a subjective feeling that they are understood. Feeling understood, while not the only indicator, is certainly a central experience characteristic of good therapy. Alongside it, some patients would also develop anxiety about being left exposed in some way. Not every patient can make this trade. At times, we push the interpretation a little too far, and it robs the patient and overly exposes them. An example from an analytic hour: Halfway through the hour, I noticed that the patient did not pay as he was supposed to at the start of the session. As it was a rather prolonged analysis, during which the patient always paid on time, I was unusually careless and participated in his parapraxis, only noticing it about halfway through the hour. As it continued to bother me, I linked the issue of the forgotten payment with something else I wanted to say as a response to things the patient said in that hour. I felt as if I ambushed him, laid a trap for him, by linking the parapraxis – forgetting to pay or an attack on the setting, whatever we call it – to other material he brought that wasn't related to it. The interpretation was over-saturated. The patient quickly responded with an interpretation of their own, but instead of stopping at one interpretation and an apology, he entered into a spiral of analytic self-flagellation for the possible reasons he forgot to pay this month. The more wisely he interpreted his parapraxis, the more I felt my intervention led him away from the surprise caused by the encounter with the unconscious. There was something exaggerated in both of our reactions to forgetting the payment, as if we were both overtaken by the fantasy that the entire analysis was directed towards the moment he would somehow slip and I would catch him red-handed. In this case, I somewhat regretted not letting the patient remember the payment himself.

Are there analyses where you don't interpret at all?

The therapeutic process is not limited to interpretations, and as we have seen in the previous chapter, the concept of interpretation itself can be broadly or narrowly interpreted. When we offer ourselves, place ourselves as thinking and breathing partners of an extraordinary kind in the patient's world, partners who are willing to witness and be targeted by parts of the patient's inner world they themselves only partially understand or are not even aware of – the moment we fill this function we are already in an interpretative position, even before we started interpreting systematically. Even therapists who think they don't interpret, giving themselves various rationalizations on why they don't, do so more than they account to them-selves. A bit like with art – in cinematography, the location of the camera and the way the scene is shot already interprets the scene, the script. A patient who enters your clinic on fixed days and hours starts "being interpreted" before you even say one word.

I want to consider the objection made by trauma specialists and others regard-ing interpretations when working with trauma patients and discuss it in the wider context of the theory of trauma in current clinical work, a sensitive subject that immediately brings up every demon – tamed and half-tamed, real and imaginary – from the history of psychoanalysis.

Today, many tend to discuss trauma and dissociative disorders as if they are two sides of one psychopathological or clinical entity. Some consider dissociation a pathognomonic expression of trauma. This may sound novel, but, in fact, it takes mental health back to the days before the Freudian revolution. Not only science but also clinical and cultural studies are affected by trends and fashions. Scholars of various fields are eager today to incorporate the concept of trauma in any psy-chological, literary, artistic, political, moral or historical discussion. I believe that exaggerating trauma in psychological, historical or political interpretations con-tracts the range by which people, political processes, texts or art can be understood and experienced. I also don't find it very analytical to automatically categorize patients who suffer from eating disorders or alcohol, drugs or pornography addic-tions as trauma victims. Some contemporary versions of the theory of trauma have very little in common with psychoanalysis in its Freudian or Kleinian sense. Their deterministic aspirations are much closer to what Wilhelm Dilthey termed the natural sciences, where we seek to *explain* phenomena in terms of cause and effect, or the general and the particular, rather than the human sciences, where we seek to *understand* phenomena in terms of the relations of the part and the whole.

The traumatogenic or traumacentric perception has at its heart an almost obsessive desire to identify trauma born of external reality as the origin, to create a link of apocalyptic causality between the beginning and end of psychic life. Speaking through the prophet Hosea, the Lord said to the people of Israel, "I did know thee in the wilderness, in the land of great drought" (Hosea, 13:5). This teleological and deterministic perception of psychic life as a wasteland, overgrown with environmental lacks and parental failures from which the therapist rescues the patient is, as I understand it, a complete reversal of the Freudian psychoanalytic perception of humanity.

Certainly, any psychoanalytic theory, from Freud to current ones, puts a large emphasis on infancy and childhood and early object-relations. All central psychoanalytic models are also interested in how phylogeny, inter-generational transmission and culture influence the process by which the internal world forms. Classic psychoanalysis, however, is unique in that it does not refute the subject's liberty and the dynamism of psychic life as open to continuous and lived-through re-interpretation of the past. In its maximalist version, the theory of trauma tends, I believe, to explain too many human and clinical phenomena. But most importantly, trauma-centrism warps the way the psychotherapist's role is perceived, placing them in a tradition of secular prophets under a scientific pretense.

Practicing psychotherapists have become accustomed to regard the ability to think and feel as belonging to a privileged few exceptional individuals who enjoyed fortuitous autobiographical or historical circumstances (Green, 1998). In any case, we live in a golden age of patients diagnosed with post-traumatic, dissociative and autistic spectrum diagnoses. The prevailing therapeutic discussion today emphasizes – in children as well as adults – the most archaic and deepest pathologies, early mental states and "white psychoses." One "byproduct" of this conversation is creating an almost absolute identification between early mental states and early mental trauma. In the imagination of the dynamic therapist, patients have all become infants neglected in the crib, or even before being born into the world, by an environment that misread their special needs. This discussion justifies itself by emphasizing various new therapeutic strategies. I sometimes read case reports submitted to my institute's training committee by junior analysts and wonder, where did all the neurotics go? Where are all the borderline and psychotic patients? Doesn't any patient ever come in with a symptom, hear interpretations, resist the transference for a bit, then a little less, react? I believe at this point that a certain theology is taking over the popular discourse and professional community, encouraging therapists to think of too many patients as empty husks, children who were raised in the lap of a "dead mother" (Green, 1983) or as "high functioning autistics." I have no objection to expanding the psychoanalytic field of view and scope of treatment, but I believe this trauma-centrism is at the expense of patients who can definitely use interpretations but are not receiving them. Even patients with deep psychopathologies are not fetuses. Just as no patient is completely psychotic, there is never a "pure" injury – patients have injured parts and neurotic parts. Even a patient diagnosed with chronic schizophrenia has a part of their ego outside the psychotic order, observing the psychosis from the outside. Much of our analytic knowledge originates in treatments of psychotics with whom analytic work has been done – starting with the Wolf Man, who was a low-functioning borderline when he came to Freud, and through the severely ill patients described by Bion, Riviere, Hanna Segal, Searls and Frieda Fromm-Reichmann. For this reason, I believe that trauma, post-trauma or dissociation are not "absolute contraindications" for interpretations. Dissociation is a relatively common defense mechanism. It is seen even in healthy neurotics who encounter a reality that causes unbearable physical and mental anguish. We see it in prisoners of war, concentration camp survivors and victims of torture. I encountered it recently in my work with survivors of the October 7 massacre of Israeli citizens by Hamas terrorists. We see it in complex grief situations and psychosomatic disorders, sometimes even in a bride or groom as they make their way down the aisle. Technology, the prevalence of screens and video games also influence the growing frequency of dissociative experiences in our younger patients. That doesn't mean we should avoid interpretations, but that we should learn how to offer interpretation in a way that our patient could use them to integrate splits rather than break apart. An experience of closeness and understanding can also flood patients and put them into a dissociative state. For some patients, anything in the analytic situation is "too much reality." Even the rumbling of the analyst's stomach or the murmur of the water running through the pipes unnerve them and stimulate the death drive, which turns against and attacks mental representations (Green, 1998).

I'm reminded of a patient who asked me, just before saying goodbye at the end of the hour, where she could find a certain bus line she needed. I gave her brief instructions on where to go. It almost ended in disaster. This concrete intervention I made in reality, the nonchalance in which I intervened in her life and told her which line to take, resulted in her being lost in the streets for hours. I learned the hard way that there are some things this patient simply can't accept from me, as a separate person, right now. With some patients, we would feel a stronger pressure to put numerous elements from our clinical experience into the theory, which might result in the experience of reinventing the theory, especially for them, or even "re-birthing them." It is completely fine that a therapist feels this way towards a severe patient they're dedicated to treating. I hope that the therapist will examine this special experience among other countertransference reactions the treatment invoked in them. Our concepts and structural terms, Paula Heimann once wrote to Theodore Reik, are "approximate landmarks, nothing more, much less the mind itself. When we navigate the seas on a designated route, this may well bring us to our destination. Yet in doing so, does that mean we know the whole ocean?" (Heimann Letter to Reik 7 February 1933 cited by Rolnik, 2005).

Hence, as a theory-loving analyst, I find it important to remind both you and myself: Not everything that works with a patient should find a concrete place in the theory, just as not anything that fails with a certain patient should be ejected from the theory, to serve as the cornerstone for a new one. With any patient, use what works with them, but remember that this pragmatic stance doesn't mean you have a new theory of psychoanalysis or that the specific patient is a rare breed for whom the entire theory has to be reinvented. Therapists who use a different approach would almost certainly have given your patient something you don't know how to give them, and the patient would have used that, too. It may even be that what the patient is unable to receive and utilize from one therapist, they would be willing to receive from another. It sometimes happens in a clinical discussion that a therapist justifies acting out in the countertransference by saying, "Even Freud gave his patients advice and presents, not only interpretations. Even he fed the hungry Rat Man." Well, if you don't accept the recommendation to avoid satisfying the patient, you are welcome to offer your patients coffee. I believe that in most cases, it would stand in their way of using you, but most of all, I want to emphasize that deliberating the question of whether or not to give the patient advice and coffee engages with a small, rather fringe part of Freud's, or any other serious analyst's, theory.

I would like to bring into our discussion John Steiner's distinction between interpretations that focus on the patient's experience of what is happening in the therapist's mind to ones focused on what the analyst thinks is taking place in the patient's mind (Steiner, 1994). In complete agreement with Steiner, I believe we should incorporate both kinds of interpretations. We combine "therapist-centered interpretations" with "patient-centered interpretations" in order to produce a motion between "understanding" and "being understood." This technique works particularly well with the kind of patients Steiner taught us to identify: Those trapped in a psychic retreat.

Therapist-focused interpretations are ones of the form "you're experiencing me like this" or "you're anxious of me being like that" – they give the patient the feeling that they are understood. This notion corresponds with Betty Joseph's (1983) paper *Understanding and not Understanding*. Alongside those, there are also patient-centered interpretations: "You're trying to make me feel," or "You're anxious now because you attacked me." These are patient-focused interpretations, which some patients would not be able to bear or would not be able to use in one stage of the therapy or another. The issue can be linked to the patient's movement between a depressive and a schizo-paranoid position within the hour, but it doesn't have to be. While the patient is controlled by a pathological mental organization and entrenched inside the primitive defenses that the psychic retreat offers them, they are unable to receive interpretations that are heard or experienced, as if the therapist is blaming the patient for being so captivated. This is also related to the difficult relationship certain patients' super-egos have with their egos, which makes it difficult for them to remain in a depressive position – without which the analysis cannot proceed. Remember that for a number of key psychoanalytic concepts, a large chasm separates how much we like them and how much the patients dislike them. The concept of *omnipotence*, detested by most patients, is one of them.

Contemporary Kleinians have their own way of expressing some reservations about traditional Kleinian interpretations from the first half of the 20th century. They do so by distinguishing between patients for whom interpretations of the attack on the object are desirable and those with whom that interpretative line is best kept to a minimum. The pioneering work in identifying these patients was done by Herbert Rosenfeld in his seminal paper on narcissism, read for the first time at the 1977 International Psychoanalytic Association Conference in Jerusalem. Rosenfeld described patients who can't bear interpretations that refer to omnipotence, attacks and the death drive because they only enhance the same death drive and omnipotence (Rosenfeld, 1978).

I think that . . .

With some patients, it's best to avoid the phrasing "I think that . . ." They need to receive the interpretation as if from within. If there aren't two people in the treatment room yet, the therapist better avoid speaking of themselves in the first person. If the patient is missing the degree of separateness required to use an interpretation that emphasizes the mental separateness of the therapist, forcing this recognition prematurely is unproductive. We use the word "I," but saying "I think that . . ." sounds to me too difficult for a psychotic patient to process mentally. Psychotherapy of borderline or psychotic patients has long stretches where the treatment room is inhabited not by two people but by one, with another inside them.

I will use the example of a borderline patient. At the onset of analysis, she is regressing in the worst way imaginable: She sleeps on the floor, doesn't shower or use the toilet, but washes herself in a large pail and collects her excrement in plastic containers. During the hour, she speaks constantly. She evacuates through speech. Suddenly, I sneeze. She says, "You just thrown me out of here," gets up and walks away. Me sneezing is perceived as a traumatic severance of the merger between her and the object. While she speaks, she is inside me, evacuating the products of her unbearable mental activity into me, just like a fetus in the womb. Hanna Segal (2007) might have said that the patient has fallen into the "symbolic equation" as a reaction to my sneezing. Because if she's inside me, and I sneeze, then in her fantasy, the container she evacuates into exploded and she is blown out of the room with everything that was in it. And that was what she did. Got up and left. I learned then that with a patient in that state, it is not advisable to say, "I think that," or "I heard you telling me that . . ." It is true that no one is completely psychotic all the time, not even the most injured schizophrenic patient, so patients usually "forgive" us for talking to the wrong level. But we want to be in touch with the level from which they communicate with us right now, not "bump" them to a higher level, even if the higher level, or the depressive position, partially exists within their mind.

Just a moment ago, I suggested that we should not be afraid of suggesting interpretations to patients who experienced early trauma. I also said that post-traumatic patients are not fetuses. And now, I advise you not to direct the interpretation to the higher levels but to search for the lowest level from which the patient communicates with you. Is my technique inconsistent? Perhaps. But that is how I understand psychoanalysis. I find it rather rare that our preferred theoretical perspective is absolutely consistent with the clinical theory that guides us within any therapeutic hour.

When I want to stay in the depths, I attempt to speak "psychotic," i.e., speak as if I'm inside the patient's head. If I think that my very regressed patient can make use of a "neurotic interpretation," I will offer them one, even if it may trigger their dissociation. In the case of the borderline patient from the previous example, I sometimes do one and other times the other. At the beginning of the analysis, when the schizo-paranoid position was dominant in the transference, I talked to her as if I were inside her head. If she had been lying on the couch for a long time, saying nothing, and I could already hear the oncoming thunderstorm of her breaking down – it was a matter of minutes before something in what I said or didn't say or some noise from the street, would drop her into the "symbolic equation" and make her storm out of the room – I might say, "You weren't here on Monday and I hated you, and now when I'm lying here I'm scared that if I talk my anger would bubble up, flood everything and kill you." I would speak her thoughts, or at least what I imagined was happening in her fantasy while she was on the couch. Another difficult patient, who is now much closer to a depressive position despite his difficulties in mentalizing, wouldn't stand me talking to him that way. It would sound intrusive and pretentious to him. With him, I would try to use the third person when he is entrenched inside a long silence after a week's break in therapy: "I guess you don't have the good analyst here today, only the horrible one who wasn't there when you needed him."

With normal neurotics, we're not as preoccupied with these types of deliberations. The movements between positions or between the neurotic and psychotic regions are more subtle, and we just sit and talk to them, like I'm talking to you right now, even though I know that while you're watching the screen and listening to me, you're also somewhat dreamy and the degree to which each of you is separated from me and your internal object is not uniform, but in constant flux.

Therapists learn to use the patient's words, their language. They speak about their friend David, and you, in your intervention, also say, "David." I'm not convinced that's always the right thing. I would sometimes use "your wife" or "your daughter" when talking to a patient, even though I know their names, even though the patient calls them by their names. This preference can have many reasons: I might think it's better that I place myself at a different distance from the object than the patient. I might feel that my intervention would have more weight if I give it a slightly higher level of abstraction or generalization: "Your wife," "the children." Think of it as plating a dish. The same interpretation served differently. The principle of adapting ourselves to the patient's linguistic range and repeating their words is all well and good, but there are times when it's best avoided. The perverse patient would drag you to speaking in graphic terms about their sexual practices because they need enactment of the perversion even in the treatment room. They yearn to hear their therapist saying, "Fuck them in the ass." They're excited to hear you repeating graphic descriptions of the sexual deeds they tell you about.

You should interpret that to them. It's no small feat to get a perverse patient to start sparing you some of the details of their sex life. It signals that the patient can start to contain the enigma of sexuality and intimacy they experience with their partner or that they don't need the fantasy of you being as excited as they are about the descriptions of what takes place in the BDSM clubs or "massage parlors" they frequent. When building the interpretation and adapting it to the linguistic structure of the patient or the position the patient is in, we sometimes have to make exceptions in our language and our use of it.

The couch

The analytic couch works in mysterious ways. We sometimes meet people who, in terms of intelligence, curiosity and ego strength, seem like excellent candidates for analytic therapy. Yet, once they recline on the therapy couch, we start regretting we ever offered they use it. The analytic couch and its place in the clinic can also be regarded from a historical point of view: Like numerous other scientific discoveries, the road to many of Freud's insights was paved by almost accidental discoveries. While the Oedipal complex Freud discovered by analyzing his own dreams, he would have never discovered psychoanalysis without treating numerous people reclining on a divan in his clinic. As early as 1898, he treated ten people every day, all reclining. Some things can only surface and be experienced while reclining. There is something about lying down – the relative physical relaxation it allows, the lack of a focused look, the release from the visual image – that stirs up the residents of the bottom levels, these "half-tamed demons," as Freud called them. Therapists often complain that sexuality disappears from their clinics. Well, where there's a couch, sexuality would very quickly find its way to speech. At times, it is enough that an analytic couch be present in the room to create a therapeutic space that has the potential to delve deeper, even for those patients who don't use it but rather sit. Reclining on a couch – perhaps to a larger extent than the "fundamental rule" itself – promotes associations from the regions of infantile sexuality. If you want to see how a patient contains anxiety, what they do with transference, in what ways and to what extent they defend themselves against it, how predilected they are to act out or how they manage the setting, suggest that they use the couch for three months, and see if it works. Some patients find it hard to lie down. Some would leave, at first, one foot on the floor as a kind of symbolic "grounding," thereby regulating the anxiety that rises when lying. For some patients, not lying on the couch but rather getting up at the end of the hour would expose them to significant emotional flooding. Some need to linger on the couch, some look for the analyst's eyes before departing and some prefer that we let them get up and leave without looking us in the eyes or saying anything (Ogden, 1996).

Regarding the use of the couch by therapists who are not trained psychoanalysts – this would undoubtedly strike you as formalistic, but I don't recommend that psychotherapists who lack psychoanalytic training treat patients on the couch. Psychoanalysis is not just a body of knowledge. The analytical praxis takes place in relation to certain historical structures and signifiers, such as "psychoanalytic train-ing," "psychoanalytic institute" and even "International Psychoanalytic Associa-tion." An analytic training and analytic institute can be seen as providing the setting for the analytic setting. They fulfill a significant role in the analyst's unconscious as a third, whether the analyst identifies with them at one point or another in their career and whether they have mostly bad things to say about them. A technique of using the couch once or twice weekly is also problematic, in my experience – in particular for patients who did not experience high-frequency analysis beforehand – since lying down supports the development of regression and strong transference on the one hand, and on the other, the setting doesn't meet the needs of contain-ment and holding when they arise very powerfully. In any case, I believe that today, the problem is reversed: Even certified analysts seem to prefer to hold sessions on chairs. Even analysts are afraid of psychoanalyzing.

Note

1 An English translation, by Yael Lotan, is available in Joseph. D. (Ed.). (2002). *The Heart and the Fountain* (pp. 255–261). New York: Oxford.

Chapter 10

The carp of truth

On listening to associations as we do to dreams, and on discussing countertransference as a form of worship. On the therapists' esprit de l'escalier. On interpretation as an action, on enigmatic interpretations, on the patient who thinks their analyst is a genius, and why do patients ask us to repeat what we just said?

I want to open with a passage from a 1939 paper by Susan Isaacs, which is both beautifully written and enlightening. It reminded me of how simply and touchingly therapists used to write, even in years when the world around them entered an existential crisis:

> We find ourselves evaluating directly, by unconscious process, his [the patient's, E.R.] mood, his affect, his attitude to ourselves. If our own minds are working freely so that we are alive and sensitive to the transference situation, not inhibited in our memory and our judgement of the present material or of the patient as a whole, if we can identify ourselves with the patient, with the whole patient, but not too closely or automatically with the particular facet he is presenting at the moment, the meaning of his words and conduct becomes plain to us. Exactly in the same way as the patient's associations to the manifest content of the dream, bringing up new thoughts, new memories, new affect, new phantasies, break down the manifest content into apparently disconnected fragments and then rebuild these into a very different whole of dynamic significance, so does the material of the whole hour, or whole phase of analysis, yield fragments of meaning, of past and present significance which, as the hour or whole period unfolds, gradually form themselves into a new and more deeply significant whole. Sometimes it is a single remark revealing a specific phantasy or memory or attitude of mind, a single comment on a real situation, which gives the meaning to every detail of what has gone before, all the rest of the material then falling into place and becoming an intelligible whole. Sometimes this emergence of meaning is a gradual and cumulative process.
>
> (Isaacs, 1939)

Isaacs remains faithful to the Freudian tradition here. She puts emphasis on the relationship between the act of interpreting the patient's speech, their mannerisms

DOI: 10.4324/9781003528470-10

and behavior and the interpretation of dreams. As mentioned, the basic model of an intervention in a therapeutic hour is that of interpretation of dreams. That is how it was perceived on the eve of the Second World War, and one can only wonder why this cornerstone of classical Freudian analysis, which has been repeatedly lost and re-found, is celebrated in contemporary psychoanalysis as "post-Freudian" or "Bionian," or even implicitly accredited to relational and intersubjective theory. Free associations promote transference, which also contributes to maintaining the dream-like state of consciousness the patient is in. In a good analytic hour, the patient comes closer, mentally, to the state they are in when dreaming. We can, therefore, draw a comparison between the analytic hour and a dream, something told more or less fluently, something the patient is reminded of gradually, that is gradually unrolled while the patient moves forward and backward in time, just like in a dream. What might differentiate the dream from an analytic hour is the role played by resistance. In dreaming, resistance takes part in forming the dream without the patient being aware of its action. Consequently, the dream is being dreamed freely unless the dream-work fails to neutralize the anxiety. In contrast, during the analytic hour, the resistance is very present in the patient's experience, leading them to filter what they say or don't say or stray away from the anxiety-provoking thought. If the therapist is in a state of "evenly-suspended attention," they are closer to a good interpretative position, one that constantly "adjusts the shutter." some therapists would use expositions: "I'm telling you this because in what you just said I heard that . . .," or "Maybe what you are saying to me now is . . .," thereby attempting to make the patient part of the process of preparing the interpretation they are about to offer them. They don't quietly produce some intervention and serve it, peeled and diced, to the patient, but show the patient how they cut, mix, season and serve their ideas.

Whether working with a clean pharmaceutical technique or a more "dirty" one, a sort of "open kitchen" for the patient, I still think there is a similarity between working on a dream and an interpretative work that holds the tension between wanting to interpret correctly – believing that there is such a thing as a correct interpretation – and being willing to make mistakes and contain a large degree of uncertainty even after interpreting. Just like the dream you might have analyzed beautifully today, it could also lend itself to another interpretation later this week.

As mentioned, a patient's reaction and the continuous unfolding of their speech are the criteria by which we distinguish a good interpretation from a mediocre one. Having offered a tentative interpretation of a dream element, if the patient suddenly remembers another detail, we are on the right path. The opposite can also happen: We offer something good and feel the patient responding with an increased resistance to working on the dream. Isaacs tells us something more; she explains that the birth of the interpretation in the therapist's mind has always been a process: "We find ourselves evaluating directly, by unconscious process." That is, we lend ourselves to listening as impartially as we can and trust that at a certain point, our mind will produce in us, through primary thinking, an idea that is worth sharing with the patient. At another point, we can suddenly feel a lack of thought, emptiness or boredom, as an expression of an unconscious happening. Trapped aggression, for example, can be experienced as a cognitive vacuum since it attacks and shatters the internal objects' representation.

During the second half of the previous century, we started noticing the countertransference as a source of knowledge on the patient. But some countertransference is obstructive, destructive. It prevents listening and blinds us to a certain aspect of the patient's material or personality. In both Freud and Klein, the concept of countertransference had a negative connotation. Certainly, the therapist transfers to the patient – it is their duty to identify that and do something with it. Isaacs discusses that in the paper, which is why I say we should also pay some attention to the negative connotations the countertransference can have. Today, we all preach "countertransference working-through" and processing, and rightly so, to a large extent. But clinical discussions made through the prism of the countertransference sometimes also have a protective, narcissist, even kitschy quality: "I wonder why I can't love your patient," a participant in a clinical seminar complains to the analysts presenting a case.

Isaacs certainly has an ideal of the analytical therapist as an interpreter who strives to be free. The aim is to be equally open to receiving frequencies, messages and other modes of communication from the patient. In the words of Anna Freud, we should place ourselves at an "equal distance" from the patient's ego, superego and id without rushing to prefer one kind of communication, a certain aspect of speech, over others. It is not enough that we be patient; we should have years of successful personal therapy to allow us to sit quietly. Not for nothing, we wait patiently, either because we have nothing to say or because we haven't understood yet; we are waiting because we learned that the correct conjecture comes to us by itself. It may not come fully; it may come warped, but we can't "induce birth." The better and deeper our familiarity with the patient is, the easier it might be for us to identify a certain transference configuration: We can already catch the projections as they fly through the room; no special effort is required to identify how the patient activates us. We are familiar with the field and already have a few interpretations "at stand-by," even a private "secret language" with a long-time patient that allows us to use code words and avoid lengthy interpretations. With such patients, I can ask: "What do you think happened to you here yesterday that made you go back and cast brown-shirt Nazis in your dream tonight?" To be able to speak like that to a patient about a regression in their mode of dreaming, we need long years of familiarity and trust in the analytic process as a partner in the formation of the dream. However, this is precisely where the new material is often hidden – inside the plowed field, inside the sadomasochistic fantasies repeated ad-nauseam, inside your repetitive back-and-forth with a patient who habitually drones about their boss, in the recurring dream of the statistics professor about failing a math exam in high school. This is precisely where some word, some undertone in the transference, will be hidden and these are the real pulse, the heart of unconscious communication.

During the hour, the patient can say myriad things. As far as the unconscious system is concerned, they will usually mention one, maybe two, central points. We have 50 minutes to find this "Ariadne's thread" that runs through the session. That's quite a lot of time. We don't have to regard the patient as if their speech constantly lays golden eggs while we chase it, trying to find the treasure and declare it found.

It also happens – this strange phenomenon always interested me – that only at the end of the last hour of the week, as we walk the patient to the door, we suddenly understand what the poor soul was trying to tell us all this time. Something similar happens in early births, where dilation started but no contractions were felt and just after the doctor decides to discharge the pregnant woman, as she gets up to leave, labor starts. Something in the motor movement, perhaps enabled by the oncoming separation, extracts some thought that was "lodged" and couldn't be verbalized. We then get an *esprit de l'escalier* – one minute before, or maybe after, we say goodbye, we suddenly realize what happened.

There are times we can share it with the patient, even while standing by the door, and sometimes, as problematic as it is to part with a patient that way, it's better to do so. I keep it as an option and would sometimes prefer to say something rather than end the hour with a feeling I didn't give off any life signs. After all, some patients would say the most important things only when they enter the room or leave it. Freud discusses them in his paper *On Beginning the Treatment.* He explains they are trying to create an extra-analytical "cordon sanitaire" and recommends that such instances be treated as if they were said from the couch. These "last words" are saved for the hour's end to keep them out of the therapeutic process and to render the therapist impotent and unable to respond. However, we can bring these comments into the following hour as the focus of much productive work (Gabbard, 1982). Perhaps having the understanding dawn on a therapist only after the patient gets ready to leave is also an expression of the therapist's own resistance to understanding or interpreting.

I'm interested in examining when young therapists are threatened by talking to patients in a lengthy, detailed manner. The problem with the interpretations I hear from young therapists – and this is obviously also a matter of personal preference and style – is not that they are "inaccurate" but that they are overly sophisticated, too curtly phrased and too rushed. Like a quick pinch. I prefer an interpretation or intervention that is a continuous, ponderous verbal movement, like pushing a refrigerator or a heavy piece of furniture. It is a prolonged push, not a short one, and when it is over, thought should continue moving on its own. My interpretations are usually a rather long movement. I think they are more useful for most patients than a quick and sharp ping-pong strike. I know some brilliant, enigmatic therapists speak like the Delphic oracle. But I suspect their interpretations sound better written down, particularly in French, than they sound in real life.

Following Isaacs's words, dynamic psychotherapists are trained on the distinction between content and process when identifying the therapeutic occurrence, between what is happening and what is being said. I think that the content-process distinction, its value notwithstanding, can show itself to be problematic from a psychoanalytic point of view. If we really are attentive to the process and seek ways to direct our interventions to a certain mental form of functioning or the predominant unconscious fantasy operating within the patients' mind or whose existence they disavow, then the division between content and process is much more complex. It might, therefore, be better to discuss a continuous movement of listening – between content, tone, words and music, to emphasize the process, what Betty Joseph termed the "total situation."

There are times when some small detail in the speech, one word or physical gesture, helps us understand what is taking place in the process. Sometimes, the content hides the key to understanding the process. I think, in this context, of the patient whose analysis was accompanied by an intensive fanning. Alongside her repeated complaint, "God, it's so hot in here," I learned to listen to the strokes of her fan as a rather complex counter-point to the occurrence in the transference.

Other times, it's the opposite action we have to take: Let go of the tiny details and verbal noise and move to a "lower level" – also an expression by Betty Joseph – to find the pulse of the analytic hour. I want to offer you an image from the field of medicine: You might know that when a physician measures a patient's pulse, they never use their thumb to avoid measuring their own pulse by mistake. The same is true for a therapeutic hour. As mentioned, it is sometimes worthwhile to bring to a consultation or a clinical seminar our "easiest" or "favorite" patient, the ones we particularly identify with. Those are precisely the ones with whom we are a little too involved, the ones with whom we are most likely to measure the wrong "pulse" when trying to understand what takes place in the patient's inner world.

Interpreting is important not only because it advances the analytic process. Not interpreting is wrong and even harmful. If you only let the patient's words disappear into the air and find it difficult, for some reason, to "put yourself out there" and interpret, there is a possibility the patient will experience you as not wishing to understand them. That may make them act out something outside the analytic hour. If the patient starts behaving somewhat oddly outside of treatment, they may be reacting to a lack of interpretations. When free associations are not met with the therapist's words, they can create serious pressure for acting out. An interpretation – right or wrong – binds to itself the energy released from the id. It produces a movement in the psyche, brings up memories and expands the range of the experience. Even when it is hard to process and not directed at calming, an interpretation would change something in the transferential configuration. Successful transference interpretation would certainly change the image of the analyst from a persecutory or disapproving object to a benevolent, compassionate and nurturing one. The patient transmits – certainly in intensive psychotherapy, but also in standard dynamic one. Even if you think they are not working very seriously, they came in for treatment, they brought their unconscious, or "inner child," and fantasies to treatment and they invest their id energy in you, even if they don't show it heavily in transference. If all the psychic investment done by the patient's inner world doesn't meet an interpreting therapist who doesn't only block the development of the fantasy or slows the therapy, it produces anxiety, it builds a dam. Some patients are intolerant of that state and stop treatment. You rack your brain trying to understand what went wrong, what flew under your radar. The explanation may be simpler than it sounds from the mouth of a patient who provides various explanations of their decision to forego therapy. Maybe you should have made an effort and offered the patient interpretations that would keep them in therapy – not interpretations directed explicitly at the resistance to therapy and the will to stop it. Patients tell us they leave us, so we start aiming at their legs, furiously interpreting their "fear of change." Don't be quick to interpret the will to leave therapy as evidence of "fear of change." Most people seek therapy because some symptom or defensive organization stopped fulfilling its role and no longer protects them from anxiety or psychic pain. The will for a change and anxiety or guilt brought about by change – the so-called *negative therapeutic reaction* – appears in much later stages of the work when the patient is required to exchange the old status quo for a new one. I believe it is better to recap, formulate and interpret what happened three hours ago when the patient still wanted to be in therapy. If you don't interpret it as "resistance to treatment," there may still be a chance to repair your working alliance with your patient. And in any case, it is best to remember: Unconsciously, patients want and love to be in treatment, and they are aided by it even as they complain about the therapist's shortcomings, even when they deliberate vocally on their desire to stop treatment and even when they resist treatment and skip some sessions. Naturally, dynamic therapists have expertise in identifying defenses and are very alert to any display of resistance to therapy, but therapists also have a tendency to listen and react too concretely or forcefully to a patient who expresses their wish to stop treatment or reduce frequency. I don't suggest you ignore everything you learned on the importance of providing an interpretation to resistance to treatment, but I also recommend that you listen to that silenced and embarrassed part of the patient that is interested in the therapy and try to communicate with it to the very last moment.

When treating children, you can clearly see how much credit they are willing to give you. Children can remember forever that you "owe them" an interpretation. You can tell a child, "So, before you went on vacation with mom and dad, you told me this or that, you wanted to tell me this other thing. And now I think I understand what you felt then . . ." and the child lights up, you can see how grateful they are that you remembered something that happened to them last week and didn't discuss and that you're still thinking of what they have been through and trying to understand them. With adults, too, we can, and sometimes should, give "late interpretations," outside the transference, about things that happened in therapy inside the room last week or two weeks ago.

We now continue to Betty Joseph's 1983 *Understanding and Not Understanding*. It is not a recent paper but one that is part of a different era of the psychoanalytic conversation. We will use it mainly as an opportunity to think about the relation between interpretation and action:

All of us, I assume, have had the experience at times of listening to our patients, believing we understood the material and its unconscious meaning, its symbolic content, only to find that our subsequent interpretations seem to fall flat, or that we are getting bored in the middle of an interpretation. If I am bored I stop, assuming I am talking about material but not to the patient. This highlights a point, which in a sense is only too obvious, that analysis to be useful must be an experience, in contrast, for example, to the giving of understanding or explaining.

It also helps to clarify an issue often raised in discussion on technique – does one interpret only in the transference, or also about other areas of the patient's life? I don't think it is only/or, but rather whether one can focus one's understanding and therefore interpretations on what is being lived and experienced.

(Joseph, 1983)

As the paper progresses, Joseph presents two clinical cases and concludes:

The analyst, in order to understand, has to tune in to the patient's wavelength, which is a wavelength of action rather than words, though words may be used. All these patients are, to a great extent, using projective identification, either as a method of communication to achieve understanding on a deep nonverbal level, or to maintain their balance, in which case they are not interested in, or are inimical to, understanding as we understand it. If we approach such patients with the notion that they want us to give them real insight, we lose touch with the patient as such, and in any case much that these patients are conveying and projecting will still be beyond our understanding.

(Joseph, 1983)

These lines offer a very useful theoretical and clinical "oxymoron" because they encourage interpreting while, at the same time, warn us against the inadequacy of interpretation, sometimes encompassed in the very invitation to do so: While the patient may have talked and talked, for them, words are actions. This is a patient not in a depressive position, so not only can they not understand what we are telling them, but their whole communication aims, through projective identification, to invite action. We spoke, but not really, to the mental regions they deny and have difficulties with, which are where the problem in mental development and functioning is.

I have no doubt that this maxim raised, and will continue to raise, controversy. We will often deliberate what patient we are really treating. Is it a patient whose words cannot be interpreted, and we should rather interpret the enactment in their words? Either way, we regard the act of interpretation on an additional level, being sensitive not only to the structure but also to the constant movement within the hour between various levels of mental functioning. The interpretation can be formally correct but not speak to the right "level" from which the patient is speaking to us right now.

I remember an analysis where I took too long to identify that something peculiar was taking place. Often, the hour would start with a beautiful, clear and enlightening dream. The patient could interpret those dreams as well as I could. We worked on them together, like a trained pair of acrobats. And then the hour would suddenly die. Instead of the good work made with the dream serving as an opening chord for a good analytic hour, what repeated was an architecture in which the first ten minutes, which seemed very good and analytically rewarding, were followed by 40 minutes of deep, frozen wasteland. He would continue to talk, but to me, it would be exhausting, as if the analysis of the dream was a kind of "idolatry." Through the dream, a part of him communicated something symbolic that could be verbalized, conceptualized and interpreted, but at the lower level, an undeveloped child was left out of our conversation.

The bait of lie

In his paper *Constructions in Analysis* (Freud 1937), Freud discusses the presentation of a false construction. He wonders – when considering the question of how to validate an interpretation – whether the patient's "yes" or "no" is the measure of the quality and validity of the interpretation. He believes no disaster would happen if we made a mistake in interpretation or construction. These are dismissed as if they were never said, and at times, we may even get the impression that "our bait of falsehood had taken a carp of truth" (*Standard Edition*, vol. 14, p. 262). In other words, an incorrect interpretation has value. It brings us closer to the truth. Psychoanalytic literature often discusses mistaken interpretations or imprecise interventions. We should distinguish partial interpretations – which are, fortunately, most of our interpretations – from ones that are plainly wrong. I think that a wrong interpretation achieves its aim mainly by reminding the patient of the limits of the therapist's understanding. It bursts the fantasy of the all-knowing therapist, and I would even say the fantasy of the therapist who can understand everything without the patient telling them anything – a dyadic merger fantasy that I need only recline on the couch for the therapist to understand me. At times, the fantasy is even more detailed: The patient fantasizes how the therapist enters into them – either frontally or from behind – or directly into their mind, where they gain access to all the files in their head.

Detectives and police interrogators use the same technique: They start by describing something completely absurd to the suspect, confronting them with some evidence, completely unrelated to them, from the crime scene – and the suspect is put at ease and unwittingly gives away some detail they had better not divulge, thereby giving the detective a new line of inquiry they hadn't even thought about. You shouldn't pretend or play dumb, but it's better that the patients think you're a tad bit less witty and clever than you really are (don't worry, they mostly think so anyway). The patient who thinks their therapist is a genius is, I believe, in a less advantageous position for meaningful therapy than the one who thinks their therapist is fine, perhaps a bit wooden. Some patients would immediately pump, through projective identification, their idealization of the wonderful therapist you aspire to be, which fuels your narcissism but also blocks the possibility of getting to know the patient. Those willing to learn from the early analysts would find they used rather simple language and sentences to talk to their patients. They didn't feel the need to show they understand wordlessly, can read minds or have a brilliant sense of humor; they didn't cite poetry or recommend shows and movies to their patients. Brilliant analysts entice the "gifted" areas in a patient at the expense of the ineloquent or less developed parts. A witty and overly clever therapist would recreate in the patient a fundamental experience of an excited little boy who can't understand the adult world. In this sense, a therapist who makes mistakes and lives peacefully with the limits of their own understanding is also a therapist who reduces stress and resistance. The unconscious also feels more relaxed in their presence. It's okay to tell a patient, "I might have misunderstood you, but I think I heard you say this and that"; it's a way to get their cooperation.

If the patient takes the misinterpretation and uses it to displace their neurosis from a region of psychic pain to a region they are more comfortable with, they would, in fact, be using our mistake subversively. They say "yes, yes," "right, right," and unconsciously go a considerable way with the suggestion. They are more influenced by the suggestion, like a hypnosis patient. Patients can find various uses for a misinterpretation we offer them. This has to do with the relations the patient has with the truth, and relations with the psychic truth are never strictly "utilitarian." At times, the very acceptance of a correct interpretation would raise resistance, even if the truth encompassed in the interpretation does not seem to cause the patient envy or psychic pain that is really difficult for them to withstand. A patient may reject an interpretation that can relieve the burden of guilt they carry with them for many years because it undermines some masochistic status quo their personality was organized around. The patient's masochism – and let us not forget that it is masochism that helps us bear the pains of living – can also take part in their extraordinary willingness to accept a wrong interpretation. Some people would eat everything you put on their plate, only to say later, "I didn't like that too much." There is a whole world of unconscious fantasies and wishes in people's willingness to accept a bad interpretation or prefer poor treatment in general.

Any interpretation, any interpretative position, must have a measure of commitment, even stubbornness. Our job is a difficult one. No one would wait for you to give a good interpretation or cheer for you after you have given one. To interpret is to knead and till and process over and over and over again. Paradoxically, it is talented interpreters who tend not to let go. They chase the patient's associations, taking their beautiful interpretation up to their front door, and for all their effort, reap only grief. An interpretation should be allowed to skip over the surface a few times, even sink; it should be left in the patient's pocket without too much noise and fanfare. If we keep on flourishing the interpretation, we don't really hear the reaction. We need some silence after the intervention to see what we changed in the structure, the speech, the architecture, the tone. If we are captivated, we become captives of our words (and we do sometimes get a little euphoric when speaking, we too are enlivened by the interpretations we suggest, we see the light, want to add just one little thing, another small thought, another brushstroke and we suddenly can't shut up) – we end up choking the interpretation, bringing the intervention to a too-saturated level, and damaging its ability to be absorbed.

An interpretation is meant to unsettle. It's not really the last piece of the puzzle. It is supposed to undermine the status quo and rattle the internal structure without collapsing it. If we don't listen, don't "take rebounds" – we lose a good interpretation. We lose the movement it could have created. Some patients would know how to press us into this sort of compulsiveness – "Say that again, I didn't understand," "Can you repeat that?" "Wait, what did you say earlier?" "No, no. What you said before, because that was interesting." "No, that word you said I didn't understand, the one before." That's resistance that is deserving of its own interpretation. Our patients attack the link that our interpretation is trying to offer them. They might be suddenly busy with the question of "Where does milk come from?" and instead of accepting the products of our mind – our interpretations, our insights – use them to think and feel, experience some sorrow and even gratitude – they find it difficult to accept from you something they can't give themselves.

Chapter 11

The psychoanalytic object

What therapeutic praxis embodies other than the therapist's theory and technique. Internalized object relations and the therapist's unconscious fantasies regarding psychoanalysis itself. What is our analytic identity composed of, and what is often exposed in a clinical seminar? Of patients accusing us that we love psychoanalysis more than we love them. How is analytic skepticism different from philosophical skepticism, why is psychoanalysis a science that does not forget its past, and what does that have to do with the neurotic relation a therapist can have to Freud? Through the concept of an "internal psychoanalytic object," even the eternal question of "What is psychoanalysis?" becomes a little less scholastic.

In describing his discoveries and the role of the analytic therapist, Freud made ample use of metaphors and imagery. Very early in his work, he discusses the psychic mechanism as a translating mechanism and the analyst as a translator of a kind. Then appears the metaphor of the analyst as an archeologist. Later still, in his *Papers on Technique*, we find a surprising analogy between the analyst and the surgeon, one that makes contemporary analysts shift uncomfortably in their chairs. I believe a fair amount of inspiration can be gained from the surgical imagery that permeates Freud's technical writing. Elsewhere, we find Freud describing an analyst as a tour guide. In *The Question of Lay Analysis,* he equates the analyst with a 'secular pastor.'

Each such image is accompanied, either explicitly or implicitly, by technical recommendations and meta-psychological insights. The image of an analyst as an archeologist, for example, dovetails with the topographical model of the interpretation of dreams, with its positivist implications on the one hand and hermeneutic ones on the other. Equating analytic therapists to surgeons serves Freud in a double role: It situates the analyst as deserving of a respectable social status; it also indicates a certain ethical position. A surgeon is an esteemed professional fulfilling a vital role and is widely accepted as deserving of a generous fee. Freud reminds us that the analyst, just as the surgeon, should not be embarrassed to require a high fee for performing difficult and useful work. The imagery of the surgeon is also meant to echo the composure and impartiality, an objective position towards a patient that should be adopted by the therapist. Psychoanalytic therapy is similar to the

DOI: 10.4324/9781003528470-11

surgical one in the sense that it requires a therapeutic position that is different from that taken by doctors who contend themselves with a cosmetic change – meaning therapists who make use of hypnosis or suggestion to remove a physical or mental symptom (Rolnik, 2015). In the second series of his *Introductory Lectures on Psychoanalysis*, Freud slips an interesting imagery and additional criterion to the controversy on the nature of analytic activity and analytic identity:

> Psychoanalytic activity is arduous and exacting; it cannot well be handled like a pair of glasses that one puts on for reading and takes off when one goes for a walk. As a rule psycho-analysis possesses a doctor either entirely or not at all.
>
> (Freud, *Standard Edition*, vol. 22, pp. 152–153)

Reading glasses are not directly linked to any particular psychic model or clear clinical position. Freud uses the imagery of a pair of glasses as if imagining psychoanalysis to be sitting at the end of the physician's nose. He then promptly denies this notion, declaring it inadequate for understanding the nature of a proper professional analytic identity. It is a criterion concerned with the therapist's level of adherence, or devotion, to the analytic point of view. To use everyday terms: The therapist's love of psychoanalysis.

The notion that psychoanalysis takes over the therapist's whole personality is far from obvious, and I believe it is one that gradually informs Freud's entire oeuvre. Analysis must undergo a process of interiorization, whereby it metamorphoses from a practice to a subject position, from a technique to an ethics, from a *profession* to a *vocation*, from a partial function of the ego to a mental and personal state that takes over one's entire personality. I will also shortly argue that the analyst's relation to his discipline affects not only his conscious theoretical and clinical preferences, his "role perception," but also the place therapy will take in the patient's inner world. A point of view that sees psychoanalysis as not only a body of knowledge and collection of practices but also an internalized object complements the perception of psychoanalysis as not only a theory of knowledge or a therapeutic technique but also a worldview or ontology.

This point of view of psychoanalysis as an internal object justifies an examination of the process by which we form as therapists, as well as periodic monitoring of the internal psychoanalytic object throughout our professional lives and throughout the various analyses and treatments we perform.

When I seek the psychoanalytic object, I have to describe what it is composed of and explore how it was born and formed in me. Some therapists would fully admit that it had taken them many years to start feeling they were psychoanalysts. I encourage you to think about what makes up the "analytic thing," which I see as a full-fledged object rather than a diploma on my wall or some minimal codex of agreed-upon practices and norms.

An introspective position is certainly an inseparable part of the internal psychoanalytic object. It is a position that is simultaneously introspective and skeptical, or even ironic, towards the concept of introspection. There is a difference in essence between intelligent psychological or philosophical musings and psychoanalytic inquiry. The introspective position, in its analytic version, is skeptical even towards introspection, the motivation to introspection, and the nature of our relations as humans with knowledge in general.

Descartes, too, thought we should be skeptical about the nature of human knowledge. So did the Socratics and Platonists before him, as seen in the famous allegory of the cave. In later centuries, Emmanuel Kant, Henri Bergson and many others still struggled with the questions of knowledge, dream and self-knowledge. Not quite – the analyst deals with the internal object. In one letter, Freud confesses: "I am not an out-and-out skeptic. Of one thing I am absolutely positive: there are certain things we cannot know now" (Freud to Romain Rolland, January 19 1930). In some cases, the analyst is skeptical even towards their own patients' skepticism. The obsessive patient wants to cast doubt on anything. Their skepticism is revealed to be a defense, a fear of knowledge. Intellectual sophistication, even ambitious scientific activity, can be achieved in the service of intellectual inhibition or other form of neurosis rather than in service of a better understanding of ourselves and the world.

For patients, intellectual speech almost always serves to distance rather than grow closer. It's not that their musings are worthless; they have value, they may be philosophy or cultural critique of the highest level, and they may be a pleasure to hear, but we should be suspicious of, or at the very least question, any speech afflicted with generalizations and intellectualization within the hour. That is not the place for generalizations, popular as they may be with both scientists and philosophers. Take a patient of mine, a sophisticated and successful intellectual who habitually brings his dreams to therapy already cut to size, packaged and stamped – neatly delivered at my doorstep. There is no work left to be done on the dream; just open the boxes containing whatever associations he had to it upon waking, mix them in a large bowl and voilà, an instant interpreted dream. The patient understands that this is not what we are here for and obviously resists sharing his dreams with me because he doesn't believe I would have anything new to add. One day, he brought in one such neatly packaged, pre-dissected dream, whizzed through his associations to the dream components, and even topped it all off with a "fresh" association regarding an old tobacco pipe stand I have on my desk, which he noticed yesterday. "You see," he added, "no sense in wasting time with a Freudian analyst on a dream that has a pipe in it. It's all so transparent."

I suddenly felt pathetic. I felt that my patient was mocking me, and I told him that it sounded to me as if he was casting his associations to his dream before me like so many breadcrumbs before pigeons, that he was showing a condescending attitude towards the work we are trying to do together – "Here, take some associations, hope you're happy with them you old Freudian fart." I think it was the association with the old pipe that suggested this interpretation. And it reached the patient, who accepted the interpretation, its unpleasantness notwithstanding.

Psychoanalytic science investigates the relationship between objective knowledge and subjective experience. Investigating the subjective, fantasmatic or drive-derivative that is associated with knowledge allows the analyst to, for example, ascribe meaning to the distinction between the passion for knowing the object and the world in their full singularity and otherness. We help our patients distinguish between curiosity and an inquisitive stance vis-a-vis the world they inhabit and subversive voyeurism originating in infantile narcissism. This is why psychoanalytic research can contribute to the understanding of phenomena such as prejudice, learning disorders, or scientific "blind spots."

Complex relations with the nature of knowledge are, therefore, part of the analytic object. So is the faith that there exists a communicative process between the analyst and their patient. Analysts think that humans, from the moment of birth and perhaps even prior to it, communicate with the world through their unconscious. It is a tool that the baby uses when communicating with its mother, and it is a tool the analyst uses to understand the patient's unconscious. It is also a sophisticated tool through which the analysand sometimes disrupts their own mind in an attempt to avoid psychic pain and impair the therapist's ability to perceive it.

An internal psychoanalytic object also comprises relations with the analytic setting, seeing it as a good contractor for achieving knowledge of the unconscious and reaching internal change. Without the setting, no transformative analytic experience is possible. The love of truth also has a central place in the psychoanalytic object. This is not in the ideological or religious fundamentalist sense of "truth-seeking," but as part of an ongoing search for a psychic truth, we see as essential nourishment for growth and development. The psychoanalytic science also acknowledges the existence of a gap, a "lack," to use Lacan's term between what we want to know and what we are able to know. I believe that it is impossible to be an analytic therapist if all you want to do is help your patient shed their pain. A measure of psychic pain, anxiety and guilt is not only unavoidable but also a condition of healthy mental functioning that allows growth and creation.

Freudian psychoanalytic theory relates the internal psychoanalytic object, composed of the elements we just described, to the Oedipal complex and infantile sexuality as the building blocks of the internal world and the world of unconscious fantasy.

Analytic identity is composed of the mental representation psychoanalysis has within us and the way we internalize it, think about it and feel toward it – consciously and unconsciously. For every therapist, a long line of introjections and identifications would gradually become a psychic structure that is more than a collection of functions of the ego or super-ego. Therapists don't merely recite therapeutic strategies or memorize rules and algorithms. They internalize, through a very long process, introjections and identifications. The concept of an "analytic object" emphasizes the fact that these internalizations include a wide range of identifications (Wille, 2008). In fact, the internal analytic object's quality is determined, to a large extent, by the kind of identifications that took part in forming it. Like other object relations, the kind of relations we have with the internal object – that is, the form of identification with the object – is, at times, more important than the quality of the object in reality. The question of whether it is a narcissistic, hysteric, mimetic or adhesive identification, or perhaps a complex conflictual one, is of great significance. The answer would determine how the therapist experiences emotional-professional conflicts as they arise during the treatment. Do I understand that I have a conflict surrounding greed, surrounding aggression, surrounding sexuality? Can I feel greedy without *being* greedy? Or without berating myself for these emotions of envy and avarice arising in me when I'm stuck at an impasse with a patient? Is it enough that I have sufficient ego strength to obey my super-ego and suppress sexual desire as it arises during an analytic hour? Tell me, "You're such a terrible analyst for having sexual thoughts about a patient"? That doesn't amount to much for the internal analytic object. It would have much value if I could also feel it without acting on it, especially if I can be interested in the desires that arise in the analytic encounter and able to explore them. Only then is there value to identification with the rule that forbids crossing sexual boundaries between patient and therapist? In such a case, arousal of sexual attraction would not threaten the therapist (or their patients) but will be identified, first by the therapist and later also by the patient, as signifying knowledge and meaning and an opportunity to explore what is taking place in the inner world.

When we listen to analysts, when we read a scientific essay or a case study, we also absorb their relations with their internalized psychoanalytic object. Along with their training and professional life, psychoanalysis becomes an internal companion for therapists. Their relations with it become rich and complex. A psychoanalyst can love, hate, despise, fear or idealize the analytic object. In most cases, the emotional blend is varied and changing. At one point in their career, an analyst can love the hatred for the "enemies" of their psychoanalysis, legitimized by their love of psychoanalysis. At another point, they might hate a certain aspect of the analytic object they internalized sometime during their romance with psychoanalysis. An analyst can have conflicting loyalties to the various psychoanalytic schools they learned. They can feel remorse and guilt for adhering to certain theoretical positions or even turn their back on the whole of psychoanalysis as a sort of revenge or disappointment from its perceived betrayal of them. Worthwhile clinical seminars are meant to do more than introduce us to various and conflicting theoretical perspectives and approaches. Seminars light up these repressed, unconscious or split regions in their participants' relationships with the internalized analytic concept. We will take part in group supervision and think: "I never believed that's what a Kleinian interpretation sounds like. I always thought Kleinians interpret unconscious fantasies bluntly, and now I hear a therapist working with so much sensitivity, and I also feel that the patient feels understood." A whole world lights up in our internal psychoanalytic object in these clinical seminars.

Certainly, there will always be those who would not like to challenge their relations with the internal psychoanalytic object in any way. They will, metaphorically speaking, continue to pray at the same church and from the same hymn book.

Examining the internal analytic object from the patient's point of view is also quite useful. Patients are engaged with the question of what their therapist thinks and feels about them. But in any analysis, there is a moment where the patient is also interested in the therapist's relationship with psychoanalysis. At times, it appears in the patient's speech as a moment of curiosity: "When did you know you want to be an analyst?" A sort of variation on "How did you and mom meet?" It can sometimes sound painful and dramatic, echoing the patient's Oedipal drama. They then say something like, "It's not me you love, you love it – psychoanalysis. You're here for it, not for me." This moment can have a healing potential despite the accusatory tone and the way it can make us want to disappear into our chairs. I think that one such moment, where the patient shares with us their thoughts regarding our relations with psychoanalysis, is also a sign that they are doing work that allows them to acknowledge the object's separateness, but also that analysis can continue to exist in their world after they separate from the therapist. They may ask us what analysis means to us, but they are already preoccupied with the question of what it means to them and how they will be with analysis without us. Robert Caper wrote in this context:

I suggest that the internal object that helps the analyst sustain his internal barrier against the patient's projections is psychoanalysis itself as a specific type of empirical investigation. It functions this way only if it is an internal object for the analyst, and it becomes an internal object for the analyst only if he loves it.

(Caper, 1997)

The patient who says, "It's it you love, psychoanalysis," is not only correct, they understood something. They understood that their therapist had objects inside them, that psychoanalysis was one of these objects, and that it was good that the therapist has love objects; otherwise, they could not be therapists.

Seeing psychoanalysis as an internal object not only helps in carrying the patient's projections. It also allows us to see the differences between therapists as emanating, at least in part, from their relation to psychoanalysis and the unconscious fantasies that were tied to it in their inner world during their development. Analysts in training develop a deep sensitivity to their training-analyst's and supervisors' unconscious positions regarding analysis. Such a patient or consultee would quite quickly place themselves in the transference, exactly where the therapist is ambivalent towards a certain aspect of their theory or analytic technique. These therapies are often revealed to be difficult, and for good reason. A patient sometimes knows you have some pain in your lives – that may be why they chose you in the first place – and will start broadcasting to where they imagine they can hurt you, delight you or otherwise excite you. The same happens when treating professionals who explore their mentors' relations with their internal analytic object in various ways. Consider the candidate who seems smitten by the idea that his therapist accepted his request to see her three times a week, at 7 AM. He also never misses a chance to tell the therapist that her dedication to her work reminds him of his narcissist and careerist dad, who has been absent from home for long stretches of time due to his work and took no interest in raising his children. In his fantasy, the patient is stealing the therapist away from her family, tearing her between loving him and loving someone else.

If relations with the analytic object are authentic and relaxed, despite their complexity, and if we both love psychoanalysis and know that it is far from perfect, when we really have a complete relationship with the theory and profession – which are "usable objects" for us rather than "subjective objects" – the patient feels that. They also feel that we are not defensive. They feel we identify with the whole and believe in what we do, as imperfect as it is. Patients perceive when we are present in analysis from an omnipotent, humble or complacent position.

The more stable the therapist's internal psychoanalytic object is, the more it can serve as a safety net, or at least a shock absorber, in cases when the therapist slightly misses on his monitoring of the countertransference or is even tempted to act out in the countertransference. In some analyses, this is unavoidable.

Psychoanalysts who share the same theoretical persuasions often underestimate their possible divergences regarding the true nature of their analytic object. Therapists often "fight shoulder to shoulder" in the name of a theoretical position, while in truth, they have little in common with each other as happens in groups, organizations and societies, fraternity and solidarity at the surface level. During times of crisis, the basic positions – on life, principal questions of morality, conscience and ideals – are revealed to be very different. This is why I think that properly run clinical seminars are an opportunity not only to expose the presenter's analytic object, or what Joseph Sandler (1983) termed the "private theory" they follow, but also to allow other participants to experience partnership and learning despite the difference in clinical perceptions. Good clinical seminars reveal something fundamental in each of the participant's internal psychoanalytic objects. When we discover what we lost by being absorbed, sometimes for many years, in one particular theoretic position, how we forfeited instructing encounters with good analysts or other theories – hate and guilt develop. Splits in analytic societies, sometimes very painful and dramatic, can be traced back to such awakenings that blur the distinction between personal and theoretical disagreements.

An inseparable part of the relations patients have with their internal analytic object is related, I believe, to the signifier we call "Freud." Every therapist has a Freud file in their unconscious archives, and it is advisable that they have access to this file. The handing down of Freud's thoughts from one generation to another has a continuing effect on analytic identity, on the analyst's internal analytic object, and no less important – the trajectory in which the discipline develops.

In his lecture *Science as a Vocation* (1918), Max Weber argued that science, by its very nature, "cries out to be surpassed"; that a scientist cannot do their work if they do not hope that others would make their discoveries obsolete. American philosopher Alfred Whitehead also argued that "A science which hesitates to forget its founders is lost." (1929, p. 120). The psychoanalytic science no doubt develops as well, but I'm not convinced that its course of development as a science is teleological, as those of the exact or natural sciences. I find it hard to imagine a dynamic therapist or an analyst listening to patients without being familiar with the way Freud's thought developed or how psychoanalytic thought developed in the last 130 years. A therapeutic situation is constructed from many layers, and the ability to establish it is linked to the ability to use it to the benefit of the patient. Familiarity with the history of the discipline and the genealogy of its basic concepts is essential for understanding the dialectic between goals and means in dynamic psychotherapy and psychoanalysis. I don't mean history in the rigorous or dry, chronological sense: "In what year did Freud dissect eels? When did he write Fliess that letter about the Oedipal complex?" What I mean is a functional historical perspective, most importantly experiential, on the genealogy of the psychoanalytic subject and on issues that are fundamental in the clinic and theory of psychoanalysis. Such a perspective allows the therapist to listen to how they listen and think inside the therapeutic hour. If, while reading the Wolf Man case study, you have not experienced something of Freud's clinical and theoretic deliberations with the historic patient Sergei Pankejeff, you will find it hard to fully understand the meaning of the concept of *primal scene* and place it in your clinical thought. If you did not read *The Interpretation of Dreams*, you will find it hard to internalize the special place dreams have in the analytic clinic (Rolnik, 2015).

The demand to regard past doctrine as valuable for present one is not unique to dynamic psychotherapists. The most original philosophers were thoroughly familiar with the history and genealogy of the particular problem to which they raised a substantial contribution. While there are areas of knowledge where every so often a breakthrough results by the work of an incidental genius, lacking formal education, who was free from the shackles of the dominant paradigm and able to revolutionary examine old problems, the chances of the same happening within the treatment room are low. Not only does establishing a therapeutic situation require long training, but it takes years before we are able to assign meaning and significance to what is happening inside of it, both from a scientific-objective point of view and from an experiential-subjective one. That is why I think that the concept of an "internal psychoanalytic object" connects not only the discipline's past with its present, in the sense of "development of theory," but also the experience of discovering psychoanalysis in the past and the present. A vital and authentic psychoanalytic object has the power to accompany the single therapist in the room with a chorus of voices from the past, near and far, personal and collective, that echo into their clinic.

I sit in a clinic with a patient and suddenly experience and understand the dilemma of trauma versus unconscious fantasy. It is happening now, at this hour, with this specific patient. If I have in my mind an analytic road map to accompany the emotional journey the patient travels with me, I won't rush to think in exclusively trauma-centric terms. I will encourage the patient to think about complex concepts in the story of their mental and emotional becoming. I won't "feign empathy" or sell the patients ready-made cliches. One child is standing by the door of his kindergarten, screaming. In his fantasy, his mom is being eaten by a wolf. For him, it is taking place right now, as she is running late to pick him up. His twin sister happily plays on, even though her mom is just as late. She has a stable, comforting internal object, and her primal fantasy may not be so saturated with such an anxious persecutive hue. If this child is in psychotherapy right now, we can use complex thinking from a different vertex because our analytic object allows us to think about the patient openly; it doesn't push us to recite ready-made schemes and formulas on "good enough mothering," which the patient did not have the benefit of experiencing, or "empathic failures" he suffered in early childhood. We will offer other interpretations and the entire transferential configuration in the room will be different thanks to the polyphonic and polymorphic qualities of our analytic object.

A more recent example: For over a week, Mrs. A. has been describing, in very graphic details, acts of sexual violence committed by Hamas terrorists on October 7, 2023. I notice that it is becoming increasingly difficult for me to listen to these atrocities. I wonder why I am feeling attacked, indeed violated by my patients' associations. Pondering over the familiar dilemma between actual external trauma and unconscious fantasy, I begin to suspect that the provocative, eroticized language that the patient's father spoke to his daughters is conflated in the transference-countertransference scene with the horror at the sexual atrocities of Hamas terrorists. Having realized the presence of the intimidating father in Mrs. A.'s associations, I started to work-through her projections better in the countertransference. Starting to listen to Mrs. A. as re-enacting with me an event from her past rather than an event from our mutual present as Israelis took a great deal of discipline on the part of my internal analytic object. The human mind is always both victim and perpetrator of psychic trauma. Sometimes, we encourage the patient to explore how they use bad external objects to reaffirm the existence of their bad internal objects or to deny intolerable guilt about their attacks on the good object. With another patient, we may notice a conspicuous denial of external reality in the face of a real danger.

Psychoanalysis's canonical texts have an added value beyond the theoretic contents or technical points they express. I believe it would be a mistake to compare them to scientific essays in neurology or biochemistry, which have become obsolete and do not merit citation or inclusion in curricula. Classic analytic texts fertilize our internal analytic object. They allow the therapist not only to familiarize themselves with the "primal scene" in which dynamic psychotherapy was cultivated – the historical, philosophic, cultural and autobiographical contexts in which the great theoreticians acted – it also enlivens analytic listening. Good analytic listening always includes an oscillation, or suspension, between what can be understood from its context in the patient's history and biography and what can only be understood from within itself, from the passing moment in the patient's speech and transference.

In the years I spent translating Freud into Hebrew, I developed a sensitivity to his use of the German language. In the translator's note I wrote for the Hebrew translation of *The Psychoanalytic Treatment,* I specifically discussed Freud's ability to create a rich, polyphonic and rhizomatic theory of human experience and activity without requiring adjectives such as "paradoxical," "dialectic" or "enigmatic" which have become so widespread in current day psychoanalytic jargon.

Freud achieved that both by using literary and rhetorical techniques that activate the reader's primary, unconscious, thinking process and by making free, often absolutely wild, use of concepts arising in a horizontal, matrix-like structure through various focal points in his writing, changing their meaning in accordance with the specific theoretical and clinical concepts they are discussed in.

Freud's thought does not grow in a hierarchical, scientific, logical structure. He himself is aware of that and remarks on it in letters. His thought develops horizontally, like grass expanding from several foci at once, like a mangrove forest that expands over wide expanses on the cusp between land and sea. Yehuda Alon, using Freud's concept of "identification," demonstrated the notion that once one understands the rhizomatic process by which Freud's concepts develop, the inconsistency sometimes ascribed to him dissipates (Alon, 2013). The process by which the "psychoanalytic reserve" forms as a modern intellectual and scientific achievement resembles, therefore, the process of creating a collage: Fundamental concepts change form and absorb new meanings, all in accordance with the theoretical and clinical context they are discussed in. The same is also true, I believe, in the process by which psychoanalytic language and principles of psychoanalytic psychotherapy are learned and internalized during the therapist's training and the process by which an analytic insight and interpretation dawns in the mind of a therapist during the hour.

When listening to a patient, I am attentive to the movement between a depressive position and a schizo-paranoid one within the hour. This movement takes place not only in the patient but also within us, in relation to our internal analytic object: At times, we feel disputed with the internal object, feel let down by it, bummed out by it and screwed by it. We feel that we are not the right therapist for this patient, that we don't understand them. This will have many qualities, at times depressive, at times projectional.

We often use a mimicry of the theory, a stencil image of it. We distort concepts, and creativity becomes nihilism or recklessness. We invent psychoanalysis in our own image, invent theories. In some clinical seminars, the participants are busy identifying the therapist's real theory, the one active at any moment. I also assume that among this seminar's participants, some felt that I did not faithfully represent a certain theoretical way of thinking. Perhaps they understand Klein, Bion or Winnicott differently than I did. "My" Freud can – and should! – be challenged as well. Every great theory in psychoanalysis has a rather wide berth for interpretation, only augmented by professional sociology, which creates hierarchies between various interpretative traditions. For Lacanians, it is practically built into the discourse. Every other sentence in a clinical seminar starts with the phrase "Lacan says that . . .". As if it is enough to cite Lacan in order to prevent any possibility of misunderstanding or re-interpretation of a theoretical text or clinical material. The Kleiniean conversation is particularly sensitive to questions of clinical and conceptual "purity and impurity." In that, Kleinian discourse re-enacts the emphasis Klein's thought puts on the processes of splitting, introjection and projection of parts of self and object from the mind.

In some hours, the "other theory," the one not on the official cargo bill of the analysis, has had enough of its position as a stowaway in the therapist's mind and suddenly starts making itself heard. This happens when a patient is out of control, and we feel that we are losing touch with them. Then we suddenly start airing to the room voices of the kind we usually rather loathe. Voices of therapists or theoreticians we didn't value before, perhaps even looked down at their clinical ideas. Suddenly, when pressed against the wall, we try those too. Sometimes they work. Sometimes, it looks like we were saved from some inferno thanks to an interpretation we offered our patient, albeit in a "foreign accent," that was contrary to all we believe in and the patient is used to hearing from us. Astonishingly, the patient calms down. There can be many reasons why a patient may react well only to interventions from a therapist who seems to be cracking up or sounds loss for words. I believe patients in those cases also react to what they experience as the analyst's willingness to change for them, or else they react to the particular affective tone of it, the glimpse they get, due to our narcissistic crisis, to regions that are, for the most part, hidden from them.

As mentioned, some patients would place themselves exactly where we are ambivalent towards a certain aspect of the theory or analytic setting. After all, our theoretic identifications are also essentially compromise formations. So the answer that should lead the therapist is not whether their identification is now colored in a conflictual shade, but why is this conflict flaring up in them right now?

We should pay attention to when a less familiar part of the internal psychoanalytic object "lights up" and starts leading our listening. We already discussed the distinction between a selected fact and an overvalued idea. A patient may start the hour with a dream or speech that sounds like it was written on a "Freudian scale." They will repeat the same word several times or mumble it, thereby attracting the analysts' "Freudian ear" to such repetitions or slips. The therapist can go a little farther with that type of listening to the patient, but if inwardly they are dedicated, slightly neurotically, to the idea that they are not Freudian but relational, the result may be that they will unconsciously recognize the Freudian scale or material in the patient's speech but also resist it. They will then try to counterbalance it or even insist on shifting not only their attention but also the patient to another scale that they might feel is more appropriate or that they have better mastery of.

These conflictual focal points are also where stereotyped versions of theoretical positions are "libidinally invested." These investments serve to stabilize the analyst's internal analytic object, which may be experienced as threatened at a certain hour. As mentioned, some patients, more than others, would challenge our adherence to a preferred or accustomed theoretical way of thinking. They will demand that we convert or move us to a fantasy that they would have been better treated by someone else with a different approach. I think that processing these projections – of the patient's and ours – on the internal psychoanalytic object requires not only the capacity to contain but also a good familiarity by the therapist with their own internal psychoanalytic object with all its whims and fancy. Such familiarity can help them arrive at the conclusion, somewhat far-reaching, that they don't have what that specific patient needs.

Our particular internal analytic object means that we can treat some patients while others are impossible for us. We should recognize that. Of course, as psychoanalysts our tendency would be to translate even an experience of "incompatibility" between us and the patient to unconscious communication, some sort of enactment, or a transference enactment of the patient's history and inner world. But, as mentioned, a therapist has to recognize their limitations as a person, and the boundaries in which they can work with their patients.

Patients also have an internal object. Perhaps it's too early to call it a psychoanalytic object at the onset of therapy, but they do have a mental model, which also includes a theory of cure. I think patients have some fantasies about what treats them, what would help them and what they need. With some patients, you can offer wonderful Kleinian interpretation until you're blue in the face; it won't get you anywhere. They can't take root in your patch because your therapeutic persona is incompatible with theirs.

We often insist, and then things get messy. When there is some deep mismatch between your patient and what you are able and willing to give, if our patient has to stretch too much to fit us, or vice versa, then I believe the risk of crossing boundaries in treatment rises sharply. It doesn't have to be a dramatic transgression, the kind raised before ethics committees, but there are various forms of acting-in-inside treatment that are expressions of problematic relations we have with our internal analytic object. Sometimes, it's a chronic problem with us, and sometimes a temporary one – illness, fatigue or a life crisis – that makes the therapist's psychoanalytic object rigid or bizarre or leads them to react too strongly to a certain patient. What comes to mind in this context are phenomena and concepts in the field of immunology, which in certain cases can also be useful in describing mother-baby relations, such as an "allergic reaction" to an encounter with otherness or an "anaphylactic shock" as a reaction to strangeness.

Just like athletes or musicians, our work suffers after a prolonged vacation or leave. We lose some sensitivity after a long time away. A psychotherapeutic practice is quite a radioactive work environment. The 'analyzing instrument' – to use Otto Isakower's (1992) beautiful term – can break down over the years, and our ability to do good work is thrown off. In this case, whatever knowledge and experience the sensitive and experienced therapist may have accumulated would not save them from arrogance or complacency.

Does the willingness to be taken over by psychoanalysis involve surrender or submission?

This question is inspired by Emmanuel Ghent's (1990) distinction between surrender and submission in object relations. And this might be a good time to clarify – if you haven't noticed it already – that when I say "object," I mostly mean an internal object. I'm not sure the same is true for Ghent, although it has been some time since I read him. In the relational school, the concept of "object relations" refers less to the unconscious fantasy and more to the relation with the object in reality. In Freud, too, it is not always clear what is meant by "object." While the internal object and the object, in reality, are seldom congruent, the state of the object in the fantasy and unconscious is related to our relations in reality with people, flesh and blood. Processes of projection and internalization form the matrix of psychic development. Today, my psychoanalysis is not as spiritual and mystical as Ghent's, Eigen's or late Bion's. I'm not a fan of psychoanalytic mentalism, and apparently less ambitious in my therapeutic goals than clinicians who discuss "object transplant" in patients with an autistic personality organization. I'm also probably not as enchanted by paradoxes as I was 20 years ago.

"All humanity rests upon reverence before the mystery that is man," Thomas Mann said in a lecture given at Princeton in 1939 (Corngold, 2022). I recently came across this text and thought about how it reflects my understanding of literature, as well as the therapeutic act. As an analytic therapist, I try to come closer to an understanding of that mysterious part of man, mostly through an examination of the twists and turns of the patient's internal object and unconscious fantasy. I do so by using various transference phenomena and exploring the messages communicated from one person's unconscious to that of another. I think I read these words by Thomas Mann in the spirit of Freud and his followers when I argue that "reverence before the mystery that is man" does not mean an idealization of lack of knowledge or a complete discarding of the journey towards self-recognition as a means of gaining a better recognition of the world, but a recognition of the interminability of the journey and the inevitable incompleteness of our ability to know ourselves and others.

Imagine the incident I recounted in Chapter 2, Unconscious and the Death Drive: A long-time patient sits next to me on the bus. Despite having met me four times a week for years, he doesn't recognize me. I can greet him, and he would smile and affably return the greeting. I have no reason to think he isn't truly excited and surprised to meet me there. But I'm still interested in the influence the internal object has on the patient's, and mine, ability to notice or deny something in the external object's reality. Perhaps the degree of separation from the internal object or some idealization did not allow the patient to recognize me today as a person taking the bus and sitting next to him. The unconscious system operates on the pleasure principle, which requires that it be very selective in accepting information received from the senses.

You might also have a few somewhat irritating acquaintances who are always surprised to meet you and ask, "What are you doing here?" as if it is any surprise that you are walking down the street. I'm sure you know that moment when a patient suddenly compliments the new carpet in your clinic, the one that has been in the exact same place for many years. When we encounter such a "sensory illusion" or a "negative hallucination," it's worthwhile to search for what else is new in the patient's internal world. What makes the familiar seem foreign? All of the examples I just noted are simple demonstrations that a thing-representation in the inner world can be very different from what the object is in reality on the conscious level since attention and the ability to identify and experience something in external reality is dictated first and foremost by internal reality.

Returning to your question regarding the distinction between surrender and submission, I would welcome it and consider it useful when examining the therapist's relation with psychoanalysis on the conscious level. However, it sounds more descriptive than dynamic-analytic. It describes something on the level of the therapist's experience, while the great drama of the object world takes place on the deep layers of the psyche. We can examine the issue of surrender versus submission or the use of psychoanalysis as an object from another angle, that of being able to learn something new. I recently found myself leafing through the pages of an old anatomy atlas I found in my bookcase. As I was doing so, various notes in my own handwriting fell out of the pages, notes I now had trouble deciphering. I thought that if, for some reason, I had to learn again the cranial nerve pathways or the names of the bones in the human palm, I would staunchly refuse. No one forced me, in my youth, to study anatomy. I used to love anatomy and could direct my libido to the field and submit to it. Today, I won't. In any learning, even of a profession we chose and love – there is a certain degree of anxiety from meeting the unknown or unconscious. I remember how anatomy studies excited me 35 years ago. It started as an anxiety-inducing mental and cognitive challenge and became a truly spiritual experience. Now think how much can psychoanalytic practice and theory rock us and engender resistance in us every single day.

Narcissism is also involved, and narcissism has quite a number of forms. Does it allow us to become curious, rub against and internalize something strange and new, "play with an idea," or would it make us respond to a new idea as a bad or intrusive object that endangers us and accordingly requires that we defend ourselves against it? Ronnie Solan emphasized in her works the role of memory schemas in the narcissistic system, which acts similarly to an immune system in protecting the internal object and what is familiar in the encounter with strangeness and otherness (Solan, 2015).

It is hard for a person to learn from their own personal experience and even harder to learn from that of others. I sometimes ask a consultee, "Why are you being stubborn? Why don't you try to apply the clinical advice I offered you?" I try to discern with them what the analytic theory or point of view I'm offering them is particularly difficult to process and internalize. It's important to help novice therapists or analysts – in training be faithful to themselves and develop according to their own inclinations (Rolnik, 2008, 2019b). But if the students' narcissism makes them feel that they "surrender" whenever they use something unfamiliar suggested by theory or their teachers, then we have a problem. Experienced therapists don't just seek supervision with a colleague; they also get together, sometimes for decades, in "reading groups." This is a unique tradition that accompanies the "analytic life" of many psychoanalysts since Freud's time, reminiscent of a much older Judaic tradition of learning texts with a study partner. Perhaps we need this learning companionship in psychoanalysis both because the analytic knowledge is always at a state of multiplicity, addition and composition and because the discovery of an old knowledge in analytic canonical texts surprises us every time anew, elicits anxiety and requires constant maintenance.

Chapter 12

Vacations, separations and endings

In what way do separations and terminations reflect the theories, implicit and explicit, we follow? Why do most therapists write about separations only in their old age, and how is that related to denying separation as an important engine for mental processes of separateness and growth? On the acceptance of veteran patients for repeated treatment, and a therapist who avoided greeting a patient of hers 40 years after his treatment ended.

The lives of dynamic therapists resemble, in some ways, those of farmers. They don't cancel sessions even when they have a cold, take a few vacations and are afraid to leave the fields and flocks unattended. The subject of separations in treatment is close to my heart, perhaps because, over the years, I separated from three analysts. There is a rather large gap between the degree to which we are engrossed with this issue in our daily lives and the relative paucity of writing about it. The gap embodies, naturally, the same resistance we also meet in the clinic – resistance to giving separation a place, to recognizing the ephemeral and transient nature of a therapeutic encounter, whether it is years-long or short-lived. There is also a constant tension between the effort the therapist puts into establishing the analytic situation, strengthening the setting and producing the most from the analytic situation and a certain nonchalance we encounter in our conversation regarding separations and termination of treatment, whether these express the therapist's will or are forced on them. Interestingly, it was theoreticians of short-term psychotherapy – some of them trained analysts – who realized the deep meaning of the end of treatment and incorporated that insight into their theory and technique. And here we are, dynamic therapists, keeping the matter of separation as professional lore, directing young therapists' attention towards holding the treatment and continuing it, with the termination of treatment usually considered, whether with understanding or criticism, as a regrettable inevitability or downright failure.

Perhaps therapists tend to deny the ending and separation because they did not experience a separation of the kind a large part of their patients do. By that, I mean that we stay in the profession even after our therapy ends. Moreover, it is possible that our choice of profession is itself the result of some treatment, that our very choice to work in this profession is a way of dealing with separation from

DOI: 10.4324/9781003528470-12

treatment, whether successful or not, in our childhood or youth or in whatever age we chose this path. That is a speculation of mine. In practice, we know that analysts only rarely completely lose touch with their training analysts or supervisors. They often continue to hold rather intensive collegial or even friendly relations in their professional lives. All of these options do not exist for a patient who is not in the profession. They might go back to treatment with the same therapist or call to wish them a happy new year, but their relations go through a very significant upheaval at the end of treatment. The patient undergoes a very intensive and meaningful process through their relationship with the therapist, and then they disappear from their lives. I don't believe this kind of separation can be compared to those of patients who are themselves therapists and have something very clear and easily identifiable in common with their therapists – the profession of psychoanalysis.

I think an interesting expression of a therapist's resistance towards considering the issue of separation and termination, and the way it can hide in seeming willingness to do just that, can be seen in the following example: In a conference of the European Psychoanalytical Federation, Betty Joseph presented a clinical case she titled *Ending Analysis* (Joseph, 2018). Wonderful, I thought; a case study by Joseph dealing with separation is bound to be original and clear. The presented patient, a woman in her 30s, was apparently one of Joseph's last patients. As her decades-long career, in which she separated from countless patients, draws to an end, the therapist, an important Kleinian theoretician, dedicates a paper to the issue of separation. The paper ostensibly deals with the anxieties separation elicits in the patient, but I believe it suffers from a blind spot: Joseph conflates her own "end" – old age and separation from the profession, which are certainly deserving of a paper in their own right – with the younger woman's separation from her as a therapist. I wondered why Joseph dealt with the separation from the point of view of her own "end of career" rather than that of any patient who simply separated from treatment while knowing that their therapist would continue to live and treat others even after their own treatment has ended. Joseph's patient is also preoccupied with the age of her elderly therapist and guesses she is about to retire, but Joseph has conducted dozens, if not hundreds, of analyses; some must have had fascinating endings. Kleinian thought and theory could be applied to this important part of analysis. Thinking further on Joseph's paper on the end of treatment, I was reminded of an interview held with her many years ago. Among other things, she mentioned that at the end of her training, she informed the teaching committee at the British Institute of Psychoanalysis that she believed she was not yet ready to finish training. Perhaps even as a young analyst, Joseph had difficulties with endings and separations.

This phase of analysis, end of treatment and separation, used to be discussed under the less-than-friendly title of *termination*. Even then, the clinical literature on the subject was rather meager, and it strove to somehow correspond with Freud's famous paper *Analysis Terminable and Interminable* on the meta-analytic level. In this paper, Freud is concerned with the question of whether "termination" is an applicable concept for psychoanalysis, which is, by its nature, a never-ending process. When does analysis end? Freud asks, and answers wryly: It ends when the patient and therapist stop meeting. Freud prefers to ask the larger question: Does analysis ever end? Little is written on "smaller" questions, such as at what point it is best to end therapy or how one prepares the patient for separation.

The question of the terminability of analysis is similar, in some regards, to the question of "What is love?" Both are good and worthy questions, but they can also be used as a way of denying the very existence of termination or love. I am saddened that such a central concept is left for the moment when important theoreticians, Freud or Betty Joseph, assent to give a place and some thought to their own end. Freud discusses the forced termination of the Wolf Man's treatment; Hanna Segal, Nina Coltart and Eric Brenman also wrote on ending analysis, but for some reason, analysts write on ending analyses when they are already rather old themselves and are busy with the question of the terminability of their own lives. The end of life and the end of analysis are still different subjects.

I'm reminded of another example of that "blind spot" the discipline has around separating from patients and post-analytic relations with them. To what extent does an analyst's perception of their role – as one who forever remains "the analyst" – is present in the habitus of a certain generation of therapists can be seen in the following anecdote: An elderly psychoanalyst sometimes meets, in professional conferences, a renowned psychoanalyst who she treated when he was young. It has been over 40 years since that historical treatment, but she never acknowledges him with more than a nod, never engaging him in conversation. The analyst is somewhat offended but mostly curious as to why a 90-year-old analyst so strictly adheres to "analytic relations" with him so many years after the termination of his analysis. He asks a colleague, who gives his opinion: "She doesn't want to prevent you from going back to treatment if you ever need it." I believe that had Freud heard this story. He would have been very perplexed by the way the older analyst interpreted the concept of "analytic relations" with a psychoanalyst who she treated over 40 years ago.

Love, separation, loss and thinking are intertwined in the inner world, in different ways and to various degrees. Patients are not always aware of the influence the form of emotional investment in the object has on their mental and emotional functioning or the movement that exists in the inner world between the object's presence in reality and its absence from it. There is something about breaks from mental therapy, taking vacations, sick days or prolonged maternal leaves that instantaneously light up not only the patient's object relations and their transference relations with us but also expose less known aspects of the patient's mental functioning. This is different from the slow and drawn-out process by which we are familiarized with the patient's inner world. It has a tremendous potential for self-recognition, growth and mental development for the patient. But separations also have "dangerous turns." Therapists are apprehensive about the intensity in which object relations flare up in the face of a separation. So much so that many therapists seldom take vacations. Not because they are greedy and not necessarily because they can't afford to lose income. The main reason is that separation and vacation require hard work from us and our patients. They severely "rock the therapeutic boat," and therapists are not certain they can handle it – so they avoid it, sometimes consciously, sometimes unconsciously.

The dearth of vacations is easily justified by the importance that theory and technique put on continuity and regularity as indispensable parameters in the therapeutic process. But this argument also demonstrates, I believe, a misunderstanding of the role of the therapeutic setting. The stable setting is not meant to serve the patient and therapist's denial of separateness or of the terminability of analysis but to create optimal conditions to understand and interpret processes of separateness and merger in psychic reality. My point, then, is that vacations, separation and terminations are inseparable parts of processes of growth and change in life and psychoanalysis. This is where very important work is done by the patient, no less important than in the process of transferential attachment with the therapist. Yes, it is difficult for them – and we help them. We interpret and we encourage them to reach this regression to dependency so we can assign meaning to phenomena that accompany these breaks in the setting. Tremendous psychic work is done by the patient during various breaks in the setting, starting with the seemingly minor rupture at the end of each hour, the weekend breaks, the longer separation during vacation, illness, lock-downs and, of course, at the end of treatment. Separations have a tremendous potential for self-knowledge, which comes at a great toil for the analyst and the analysand. There will always be an opportunity to work on dreams here because dreams intensively accompany separations. It is far from rare that the patient shares a dream with you only after a separation or a change to the setting. The same holds true for the analyst's dreaming.

I took a short vacation last week. For a moment, I asked myself if, in light of the circumstances, I'd better hold our seminar while away, but I decided to exercise moderation – not only lounge by the beach on a Greek island but also hold a digital psychoanalytical seminar. Even an analyst can only enjoy himself so much. So I postponed our meeting by one week. On the first night, I had a dream I hadn't had for years. Not in quality, in caloric value. The vacation was worth it for it alone. Not to mention the yield of dreams I'm now getting from patients as we work through the events of the missed week. It's been hard work, the last two days. One wants to leave therapy, another knocks on the door outside of the hour, a third is angry and the fourth thinks that five times a week might already be too much. Why do they react so strongly to my vacation? First, it's my vacation, not theirs. Patients deal much better with absences they asked for than ones decided on by the therapist. It is easier for them to "say goodbye" and retain the therapist as a good object. That still doesn't promise that the object would not be spoiled while it is away or that the patient would not deny the distinction between the therapist's presence and their absence, but the attack on the good object would be more moderate. Second, they did not receive enough warning and not enough preparation was made. The psychic system aspires towards equilibrium and doesn't like surprises. Because of Covid, I could not be certain of taking this vacation until 10 days before I actually did, which is not enough time to work on separation, given that some patients despise mentioning it. A patient who survives a therapist's vacation always benefits from it if the vacation is used to perform analytic work. They benefit because a large part of the analytic work is performed when the analytic pair stops meeting and holds the relationship in fantasy. Of course, the relation happens in fantasy, even when they meet regularly and even during the therapeutic hour, but during separation, the patient has the chance to search for the analysis within them and see what it is for them. Is the separation experienced as a severance of the attachment to the object and causes an attack on the patient's self? Does the bad object immediately take the place of the absent good object? Does the persecutory super-ego come into action as soon as the part-self experiences itself as abandoned by the analyst – the good object's auxiliary guardian against attacks from within? Or is the patient able to miss something without that feeling being accompanied by despair, since the good object does not quickly turn its back on it or becomes oppressive? At times, separation from the therapist will show on the patient's body: They will gain, or lose, weight, develop some symptom related to their bowel movement, suffer dizziness, a dermatological problem or blurry vision.

Not only for the analysand but also for the analyst, one can expect that a symbiosis will develop between the analytic setting and primitive parts of the mind. This is also why we should break free somewhat from our therapeutic prison. Even a good therapist should sometimes step back from their patients and be with their own inner world "sans analysis." We hide in our work and role mental states, conflicts and pains, and it is better that we occasionally release them from the professional retreat and meet them "naked" outside the clinic.

As mentioned, a separation that takes place during treatment shows the object relations from different angles. When we meet the patient at a high frequency, we learn about their attachment patterns and the primal fantasies they invest in their relations with people. But once there is a prolonged violation of the known rhythms of the setting – sometimes it is enough that you change one single session for some illusion or unconscious assumption to be revealed – something is exposed in the internal structure that would not be revealed without breaking the setting. We have an opportunity to look inward and see what we were for the patient at this point in time. What are we for them? Are they in us? Are we in them? Perhaps in their fantasy, it is they who are carrying us on their backs, as the patient Eric Brenman describes in his paper on separation (Brenman, 2006, pp. 22–33). Perhaps the separation would expose that they are living in a run-down, condemned house, such as a patient of mine dreamed during my vacation. I already mentioned the analysand who didn't believe I was really taking a vacation and thought I stayed in the clinic, only telling him that while I'm away "to see how he manages without therapy." I only found out about it in the fifth year of analysis, when one day I told him I was taking a vacation, and he responded: "I think you can stop doing that, Eran. I'll be fine." I then learned that he honestly thought my announcements of taking a vacation were merely a ploy to make sure he doesn't "get addicted" to therapy. The possibility that I, just like him, needed and enjoyed vacations did not even cross his mind before that moment.

Another example: I told a patient I wouldn't be able to hold one of our hours the next week. She quickly jotted it down in her planner and then said: "You know, you're remarkably healthy. It's amazing how I've been in therapy with you for all these years, and you never canceled one hour because you were ill." I answered, "And now you're worried that I'll be spoiled for you if we don't meet, that I'll get sick." Something about that cookie-cutter interpretation I made disturbed me. It included a little too much of my identification with the patient's idealization. So I went on to tell the patient that she somehow forgot that two years ago I was hospitalized and called her several times to cancel meeting. She answered, "I remember you called to cancel and said you were hospitalized, but I didn't believe you were really sick." At that time, she preferred being separated from me as an analyst who hides the truth from her than accepting me as an ill analyst.

This kind of thing comes up when we are interested in what is taking place in the inner world as a reaction to separation. These revelations don't happen on their own. The therapist is required to be committed to exploring what takes place in the transference in reaction to the announcement of an oncoming separation, during the separation and after sessions resume. Many therapists breathe a sigh of relief after they and the patient survive the vacation in one piece and don't even bother looking for the deep currents of this important occurrence. Again, for some patients, the right thing to do would be not to interpret, not to make a big deal of a canceled hour or a long weekend. But ignoring that, not identifying it in associations and dreams – I believe that to do so is to miss something, to collide with the part of the patient that really wants to deny separateness, the nature of the analytic relationship, such as the fact that the analyst has relationships and contact with other people, not only in their mind but also in reality, that they need a vacation to be an analyst.

This difficulty exists also in small, day-to-day separations, such as when children turn on the volume when you take a rest. Fantasies about what takes place in the parents' room, the other room, are composed not only from fantasies on the link between the parents. The very fact the mother closes herself off in her bedroom elicits in the child an entire world of fantasies and tremendous anxiety. Think of the patient who can't sleep at night if his wife falls asleep before him. He has to be the first to fall asleep because she serves as a container for his anxieties, and if she dives into her own inner world and falls asleep, he loses touch with the containing object. Many fantasies and forms of mental function receive an analytic say when we process separations in therapy.

Another one: A patient was nursing her elderly mother for a long time. I noticed that she has been asking me for the time frequently, complaining that the session felt too long for her. In a few instances, she suddenly told me: "I had enough for today," and ended the session a few minutes early. I also noticed that the patient stopped wearing her watch, and the next time, she asked me for the time I wondered where it disappeared. I saw a clear connection between the watch and the elderly mother and had an idea that alongside the wish to forego separateness and unite with the object, my patient experienced anxiety over being deserted by the mother and separated from her. In the transference, she "prematurely" separated from me in order to avoid the pain of separating from mother. Through projective identification, she deposits with me her fear of separation by ending the hour early.

It is important to inform new patients that you expect to take vacations throughout the year. I think it's also sometimes important to encourage patients to take a vacation and remind them that a vacation is helpful for analysis as well. All this has to be discussed in the context of terms, of course. What you charge the patient for and what you don't. I prepare the patient for separations not because I'm concerned that they won't handle it but because I think that separation is part of life and analytic work. It's good for you to take vacations, and I recommend long rather than short ones, but that's a matter of preference. Freud's patients were used to him disappearing for three months at a time during summer. Some of them he would receive even while on vacation if he was staying a reasonable distance from Vienna.

Some patients would experience it as immensely difficult. You shouldn't think light of that. Some patients would have to be encouraged to call you even during vacation, if necessary. For some patients, it would be better that they know where you are vacationing, and for others, it's preferable to encourage them to fantasize about where you will be rather than satisfy their curiosity. There might even be those who you'd want to encourage to use a transitional object, like a child finding it difficult to separate from his mother when going to school. I don't recommend they take a chair, or even a pillow, as something to remember the treatment room by, but sometimes a patient has an interesting idea on how they can keep in touch with the analytic object, and we should help them identify this transitional object. Maybe a transitional space can serve that purpose: They decide that at their usual hour with you, say Wednesday at six, they will come do the shopping or just sit at a cafe not far from your clinic. Maybe they can use the hours freed from analysis to finally write their Ph.D., maintaining a connection with the analysis this way. The more you enrich your patient's "symbolic repertoire" to therapy in the times you don't meet, the more you help them make use of you during work and treatment and even prepare them for an important part of analysis – separation from it and life after it.

Everything I just said is not meant to calm "separation anxiety" or encourage the patients towards "regression to dependency." Regression, just like transference, negative or positive, has a function in treatment (and life). At one point in time, regression can promote the treatment, and at another, it might wreck it. Any patient in analysis would eventually experience a certain degree of separation anxiety. It is an analytical artifact we would expect to see expressed even in healthy people who don't enter a deep regression during treatment. My emphasis is not on relieving anxiety but self-knowledge and promoting the patient's interest in freely examining the relations with the analyst and the nature of these relations. Thus, I would encourage a patient to fully express her relief for not having to meet me last week or help a patient express anger at my absence, precisely when he had a particularly hard time with his boss. Your patient might report that, during vacations from analysis, they are able to come closer to their spouse. After all, for some patients, intimate relations and sex life suffer greatly from their relationship with the therapist. Don't think light of that. During vacation, they can again grow closer to their partners, thin out the transference somewhat and enjoy sex without guilt. Young patients may do dangerous or idiotic things in the time you don't meet. They may cause themselves harm or make rash decisions to recreate an experience of parental negligence. Various types of acting-out, characteristic of infantile and borderline patients, would be the purview of a relatively small group of the myriad of phenomena we see during separation. Most patients are neurotics, who react in various gentle and idiosyncratic ways to separation from the analyst based on their life story or a transference configuration that is dominant in the therapy right now. Does the patient disavow their envy, or are they happy for you for taking a vacation? Look for the unconscious fantasy behind the conscious fantasy, revealed completely at random when the patient remarks, off-handedly: "It was during the summer, while you were living it up in London by yourself . . ." "You think I went to London alone." "Yes, one of the days we didn't meet, I was in the area, and I think I saw your wife in the street."

As I said, I sometimes answer the question "Where are you going?" concretely, such as with patients with a severe impairment in object constancy. I sometimes suggest an interpretation and sometimes respond with a question: "You tell me where I am when I'm not here with you. Where do you imagine me going?" That is, I try to explore, with the patient, the half-conscious fantasy related to her question. A whole world of mental scenarios hides behind this seemingly informative question – "where are you going for your holiday?" The moment the issue of separation, or vacation, appears on the agenda, it's worthwhile to listen well to dreams and various enactments and small acts within and without the hour. The idea is not only to identify the acting and contain or mitigate it through interpretation but also to interest the patient and interpret for them the kind of fantasies that come to life in the face of separation. You might discover – I think this is a rather common fantasy – that your patient is envious of your coming vacation because, in her fantasy, you spend it with other patients with whom you have become close friends. That is, the reaction to separation arouses the patient's anxiety that they are not good or loved enough for the therapist to want to be with them alone, and also the fantasy of a different kind of relation with the patient, enabled maybe, some time, after the end of treatment.

A patient tells me of a day-dream they had in one of the hours I canceled: "I know that you spent the hour you canceled on me in Vienna, sitting at a cafe with Freud, telling him about me and that I would prefer that he, rather than you, treat me. And Freud tells you to work a little differently with me, to give me presents like he did with patients he particularly liked." Alongside the need to restore the narcissist injury inherent in canceling the hour and denying separateness – if I'm not with him, I must be talking to Freud about him – this creative day-dream is at one and the same time humiliating and uplifting, bringing the object, damaged by its declaration of separateness, both closer and farther away. The patient's way of accepting me canceling an hour is a fantasy that, with Freud's help, I would come back from the separation a better, more generous analyst, be able to admire him and love him as a good therapist or parent should. It's meaningful that in the patient's fantasy, the hour I canceled is dedicated to meeting the forefather of psychoanalysis, i.e., a historical figure with which both analyst and analysand are in a symbolic relation, rather than with a living, breathing person I know and love. Meeting Freud in Vienna means missing the meeting in Tel Aviv but still maintaining a connection to them through a common familiar object, the psychoanalytic object.

Interpretations that routinely mention the therapist's absence raise quite a lot of resistance. Patients see them as the therapist insisting on making them dependent and helpless. It takes quite a lot of time for the patient to be convinced that when we ask them if they enjoyed a long weekend or a vacation, we're interested in their inner world, not reaffirming their misery and dependence on us. As mentioned, I think that there could also be "good reasons" for a patient to be absent from an analytic hour. I don't hide that from my patients. A patient taking a vacation is a good thing for the therapeutic process as well. For some absences, such as illness, death of a loved one, and so on, we should employ clinical judgment in deciding how much to share and with who. I don't think it's right for a therapist to hide from their patient that they are mourning a relative or were diagnosed with a severe disease. But I wouldn't be too quick to share with all my patients that I had to cancel a meeting because I had a dental treatment or was invited to give a lecture at a conference. Young therapists sometimes hide pregnancies from their patients for a little too long. It's best to do some work in the countertransference and see what the reason for secrecy around pregnancy and sexuality is with one patient and not with another, for example.

From a conceptual or theoretical perspective, a whole analysis can be gathered into the subject of separation. It certainly seems like an interesting narrative and thematic axis for writing a clinical case study. How were the separations at first, and what kind of development took place in the relations with that issue during treatment? Does any absence by the good object still cause the bad object to have the upper hand over the borderline patient? Does the patient still dream of arriving at the airport without a passport and a ticket, or that during analysis, there has been some development and, at least in their dreams, they are able to get everything together and reach their destination "in one piece"? I remember a patient who, before therapy, had a recurring dream of arriving at the airport without a suitcase, with only his toothbrush. Before the first summer vacation during analysis, he dreamed of shaking my hand and having that hand detach from my body and stay with him. Another patient used to dream of going on vacation, but having his luggage take up all the space in the taxi, and having a terrible argument with the driver, who refused to let him in.

Tracking dreams and transference phenomena around vacations can demonstrate progress in using a more developed defense mechanism, a decreased intensity of splits, an ability to maintain contact with the internal object from a depressive position, acknowledging separateness, a decrease in level of envy, improvement in willingness to be happy for the therapist for taking a vacation. It is very worthwhile to continue listening to what the patient is going through during separation, even after meeting them again. Don't pass it over; don't ignore the connection between anything that happens in a patient's life and the vacation you took. I give that plenty of attention in my transference interpretations.

With some patients, our vacation may catch them at a too-early stage of the treatment. They won't stand it and won't give themselves a chance to find out what happened. They will stop treatment very soon after the separation, which they experienced as a severance. In general, I try not to take on new patients before a vacation, mine or theirs.

All things considered, we can't be too spontaneous with our vacations. It's advisable to let the patients know about them long in advance, if possible, and it's preferable that they be synchronized with the clinic's "life cycle." If you have a clinic full of patients who all started treatment last week, that might not be the best time to go on vacation. Woody Allen, in one of his earlier movies, says that every August, New York is "full of crazy people" because the analysts are all away.

As mentioned, I consider a vacation a good thing in the patient's life, not a regrettable accident they have to survive somehow. If, for some reason or another, any separation is listed in their inner world with a traumatic or catastrophic grammar, the therapist has a duty to assume it is a "depth-charge," whose echoes must be sought. If the patient is indifferent to, or completely denies, the fact that you will soon have a two-week break in sessions, you should turn their attention to that behavior. It's usually the "comfortable" patients, who act as if they have no problem with you canceling a week, who will stop the treatment soon after your return from vacation or ring your doorbell when you're not there, and perhaps, one day, even tell you about it. It's not too pleasant to see the clinic closed at your regular hour, but that is the price they pay for not being able to consider separation as a meaningful psychic event. Some would say, "Oh, no problem, just remind me next week when it's relevant, and I'll put it down in my calendar then." To which I answer, "I'm telling you now, so you better put it down now." And they say, "No, there's no point. It's two months from now; anything can happen in two months." We start a sort of negotiation around the denial. I don't expect every patient to immediately quench my thirst for analysis of separation and separateness anxiety, but the theory of mind I hold, certainly the clinical theory, suggests that I pay close attention to vacations, mine and the patient's, and anyone treated by me has to bear with my style of doing it. I would try to adapt it to patients, and not everybody needs it to the same extent, but overall, I prefer to badger patients a little than miss an opportunity to investigate this aspect of their inner world. The movement between being with the object in reality and being with the object's internal representation is very important, in my view.

If you set your mind's eye down these paths, you will find plenty of reactions. For example, people with a perverse structure would be seemingly indifferent to the separation, but their dreams, and sometimes sexual acts, will show a dramatic regression and very severe sexual acting out, evidence of a growing need to make their dependence anxiety into a sexual thrill. An announcement of an oncoming vacation is enough to wreak havoc not only in the dreams of perverse patients but also in their sexual practices. For some patients, canceling an hour is translated, in their inner world, to you being very sick, on your death bed, and therefore, they can no longer trust you to be with them. Patients would hastily terminate rather successful treatments midway through the year, only to avoid having to separate from you during the summer holiday. For some patients, their death drive would quickly offer itself to transform dependence anxiety into an omnipotent bacchanalia of death and destruction or merely a sexual thrill.

The more the end of treatment draws near, the more clear the affinity between the terminability of treatment and that of life – since the relations with the analyst have become such an integral part of the ongoing function of the mental mechanism, to the point that certain patients may fantasize that without that relation, without analysis, there would be no psychic life, which is akin to death. The fear of emptiness and loneliness as a function of the relationship between the life and death drives is refueled towards the end of treatment. We might see, at that point, various maniform attempts by the patient to push away the pain of separation.

Analysis should reach a natural death

Criteria for terminating analyses and dynamic therapies are often worded using the same concepts and models by which we understand the psychopathology of the patient and the analytic situation. Some therapists would identify the point at which we can already discuss the end of analysis with the disappearance of splits and the development of a sustainable integration between the persecutive introject and the idealized one. Others would emphasize the central place the patient's grief work has in the process of separating from the analyst. Some thought that it's best that the patient undergo the separation process with a different therapist, i.e., in their next therapy. Hans Loewald (1998) believed that, in some cases, the "last" question to come up in analysis, whether to continue or terminate the treatment, would paradoxically be the first to allow the patient's transference neurosis to unfold in full.

In 1928, Ferenczi wrote that "The proper ending of analysis is when . . . it dies of exhaustion, so to speak" (Ferenczi, 2018). He adds that even then, the therapist should remain suspicious and consider whether the patient's desire to leave has to do with their will to save something of their neurosis. That is, he recommends that even the desire to end a prolonged and successful analysis be viewed as an expression of resistance.

Inexperienced analysts usually invest most of their energy in making patients come to therapy and persist in it. But, as a therapist's holding and containment abilities improve, so does their ability to understand patients and they become more and more engaged in deliberations regarding the timing of terminating therapies. How does one introduce new patients and release older ones? It's nice to work with a friendly, serious patient who was aided a lot by us and from whom we learned a lot about humans, ourselves and the world, but they, too, have to be let go. In most cases, we hear it in the clinical material – provided, of course, that we don't turn a blind eye to the material in which the patient is concerned with the end of treatment. We should not miss an "exit ramp" from a long and successful analysis. We can listen to the part of the patient that discusses the ending, perhaps not explicitly, but the part that is getting set for it. Patients discuss termination long before they know they are discussing termination; they bring it up in their dreams. They are preoccupied with the question of whether they could come back to therapy after terminating it. As mentioned, at the start of therapy, I already discuss its end. I say that I think termination of treatment is a process and that when the time comes, we will dedicate several months, sometimes a whole year, to it. I explain to the patient that they, not me, will choose the date, that I won't force it on them, but also ask them to try, as much as possible, not to surprise me with it.

As a generality, I would say that patients don't like to work on separations. Not on small ones and not on large ones. Many fine therapists also don't like working on separations. They prefer to separate right here and now, then get set to separation, consider it something real and tangible. I'm just now finishing a 12-year-long analysis. At first, the patient allowed herself a full year for the process but lately informed me that we would separate six months earlier. I agreed under protest.

Sometimes, the extent of our role is to help the patient properly separate from their previous therapist, who died during therapy, or who, for any other reason, did not conduct an orderly separation. A woman approached me, seeking to start analysis. During the first session, she told me that last month, she ended an analysis that lasted many years. It was a miserable separation, she says, and it's difficult for her to imagine how she can live without analysis. The role of the analyst here may not be to allow her to "start a new analysis" but rather to aid her in separating from her therapist, who, it seems, denied the issue of separation. Moreover, it may be worthwhile to encourage her to live without analysis for a while so she can again find in herself the good points that must have existed in that analysis, as discordantly as it ended. We should develop a sensitivity to the patient's "point of entry" into treatment with us. A too-sharp transition from prolonged therapy with one therapist to another may, in my experience, prove to be a problematic starting point.

I imagine that a patient who we treated in our 30s received different interpretations than patients who see us when we are older, even elderly. The difference between a young therapist and an older one is more than merely their clinical experience. There is always something in the analyst – in addition to their personality, clinical skills or the theory through which they listen and understand the material – that takes part in the transference layout of the analysis. Some patients get the young you – busy with your love life, struggling for tenure, publishing papers and submitting grant proposals, pregnancy and raising children. For others, you will listen to their associations as a grandfather or an older woman, maybe recently widowed. The heart of any meaningful analysis of any significant life is contact with growth and development, with mourning, loss and separation. Patients meet the therapist at a particular point in their life, and the analyst's own issues with separation will always be a region where they will have to do some extra working-through in the countertransference. Some of the therapist's anxieties always meet the patient, perhaps even making it somewhat difficult for the patient to make free use of the therapist. A young therapist – who may see their very ability to hold long treatments as validation of being a good therapist – would experience a patient's wish to end treatment differently. An older therapist may be interested in reducing the volume of work in their clinic. Or perhaps the opposite is true: The older psychotherapist would react with great vulnerability to the patient's wish to terminate treatment because continuing it would validate for them that they still "have what it takes," while a younger analyst may be secretly glad to unload the burden of a demanding, dependent or adhesive patient she's been seeing ever since she was a resident.

Ferenczi thought that analysis has, in theory, a natural end, a point at which the patient and therapist can say their goodbyes. Freud was somewhat more pessimistic on this aspect and saw analysis as an interminable process. On the other hand, if you remember Freud's reaction to Ferenczi's reproaches – that he did not analyze his negative transference while treating him – you will realize that, in fact, Freud refuses to revert his relationship with Ferenczi, to forever remain his analyst. He once wrote him:

> I ascertain that, in connecting with our analysis, you have pressed me back into the role of the analyst, which I would otherwise not have reassumed vis-à-vis the tried-and-true friend.
>
> (Freud to Ferenczi, January 20, 1930)

I think they were both right, in a way. Ferenczi wanted to be both a patient and a friend. He wanted to continue using Freud unhindered, as a patient does with their analyst but also wanted to receive from Freud things that, as a patient, he couldn't.

Analysis is indeed an interminable process. But, that does not mean that this specific analysis, with this particular patient, should continue indefinitely. That won't change the fact that psychoanalysis is essentially interminable. Prolonging the analysis by five more years would not necessarily guarantee better results. Moreover, many analyses and psychotherapies have, I believe, an expiration date, after which they're "idling." It's best to identify and acknowledge that state. It's not always a matter of "impasse" in the treatment. Sometimes, the whole affair has exhausted itself. Perhaps in the future, with a different therapist, it could be picked up.

One can always find signs of resistance in therapy. But, the very existence of resistance does not exempt us from considering the possibility that analysis is reaching its end. You can find telltale signs of the end of therapy in the patient's speech and dreams. They are internal, not external. That is, the fact that the patient did not get married or finish their Ph.D. while treated by you – even if that was their overt wish, perhaps even what they defined as their "main complaint" – still doesn't justify continuing treatment. You listen to the patient, and while their content may still be concerned with the same deliberations, their psychic position and form of mental function have been transformed. Continued growth may only be possible after separating from the analyst. Dreams help me identify these fine changes in my psychic position. There is a question of whether we decide that it's time to end therapy or wait for the patient. A patient of Bion's said that one day, Bion told him that it was time for him to stop analysis and get married (Culbert-Koehn, 2011). I still haven't made such a declaration, but if a patient says, "I was thinking about ending therapy," it is very conceivable that at one point, I would stop interpreting that meditation for them and offer that we set a termination date.

I think discussing a termination date is good; it's the right thing to do. It's important because a very important phase of the treatment begins the moment we don't just "discuss ending treatment" but set an actual termination date. If the patient likes, they can change their mind and continue. But the separation phase, with all it entails, can only begin if you consider the end of the treatment as a reality rather than more grist for the "analytic mill." I'm now working with a patient toward termination inside a storm that seems, superficially, like regression. As we know, regression can be benign or malignant. It can serve as a defense mechanism from emotional pain, that is – be an expression of resistance. But, it can also serve the therapeutic process in the same way it serves processes of change and creation. I understand the current regression differently than I would have understood similar behavior by the same patient during analysis. I think the patient is repeating "favorite episodes" in the treatment and his neurosis as preparation for separating from me. I don't think it is a "negative therapeutic reaction." We had that, too. But once we started discussing separation, what started is a sort of compression of all our years of analysis, a kind of sped-up rewind. After we already set a date for ending treatment, he started to thin out his arrival to sessions significantly. In the last two months of the analysis, he usually made only two of his five weekly hours and spent those on the couch, catching up on sleep. Sometimes, when I turned his attention to his absences and difficulty in discussing the oncoming separation, he told me he didn't even notice he missed yesterday's hour. Sometimes, he reports on something wonderful he read in psychoanalytic literature instead of coming to his hour with me. "For me, reading Freud," he said, "is like being here in analysis with you."

I woke him up once when he was napping on the couch and asked him, "Where are you?" He answered: "I was just thinking how weird it is that medicine still hasn't found a way to take a fetus from its mother's womb and implant it in another. After all, the mother doesn't create the baby. The fetus only needs a womb environment to grow, not a mother, so how come there's no way yet to move fetuses from the body of one woman to another?"

I realized what tremendous effort the patient was making, as part of preparing to end treatment and separating from me, to deny their dependence on me, his analytic mother. How deeply he hopes that the section between life in the analytic womb to life after birth would allow them to continue unharmed, for father Freud to act perhaps, in his fantasy, as a surrogate mother, in which he can continue to develop. I could better understand all the dozens of hours in the last months in which I waited for him and he didn't come to analysis, examining in his fantasy whether he could end the treatment as a baby born of an artificial pregnancy, who was able to bypass not only the primal scene as a fact of life, but also the pregnancy itself.

This time of preparation for separating from analysis is also used to discuss disappointments and goals not achieved. We find ways of expressing anger about what wasn't achieved, what perhaps prevented certain things from being achieved, maybe due to the therapist's limitations. Perhaps another therapist would have better understood and worked better with certain materials and transferences. Perhaps in the future, another therapist could help the patient with what I couldn't.

I don't like discussing the end of treatments in the slightly archaic concept of "resolution of the transference." Some patients don't want the transference to be resolved, and I respect that. I try to hold back and not surprise patients with various "self-disclosures" and sentimental "closing speeches." It's not really my style during analysis, so there's no point in behaving like a different person just because of the oncoming separation. Naturally, longer analyses create a certain relationship with each patient – one patient knows where I grew up and is familiar with my political position or literary taste, another doesn't – this isn't accidental, and there is no reason to change this state of affairs only because we'll soon be parting. We have a different relationship with each of our patients, and I wouldn't place myself completely differently with a patient who kept themselves from knowing various things about me; I wouldn't confront the fantasies they had about me with reality near the end of therapy. What allows a patient to see the therapist in a more or less realistic light is the use they made of the therapist and the slow and diligent interpretative work you've done with them, not suddenly exposing them to some biographical detail about you. Analysis is not a play, and the patient is not an audience to be invited to peek behind the scenes.

A good separation from psychotherapy aids the continued usefulness and effect the treatment has in the following years. This is where the interminability of the analytic process is really tested, whether the therapy continues to accompany the patient, helps them think and feel, relax, contain and fathom their mental make-up. A successful therapy remains a living, breathing object in the patient's mind for a long time. True, some therapies enter into a kind of hibernation following the end of treatment and seem to be "missing in action." But at a later point in the patient's life, they can "thaw" the analytic object that, for whatever reason, they put into deep freeze and use it. I was recently approached by an 85-year-old woman who asked me to help her find an analyst to aid her with something that has lately returned to bother her. She was in analysis in her 30s and feels that this is the time to go back for some matter that excellent analysis did not help with.

The patient's love for psychoanalysis as an internal object can be revealed as more resilient and useful than the love the patient felt their analyst had or didn't have, towards them during treatment, and more than goals achieved or not, in analysis. Not only as therapists but also as patients – do not be afraid of the anger and disappointment you have towards your therapists or the analysis you had.

The door is always open for patients we separated from. We tell them that. Part of me identifies strongly with the continued commitment to my patients even after the end of treatment. Moreover, I sometimes understand something that was less-than-perfect in therapies I performed in the past and imagine "recalling" patients, like car manufacturers sometimes do, when they discover a severe enough problem in the assembly line. I make sure to have a few hours open on my calendar in case I need to receive a past patient who needs me. Deep down, however, I don't think it's always the right thing to receive any patient who wants to come back to therapy. In hindsight, for some patients, it would have been better had I not taken them for another therapy at a later point in time. I think I made a mistake, taking certain people for a second round or even for a few hours. Some patients are suited for dynamic therapy, and some are not. For some, the right thing would be to allow them to come back for treatment with you, and for others, it would be better that they be helped by a different therapist after they finish therapy with you. We are not the be-all and end-all. More than that, sometimes, just at the end of the analysis, some big new issue arises, and it's very tempting to continue exploring it, even though we already set a termination date. That, too, is not always wise, I believe. Well, you think to yourself, if the sun is once again shining over the analysis, why won't we continue climbing up the mountain to see even brighter, greener peaks along with our patient?

Just as we shouldn't get too excited about any small regression and translate it to pushing back the end of treatment, often working with the patient would feel wonderful towards the end of treatment. And then the question arises almost naturally: If the decision to end treatment had such a good influence on its progress, why stop here? What then happens is that we keep some patients with us because they're funny or interesting, because we love them or insidiously lulled into a merger fantasy with them towards the end of treatment. Or, to the contrary, perhaps we're being faithful to patients to whom we haven't been feeling like we're helping much, or at all, for some time, but we are afraid of letting them go and accepting that knowledge about ourselves and the limits of mental therapy. So we wait for a moment of inspiration or some miracle to take place in therapy, to save us and the patient from this predicament.

Like children who find it hard to separate on good terms, to go to sleep quietly or leave with a good object, both patients and therapists "spoil" good separations. Bion writes that the good object absent is a bad object present. I believe this is true not only for those patients who completely lose touch with the good object when it is absent, but also for therapists. Therapists, too, "spoil" good therapies with less-than-adequate separations. Therapists create provocations, don't let go well, release the patient "back into the water," but fail to take the hook out of their mouth. I recently heard of an older analyst who, when asked by a long-time patient to start planning the end of the analysis, responded: "As far as I'm concerned, we have nothing more to discuss. If you want to end analysis, we can do so right now."

Other therapists adopt a different strategy to deny the end of analysis: They cooperate with the patient's desire not to separate but merely "take a break in treatment," thereby saving themselves the work of separation. I believe it's a mistake to take a long break in treatment without expressly calling it what it is – separation. Even if the analysis "fell flat" prematurely from the point of view of the candidate or experienced therapist.

The need to repair and retain the good object leads patients who found much help in us to be very scared of the therapy becoming interminable. They set off on the difficult mission of repairing their internal objects. In their fantasy, this mission is "too big for them," however, and sooner or later, it would rob them of every psychic and material resource they have. The phenomenon Freud termed a "negative therapeutic reaction" is related to the quality of the patient's super-ego and the hold the death drive has over it. It can cause the expression of very complicated object-relations and unconscious psychic structures. For example, the patient might inform you that she's not interested in ending the treatment but only taking a break for a few months to care for her sick mother, who needs treatment more than she does. Or she might object to still being in therapy at her age: "How come I've been here for all those years and never met anyone else who's also been to analysis?" Another patient may reheat the old complaint about the high cost of therapy "that only privileged people can enjoy" or express fear of "addiction" to therapy, which would never end. For each of these examples, alongside the rational reasoning for stopping treatment, we should also listen to that region of the patient's ego that might have experienced itself as hopeless or unworthy of help – whose envious of another region of their own ego, which is helped by the treatment and persists in it, despite the pain and anxiety it experiences.

Before acceding to these reasonable requests by the patient – such as lowering the cost of treatment and decreasing frequency to allow the treatment to continue – it's worthwhile to seek the conflict or unconscious fantasy that takes place in the appearance of negative therapeutic reactions at a certain point in time. Just as everything in treatment can be used by the resistance to performing psychic work, so can the resistance to terminating treatment be used by the unconscious to neutralize the treatment. As the subject of this meeting was separation, I will say that, in my opinion, it is sometimes better to take an active approach and aid these difficult patients to end therapy in an organized manner rather than push them to prolong treatment over and over, until you get to the point where they sever it.

It takes experience to decide when to stop interpreting anxiety over the continued treatment and instead starts interpreting resistance to working on ending it and separating. But, it also takes assurance that the good aspects of the analysis stand firm and could stand with the patient even without us. It is important to let patients go, let them swim on rather than get stuck with some toxic introject or chronic transference that will make their lives a living hell.

Chapter 13

Psychoanalysis as a worldview

The world we live in contains new and sophisticated technologies that aim to deceive, oppress and enslave, under the guise of pluralism, autonomy and freedom of choice. These technologies influence our object relations, as well as our perversions and addictions, just as much as they influence our relations with knowledge and authority. Meditations on guilt, democracy and politics.

In 1929, Freud evaluated his life's work thus:

> All I know is that I worked terribly hard; the rest followed as a matter of course. It could also have been very much better. I was aware only of the objective, not of myself. My worst qualities, among them a certain indifference to the world, probably had the same share in the final result as the good ones – i.e., a defiant courage about truth. In the depths of my heart I can't help being convinced that my dear fellow men, with a few exceptions, are worthless.
>
> (Freud to Lou Andreas-Salome July 28 1929 In: *Letters* p. 390)

Freud's "defiant courage" and his love of the truth have received the recognition they deserve. Many psychoanalysts identify with these properties in some way. But this "indifference to the world" Freud identifies as one of his worst traits, did it, too, become a trademark of the analytical therapist?

Whenever the question of a psychoanalytic *Weltanschauung* – worldview – comes up in Freud's writing, he takes particular pains to dismiss the need for it. For him, the need for one is an expression of narrow-mindedness, a choice of the pleasure principle over the reality principle. "The benighted traveler may sing aloud in the dark to deny his own fears;" he writes, derisively, of those who champion a worldview. He makes it abundantly clear that identifying psychoanalysis with any worldview other than the scientific is an anathema to him.

Freud's position is commonly understood in the context of his aspiration to distance psychoanalysis from philosophy and anchor it in the natural sciences. He criticized philosophers, too, for being unable to walk the world without a "travel guide" to inform them. Analysts, he believed, should be impartial and free of prejudice. They should be suspicious of ideologies, adopting only the scientific

DOI: 10.4324/9781003528470-13

worldview, which accepts the limitations of knowledge, strives to discover the truth through empirical means and avoids relying on intuition, revelation or the mandates of some superior power.

When arguing against a psychoanalytic Weltanschauung Freud's main concern was that psychoanalysis become politicized, a concern supported by an ideological interpretation given, mainly in socialist circles, to his theory of infantile sexuality and the Oedipal complex. In the 1920s, Freud openly opposed the publication of Wilhelm Reich's work, which tied capitalism with an increased death drive, and in the 1930s supported Reich's removal from the International Psychoanalytic Association, on the background of Reich's attack, peppered with psychoanalytic insights, on German fascism (Rolnik, 2006). These were the immediate social and political circumstances in which the discussion on a psychoanalytic worldview took place in the first half of the 20th century. I believe that to this day, these circumstances still hide from us the fact that the relationship with the concept of truth is an important point of contact between psychoanalysis and political theory, which we should not be quick to dismiss.

Human beings cannot be understood as acting, thinking and experiencing psychological creatures without understanding the world they were born into and are formed in. My ideas on the relations between psychoanalysis and politics were influenced by my research on the way psychoanalytic institutes regarded the Nazi rise to power in Germany, the immigration of psychoanalysis during the interbellum between the two World Wars and its reception by the Jewish society of Mandatory Palestine (Rolnik, 2006, 2007, 2012). For that purpose, I also studied the history of psychoanalysis in other countries, such as France, the USA, Argentina, Australia and Russia – aiming to gain a comparative perspective on the way a mental environment and political culture echo into psychoanalytic thought and ethics, enables its development, or in extreme cases – as happened in Soviet Russia and Nazi Germany – oppresses its practice almost entirely. There is much to be gained from familiarity with various psychoanalytic cultures and theories in the social and political context they developed in or exist in today.

Freud tended to disparage religion and applaud the achievements of science. Regarding his theory as part of a comprehensive worldview could jeopardize psychoanalysis' academic credentials. However, A position seeking to integrate psychoanalysis into academic psychology is even harder to support today. When it comes to fields of research concerned with the human psyche, science – which in general loses interest in the distinction between knowledge and truth – seems particularly intent on deepening the trend to reduce subjects to their physio-chemical system. Nowadays, the discussion of the "psyche" is conducted, almost in its entirety, through very essentialist, cognitive or voluntarist biological concepts. Psychiatry and neuroscience eagerly promote the image of a human as a naturalist being that is, at one and the same time, digital-cybernetic and, therefore, also measurable, predictable and infinitely improvable. Current voluntarist and spiritual psychology also insist on equating the mind with cognition and seem to see humans as a "beta version" of a living machine, superior in intelligence and efficiency, which is still under development. Accordingly, the behaviorist individual is "mindful" only under "limited liability." They refrain from exhibiting curiosity or being in touch with any part of their inner world that might disturb their peace of mind and even proudly present the narcissistic and psychopathic aspects of their personality as a shield, protecting them from any emotional contact with weakness, dependence, ignorance, guilt, shame or regret. In the era of the brain, "good living" and psychic pain (or psychic lack) are perceived as mutually exclusive. In general, the self of our time prefers to reside inside a fraction of itself, content with excitement and sentimentality rather than emotions (Bollas, 2015). Many of our patients give in to the intensity of the sensory experience, confusing wholeness with perfection, pleasure with happiness or satisfaction. New forms of depression, emptiness, anxiety and attention disorders, and an unprecedented increase in consumption of psychotropic drugs and psychoactive substances are among the current manifestations of the difficulty in bearing sorrow, guilt and lack of pleasure.

In the early 20th century, psychoanalysis served an important role in blurring the line between the previously dichotomous concepts of normal and pathological mental states and in expanding the boundaries of what was considered mentally normal. In our times, the psychotherapist has a role in nurturing the full complexity of the concept of mental normalcy and expanding it to the realm of political discourse. Through psychoanalysis, we can identify perverse structures in media, science and politics, set apart scientific theories and human perceptions that open up new avenues of thoughts from those that "use the truth to lie" and maintain partial object relations with reality – only with that part of the subject's reality which is liable to be measured and quantified.

Psychoanalytic thought can aid us in identifying technology and forms of information and communication that are pluralistic and expand our scope, and distinguish them from forms of communication that aim to not only recombine the wheat with the chaff, but to completely undo the distinction between addictive, evacuative chatter to deep, meaningful thought, between healthy skepticism to infantile subjectivism or relativism. The world we live in contains new and sophisticated technologies that aim to deceive, oppress and enslave under the guise of pluralism, autonomy and freedom of choice. These technologies affect our object relations, as well as perversions and addiction, just as much as they affect our relations with knowledge and authority.

I find strange the argument that because psychoanalysis emerged in a patriarchal, male-chauvinistic world, or since it focuses on the unconscious and the inner world, it is therefore irrelevant in the political or ethical discussion of our times. In the clinic, we can see a relationship between the development of authenticity and integrity and the ability to integrate drive derivatives and conflicting emotional positions in the inner world. Even the concept of an inner psychoanalytic object I developed in our previous sessions is rooted in psychoanalytic ethics. Must we ascribe dogmatism, paternalism or narrow-mindedness to a political worldview that uses the psychoanalytic idea that we, as humans, are torn between the life and death drives, between logos and eros, or between striving towards the object and longing towards emancipation from it? This conflict explains human ambivalence towards knowledge, the truth, the good or justice, an ambivalence reflected both in individual love and sexuality and in the political system, social institutions, and object-relation technologies we develop. The technological and scientific world-view alone, with its characteristic emphasis on methodology, data processing and evidence-based conclusions, would never release humanity from antisemitism, racism or misogyny. In its current hyper-technological version, modernity does not realize universalism and the values of enlightenment. It is characterized by polarized ideological positions, widening class gaps, overblown and idealized fragments of identities and identifications and, more generally, "narcissism of small differences."

Freud's thought contributed much to the children's rights movement, the women's liberation movement and the gay rights movement. It also contributed to the understanding of the various forms of the phenomenon of racism. The distilled essence of psychoanalytic thought on antisemitism and racism is expressed in a paragraph completely unrelated to that issue: In his paper *The Unconscious*, Freud likens unconscious instinctual impulses (Triebregungen) to mixed-race individuals, who belong, qualitatively, in the preconscious system, but in actual fact are in the unconscious system. It is the origin of these particular "drive derivatives," Freud argues, that determines their fate:

> We may compare them with individuals of mixed race who, taken all round, resemble white men, but who betray their colored descent by some striking feature or other, and on that account are excluded from society and enjoy none of the privileges of white people.
>
> (*Standard Edition*, Vol. 14, p. 191)

Comparing the drive to a "mixed-race individual" excluded from the politics of the ego and likening it to a psychic "mixed race" devoid of equal rights, i.e., the privileges of whites, serves as an interesting point of contact between the Freudian concept of drive and what would later be termed *Post-colonial theory.*

This comparison allows us to see racism, for example, not only as a mode of relating to the stranger and other – which is how it is commonly presented in popular discourse – but also as a mode of relating to the inherent human drive to know the other, and to the psychic unconscious in general. Thus viewed, racism is an expression of the failure to realize the desire for intimacy between humans as different from each other and preferring narcissistic, excluding and symbiotic forms of union between humans.

Historian David Ohana argues that fascism, more than a political ideology, is a *political community of experience* that draws its power from the exciting, violent act itself (Ohana, 2020). This argument does not excuse historians and sociologists from the need to examine the particular circumstances in which the phenomenon of fascism, in its various instances in historical space and time, rises and falls. As analysts, I believe we can also fill Ohana's conclusion on the fascistic experience with meta-psychological content: We know quite a lot about the mutual relations between fascistic trends and phenomena, on an individual and group level, and the way a culture or society regards unconscious psychic reality. The psychoanalytic unconscious is, by its very nature, more disturbing than that of philosophical idealism, romanticism or mysticism. The way politics and culture regard it would influence individuals and groups' forms of mental functioning, their relations to the values of pluralism, as well as their object relations both with people close to them and those who are somewhat removed – strangers and relatives alike.

Psychoanalysis does not take for granted humans' ability to distinguish their heart's wishes from reality, nor their ability to think and feel. For human subjectivity to be expressed, it requires not merely mental-individual conditions and enabling developmental ones but also social and political ones. A group of people can live and function for long periods without actually thinking or feeling and without even really dreaming.

In patients sometimes controlled by a "fascist state of mind" – as Christopher Bollas (1992) calls it – the mind would destroy parts of self and internalized object parts. Archaic modes of mental functioning, perverse or psychotic structures, may block the ability to contain doubt and uncertainty, to think and feel. As mentioned, this knowledge is not confined to the analytical clinic. Societies and groups can reach a state where they function on a schizo-paranoid level, prefer a leadership that is narcissistic-charismatic and encourages their denial of large swaths of internal and external reality to the point of self-extinction. In a totalitarian society, humans avoid independent thought and "willingly" blind themselves to reality. They deny knowledge even where it is accessible to them. In a democratic society, the distinction between prejudice and facts of life is meaningful. Facts of life (Money-Kyrle, 1971) are not only evidence-based knowledge received as the objective truth by scientific consensus but also psychological knowledge that cannot be quantified and measured and has the validity of truth, knowledge that combines the objective and subjective dimensions of human experience. Psychoanalysis has contributed much to our ability to gain such knowledge and to identify unconscious assumptions and fantasies that inhibit such knowledge. One example is knowledge of the importance of the ability to feel shame and guilt.

Guilt

Young Freud wanted to be a legislator when he grew up. Grown-up Freud, now a mental health doctor, discovered that one of the conditions for good living is to leave some parts of the inner world beyond the realm of moral judgment. It is better that the ego strive to maintain its sovereignty even when its own super-ego stands against it. Freud identified two sources of guilt: Fear of authority and fear of the super-ego. The super-ego has a number of roles: To supervise the ego, to set its ideals (the ego ideal) and to serve as its moral compass, i.e., its conscience. Authority and the super-ego demand that we forego satisfying certain drives and libidinal urges in order to not be punished or not lose our parents' love. Internalized by the subject at an early stage of its development, the loss of the super-ego's love is a death sentence for the ego. Freud wrote in 1923: "To the ego, therefore, living means the same as being loved – being loved by the super-ego" (*Standard Edition*, Vol. 19, p. 58). In the analytic clinic, a central distinction formed between feelings of guilt – traced back to an actual deed or moral transgressions – and unconscious guilt – which is rooted in fantasized transgressions and attacks on the loved object – seeking to be released through self-punishment, melancholy and various forms of violence.

Freud's discussion of guilt is limited to the anxiety over the love of the object or the loss of the super-ego's love. He was aware that his theory does not cover justified instances of guilt, such as harming the object in fantasy, but he also did not conduct a full revision of the theory of guilt after adding the death drive to his theory. In *Civilization and its Discontents* (1930), he briefly considers the distinction between guilt and remorse and argues that remorse is an expression of the conflict of ambivalence and of the eternal struggle between the death and life drives.

In describing the *depressive position,* Melanie Klein added an additional dimension to our understanding of guilt: The ability to bear guilt as an expression of a developing anxiety over the wellbeing of the object and a will to repair it. Freud and Klein disagree on the question of the origin and the circumstances around the development of the super-ego. The Freudian super-ego is the successor to the Oedipal complex, while the Kleinian super-ego is formed as the result of the splits between the good and bad objects that take place in the ego during the first year of life. Both, as mentioned, deliberated on the question of the disproportionate hostility embedded in the super-ego's relations with the ego and the circumstances in which it becomes an unending reservoir of envy, anger, wrath and indignation – "a pure culture of the death drive," in Freud's own words. Klein not only emphasized the death drive and the projections the super-ego forms, but she also described the importance of the real good object in the struggle waged by the ego, from its inception, against the bad object and the death drive.

One of the explanations given for the disproportionate way in which the super-ego tends to relate to the ego is influences outside of individual history. The figure of the murderous primal father embedded in the phylogeny of the human species is projected on the parent and creates a strict "judicial instance." As an analytical therapist, I do not content myself with the claim that aggression created as a result of trauma, early deprivations or excessive libidinal frustration is projected on the super-ego and makes a demon of it. I see guilt as evidence that the psyche is open, from its very first moments, to influences external to individual psychology and life experience, influences that originate in ancient historical times, on the one hand, and the culture we are born into, on the other.

Just as the super-ego represents mankind's far past in the inner world, social and cultural circumstances also play a part in shaping the conscientious climate in which people develop. In *Group Psychology and the Analysis of the Ego,* Freud notes that the moral standards of an individual, as part of a group, can be very different from those they internalized individually. Writing in a time of political turmoil and mass protests in post-World War I Vienna, Freud describes the two axes around which non-democratic ideologies revolve: Self-love transforms to a sense of partnership and group cohesion on the hand and to hostile sanctimony towards outsiders on the other. One of the functions that any group, organization and political culture fulfills for its members is protection from guilt. This insight was used by Holocaust historians when attempting to explain the willingness of "decent people" to obey, through complete self-conviction, murderous orders given during the War. Tracking the echoes of the Holocaust in the inner worlds of those who were not directly involved in it, as executioners or as victims, required a sharp ear. The collective repression of feelings of guilt that characterized postwar West German society attested to the Germans' inability to mourn: For the narcissistic, grandiose investments they made in the person of the omnipotent leader, for the shattered hopes they pinned on the War and for their refusal to take responsibility for the murder and destruction their catastrophic political choices foisted on them and on the world. They were "good Germans" who refused to accept responsibility because they hadn't been members of the Nazi Party. In this way, they absolved their conscience of collective responsibility, cultivated a voyeuristic attitude toward every political aspect of their life, and withdrew into a private, obligation-free existence (Mitscherlich, 1967; Bohleber, 1997; Sebald, 2003).

As mentioned, the role of the super-ego is not merely to scold the ego and police it but also to support and comfort it. The emphasis Melanie Klein and her successors put on the well-being of the good object and the drive for its reparation advanced the part that was left undeveloped in Freud's theory of guilt: Love as a source of ambivalence, guilt and remorse. Klein's concept of a depressive position stipulated both a developmental phase and a recurring mental position, where anxiety for the well-being of the object and attempts to repair it become more dominant than the paranoid anxiety about the super-ego's damaging effect. Combining the two perspectives of guilt – the Freudian and the Kleinian – has, I believe, far-reaching ramifications not only for the analytical clinic but also the place politics can take in psychic reality.

Let us start with the clinic: As psychotherapists, we could perceive our patient's guilt as emanating from an identification with a pathological-abusive super-ego, one that "locks" the self in a schizo-paranoid position. From such a theoretical perspective, we aspire to "release" the patient from the burden of an intra-psychic judicial instance that is overbearing on the self. How do we identify a person standing helpless at their own inner "gate to the law"? Persecutive guilt is typically accompanied by resentment, despair, fear and self-flagellation. We find it, for example, in melancholic depression. The ego, feeling that the super-ego does not love it but rather hates and condemns it, neglects itself. The melancholic's guilt can lead to them being unable to walk through a street without feeling compelled to take home any stray animal they happen upon. As small and overcrowded as their house may be, the guilt doesn't relent. The patient's guilt may be revealed as a defense against a mental pain originating in an encounter with parts of their personality that mercilessly attack their dependence needs. The patients would find it difficult to cleanse themselves of such guilt even if they take in every stray kitten in the world. People who take their own lives sometimes maintain that by doing so, they set their loved ones free.

This difficulty of cleaning oneself from the persecutive guilt that plagues the melancholic received poetic expression in C.N. Bialik's poem, "eating sins" (also named "repentant" and commonly interpreted as a critical satire on the Hasidic movement), which describes a man absolving himself of sin, through the ritual of Kapparot, on the eve of Yom Kippur. To break the fast, he delights in a dish of chicken, only to realize he has used the same chicken for both the ritual and the feast – metaphorically ingesting all the sins and crimes he committed in the previous year. A similar fate awaits melancholic patients, who swallow whole the same object they directed their love and aggression toward.

Depressive guilt, or "conscientious guilt," is different from melancholic or paranoid guilt. It is expressed in sorrow, concern and responsibility towards the object and the self. It might not motivate a person to adopt every stray cat in their neighborhood, but it could push them to repair the inner object and recognize the limits of their responsibility. From a therapeutic perspective, there is a special significance to the patient's ability to relate the unconscious attacks on the inner object and their relation to guilt.

Let us put into focus a different therapeutic perspective: A psychotherapist who appreciates not only the misery of his guilt-ridden patient as a testimony to an all too harsh super-ego but also the importance of guilt to the maintenance and functioning of the inner world. Such a therapist would not be quick to "cleanse" the patient of guilt by decreeing it "unrealistic," "irrational," or arising from infantile sources. They would aspire to aid the patient to explore their guilt and identify the unconscious urges and fantasies that underlie it. Naturally, the patient's guilt, as projected upon the figure of the analyst and the setting, will also be the focus of transference interpretations.

What complicates matters is that when working with patients for whom the super-ego developed in overbearing directions, we often witness a sadomasochistic re-enactment between the patient and therapist. When a patient "reveals" to us that they are "about to burst" because they have been, for some reason, refraining from using the bathroom throughout the hour, we should examine whether a similar drama is starting to make its way to the transference. As therapists, we may identify with the projections of an accusatory patient and feel that we over-restrain our own needs or withhold certain interventions for fear of the patient's wrath. For example, we would be apprehensive about ending an hour on time, hesitant to remind a patient they still haven't paid us this month or avoid taking a vacation for fear of a patient's response.

This next example shows the sadomasochistic potential of guilt in transference relations: D arrived in therapy after bringing financial ruin to himself and his family. It's difficult to tell whether D blames himself for squandering his money or his family for enabling him to burn through a large inheritance to the point of only being able to afford bare necessities. The beginning of the hour is always

accompanied by the same ritual: D enters and announces, in self-coddling contempt: "Dr. Freud, is it okay if I have a glass of water?" He immediately answers, "I
know you hate it when I call you that and ask permission to take a glass." He gives
me his mobile phone to plug into my charger and heavily drops into the couch with
the glass of water he poured himself. Once a month, D's car runs out of gasoline,
and he calls everyone he knows to come rescue him. "I've got such great friends,"
he says. "Almost always, someone comes to bail me out."

One day, I suggested to D that he start taking care of charging his phone himself. I decided to put into action what I have been feeling in transference for some
time: D is behaving like a "damsel in distress" with me, too, activating me in a way
that weakens him and controls me. I told him he would like me to help him with
the emptiness he feels and his hunger but that it is hard for him to ask and receive
from me something he can't give himself, such as mental aid and understanding.
That is the reason I became, in his imagination, someone who is strict with him and
prevents things from him. I also tied it to his continuous struggle with his weight
and the greed that made it difficult for him to retain his inheritance. I talked to him
about the fantasy that the weaker and poorer he becomes, the more others would
take care of him, and he would not have to assume responsibility for what is happening in his inner world, would no longer have to keep what he has and would no
longer feel guilt over his aggression and destructive behavior, and over the damages he caused himself and his family.

Therapeutic work with patients of D's kind taught me that one of the challenges
in therapies where the super-ego is revealed to be particularly nasty, and the ego
too weak to bear guilt and remorse, is to butter the bread on both sides: Interpret the guilt as a direct result of unconscious attacks on the object, and interpret
attacks on the object as a direct result of dependence on it and love towards it.
This is a Sisyphean task, which would sooner or later also activate pathological
parts in the analyst's super-ego. The result can be a false analysis, where the therapist defends against the patient's projection through feigned empathy, allowing the
patient a facade of cooperating with the treatment while unconsciously retaining
a passive-aggressive position towards their psychic reality on the one hand and
toward authentic relations with the analyst on the other. In D's case, matters were
complicated by the fact that his therapy was paid for by a wealthy relative, a fact
that made therapy itself a potential accomplice in his passive-abusive relationship
with his surroundings.

It is never easy for the ego to be the "master of its own domain." But the ego's
position relative to the super-ego is at times, even more difficult than its position
relative to the id. There is no direct relation between the super-ego's rigidity and
experiencing real trauma or identification with harsh and vengeful parental figures
in reality. It seems that for many patients, a disproportionate hostility is phylo-
genetically inscribed in their archaic super-ego, which is almost completely sub-
merged in the unconscious. For many of our patients, it is not the id that is the real
master but rather the archaic super-ego. It is what they find difficult to decipher
and relax, and they require constant friction with it – as the patient in my last

example did – to feel a level of control over it. These patients require help to stand up straight and face the perverse and oppressive versions of the super-ego. In the clinic, we encounter ever more often patients who have developed an opposite strategy to deal with the power of their super-ego. These patients gained various monikers in psychoanalytic literature: Bad hysterics, malignant narcissists, sociopaths and others. They fantasize about subjectivity and object-relations without feelings of sorrow, remorse or guilt.

Guilt and democracy

A clear conscience, writes Wisława Szymborska in her poem *In Praise of Feeling Bad About Yourself* (Translated by Stanislaw Baraczak and Clare Cavanagh), is among the signs of bestiality. Indeed, many of the titans of culture, capitalism and politics of our day represent, for their admirers, the possibility of a guiltless, shameless world, not only in the intra-psychic, interpersonal context but also when it comes to the relations between man, nature and environment. Having elaborated on the challenges that the structure of the patient's (and analyst's) super-ego poses for the psychotherapist, our civilization and democratic structures, in particular, are very much dependent on it. I doubt whether a perception of self and of humanity – be it voluntarist, objectivist, libertarian or fundamentalist – that aspires to abolish shame and guilt as a fact of life and as an essential component of humanity is sustainable from a cultural-evolutionary or even environmental-ecological, perspective. In a guiltless, shameless world, there is no love but idealization of technology, authoritative admiration of the rich and powerful and self-love. In a guiltless world, one cannot learn from experience. It would, therefore, be better if the concept of guilt took part in the political debate over the sustainability of civilization and the repair of the ecological system. The more we realize the harms of capitalism and industrialization on the environment as well as on our systems of government, the more it is difficult for us to acknowledge our responsibility for these damages, mourn them and gather our forces to repair what can still be salvaged.

It is still difficult to imagine the Herculean task set to a post-Covid society from the perspective of collective guilt. If we take the route leading to oppressive guilt, it would lead to seeking scapegoats, fake news, social polarization and maybe even violence on a scale known only from the first half of the 20th century. A psychoanalytic worldview can help understand how the populist onslaught on science and vaccination in our time – as well as the denial of how unfettered capitalism affects the Earth and the environment – bears characteristics of oppressive melancholic guilt. It is not skepticism and love of truth which stand, I think, behind the preference of "alternative facts" and fake news, but suspicion, disavowal and mistrust. Depressive and conscientious guilt can aid in creating solidarity, responsibility and cooperation between conflicting parts, within societies and among nations, to allow us to mourn losses and fix technological and economic models, social structures and political mechanisms. It is critical that we distinguish between the politics of responsibility and the politics of blame.

Two main types of defense exist against psychic pain: Splitting the self, which enables projecting parts of self and unbearable mental content on others, who become a subject of hatred or idealization – racism and antisemitism, or otherwise a cult of personality – or the self can rise against itself and attack the internal object and the ability to think and feel. Both mechanisms can be seen not only in the analytic clinic but also in the political, scientific and cultural fields.

Psychoanalytic ethics and democracy have a rather complex relationship. Psychoanalysis leads us to face unconscious wishes and fantasies of the kind that feeds undemocratic desires embedded in human history and psyche, desires that fascistic or autocratic regimes can augment and abuse. For example, the longing to merge with the ego ideal, the fear of the different, anxiety about working-through grief, preferring violent action over thought, or the will to avoid, at all cost, remorse and bad conscience. Fighting for democracy and against tyranny is, when translated to psychoanalytic language, resisting the temptation to aspire to perfection, consensus and "peace of mind" offered by undemocratic forms of rule, as well as some states of mind in science, culture and religion. Psychoanalytic therapy and the democratic project stand leveled – both seeing the ability to think and feel and the connection between thought and emotion or logic and desire as mental and cultural achievements that required immense effort from humanity, achievements that are frequently attacked, from within and without.

Self-deception, the inherent human tendency to avoid integration in the face of anxiety, guilt and psychic pain, and the human tendency to fantasize in order to deny and reject feelings of helplessness, dependence, separateness and envy – these are all "facts of life" explained by various psychoanalytic theories. At the base of the psychoanalytic worldview and perspective on humanity stand also "impractical" human psychological needs, such as the need for dreaming, play and creativity, which we consider essential for emotional and cognitive development, socialization and knowledge of ourselves and the world. History teaches us that the ability to create, play and dream is also very much dependent on politics and its level of commitment to truth as a universal value.

Politics can corrupt, or it can aid people live according to the truth on both the intra-psychic, inter-subjective and trans-subjective levels. It has the power to influence the kinds of defenses a group turns to when it negotiates with the truth, with the unknown, with drives, with guilt and with the demands of reality.

I want to summon Oedipus to our conversation one last time

All arts and sciences share an occupation with the idea of truth. Freud and his successors developed a complex theory and technique to investigate overt and covert instances of the human need for truth as a psychic and mental function of individuals and groups. Before Freud, philosophy never invented a comprehensive theory, not to mention a method, to explain emotional obstacles – ambivalence, love-hate relationship, the delicate balance between enjoyment, pain, dependence, anxiety and guilt – which fill a role when the individual (but also a group, science or culture) approaches the question of truth from an emotional psychological perspective, rather than a purely philosophical, rational, utilitarian and cognitive one. I opened our first encounter, in the first week of the first lockdown, with Oedipus. I wish now to summon him to our conversation one last time.

Freud deciphered the myth of Oedipus as a testament to the longing for incest by the child in the adult. But Oedipus's life was more than his relations with the sexual drive. He also portrays the essence of choice between self-knowledge and recognition of the truth and self-deception. Before bringing ruin to himself, Oedipus saved Thebes from the disease. He was able to boldly look at life's riddles head-on, think independently and solve the riddle of the Sphinx. One might say that Oedipus could have been wise, but his conflict with the drive and with knowledge and mindfulness made him vain and stupid.

Psychoanalysis investigates the subject's sense of truth, as it is weaved with the life and death drives. The political field has, I believe, a large influence on the quality of our search for truth and its many manifestations and a tremendous influence on our relations with the life and death drives. Politics influences individuals' and groups' willingness to incorporate more than one point of view into their intra-psychic and inter-subjective world. We cannot stay complacent to the political world because we also require politics in order to *become* subjects striving for the truth and attempting to live by it, even when it doesn't serve our immediate interests and desires. The patient's freedom of thought, even within the confines of the analytic practice, is much more reliant on politics than most analysts acknowledge. Politics is also what will allow or block for people the possibility of accepting the simultaneous existence of varied truths and perspectives in society without resorting to physical violence and mass psychosis.

In times of political upheaval, the therapist must not only encourage the patient to recognize their dependency, make the connection between their mental inhibitions and their childhood and generally "tend to their garden." As analytic therapists, we must also take into account that a functioning democracy plays a role in the regulation of an individual's deepest impulses and fears, as well as in a society's ability to exist and adapt to changing historical realities. Few are those uniquely gifted individuals whose humanity remains unharmed by an environment that surrenders itself to a selfish leader, devoid of any moral inhibitions, who considers himself above the law. The chances of having meaningful mental health care in an authoritarian society are negligible. It is no coincidence that the process of Germany's de-Nazification went on for many years after the defeat of Nazism. Authoritarian, corrupt regimes also take hold of the souls of even those citizens who did not support them at the ballot box or consciously identify with their actions.

Consider Plato's allegory of the cave: Plato himself says the prisoners would kill anyone who would escape the cave to return wiser and more knowledgeable about reality. But, Plato does not offer an explanation as to why would the prisoners wish to kill the philosopher who returned to the cave with this new liberating knowledge of the world. This is where psychoanalysis comes into the picture, and attempts to explain this emotional and irrational aspect of our love-hate relationship with truth, which are very seldom regarded by science, philosophy or politics. It is the role of politics to protect the philosopher, the artist and the scientist – and also the psychotherapist – to allow them to persevere in their search for truth for the benefit of all other dwellers of the cave. To reject thought, writes Hannah Arendt in the prologue to her book *The Human Condition*, does not mean to be stupid or unintelligent, but to become thoughtless, to prefer complacent repetition of empty and trivial truths (Arendt, 1958, p. 5). Through her concept of the *banality of evil*, Arendt offered a historical-sociological analysis of the loss of ability to think and act morally, which in many ways complements Freud's, Lacan's and Bion's theories of thinking, which are focused on internal emotional resistances we, as subjects, harbor against knowledge.

Indeed, Freud's correspondence with Einstein clearly shows their concern with similar processes and hope for opposite ones, even before the Nazi rise to power. Answering Einstein's argument that "man has within him a lust for hatred and destruction," Freud was unwilling to explain war solely by referencing the death drive and did not rush to make his psychological explanation for war contingent on such an ahistorical concept as "human nature." In *Why War?* Freud (1993) hypothesizes instead that war might one day come to be seen by man as debasing not for conscious, rational or emotional reasons but for reasons that are structural, organic and aesthetic. He writes:

> We pacifists have a constitutional intolerance of war, an idiosyncrasy magnified, as it were, to the highest degree. It seems, indeed, as though the lowering of aesthetic standards in war plays a scarcely smaller part in our rebellion than do its cruelties.

Freud uses his letter of reply to Einstein to implicitly hypothesize about the existence of a "second nature" in man, of a historical human subjectivity that transcends both biology and individual psychology. That second nature is a historical-cultural product and the fruit of social construction, but only when it becomes a type of biological intolerance, or in Freud's words, "pacifism for organic reasons," is it likely to constitute the basis for an authentic repudiation of war. In his response to the question of "Why War?" in 1932, Freud, the notorious pessimist, sounds more optimistic than Einstein (Freud & Einstein, *Why War*, 1932 in: Ashkenazi, BarGal and Rolnik, 2018).

I would like to end my "talking cure" with words written by Ludwig Wittgenstein over 100 years ago: "We feel that even if *all possible* scientific questions be answered, the problems of life have still not been touched at all. Of course there is then no question left, and just this is the answer" (Wittgenstein, 2012, p. 116). Psychoanalysis is not a religion or an ideology; it does not seek to answer all possible ethical or scientific questions, just as it is suspicious towards defiant interjections that "there is no such thing as a subject" or that "everything is political." As a worldview and ethics, it still retains the ability, however, to explore and touch the "problems of our life" in a unique way, both publicly and in the intimacy of the treatment room. It never stops surprising me.

References

Hebrew sources

Alon, Y. (2013). 'Hizdahoot' ve-'cannibalism' bemishnato shel Freud: Musagim hamam-chisim machshava rhizomatit minekoodat hamabat shel Gilles Deleuze ve-Fèlix guattari ['Identification' and 'Cannibalism' in Freud's Teaching: Concept Demonstrating Rhizo-matic Thought from the Perspective of Gilles Deleuze and Fèlix Guattari] Ma'arag, 4, 17–43.

Ashkenazi, O., Bargal, D. and Rolnik, E. (Eds.). (2018). Einstein ve-Freud ve-hamilchama haba'a [Einstein and Freud and the Next War]. Carmel Publishing.

Lubrani Rolnik, N. (2009). Chaim betoch sipur: teatron playback ve-omanut haimproviza-tzia [Living Inside a Story: Playback Theatre and the Art of Improvization]. Hakibbutz Hameuchad.

Rolnik, E. (2006). Tipulim achronim – hatnua hapsychoanalitit le'achar aliyat hanazim lashilton [Last Therapies – The Psychoanalytic Movement after the Rise of Nazis to Power]. The Journal of Holocaust Research, 20, 7–38.

Rolnik, E. (2019a). Sigmund Freud – michtavim [Sigmund Freud – Letters]. Modan.

English sources

Arendt, H. (1958). The Human Condition. University of Chicago Press.

Bion, W. (1979). Making the Best of a Bad Job. In: Clinical Seminars and Other Works (pp. 321–331). London: Karnac, 1994.

Bion, W. R. (1997). Taming Wild Thoughts. London: Karnac.

Bion, W. R. (2013). Wilfred Bion: Los Angeles Seminars and Supervision. In J. Aguayo and B. Malin (Eds.), London: Karnac.

Bion Talamo, P. (1997). Bion: A Freudian Innovator. British Journal of Psychotherapy, 14, 47–59.

Bleger, J. (1967). Psycho-Analysis of the Psycho-Analytic Frame. International Journal of Psychoanalysis, 48, 511–519.

Bollas, C. (1987). The Shadow of the Object. Psychoanalysis of the Unthought Known. New York: Columbia University Press.

Bollas, C. (1989). Normotic Illness. In M. G. Fromm and B. L. Smith (Eds.), The Facilitat-ing Environment: Clinical Applications of Winnicott's Theory (pp. 317–344). International Universities Press, Inc.

Bollas, C. (1992). Being a Character. Psychoanalysis and Self Experience. London: Routledge.

Bollas, C. (2000). Hysteria. London: Routledge.

Bollas, C. (2001). Freudian Intersubjectivity: Commentary on Paper by Julie Gerhardt and Annie Sweetnam. Psychoanalytic Dialogues, 11, 93–105.

Bollas, C. (2007). *The Freudian Moment.* London: Karnac.

Bollas, C. (2015) Psychoanalysis in the Age of Bewilderment: On the Return of the Oppressed. *International Journal of Psychoanalysis*, 96, 535–551.

Brenman, E. (2006). *Recovery of the Lost Good Object.* New York: Routledge.

Britton, R. and Steiner, J. (1994). Interpretation: Selected Fact or Overvalued Idea? *International Journal of Psychoanalysis*, 75, 1069–1078.

Brown, L. (2011). *Intersubjective Processes and the Unconscious: An integration of Freudian, Kleinian and Bionian Perspectives.* New York: Routledge.

Caper, R. (1997). A Mind of One's Own. *International Journal of Psychoanalysis*, 78, 265–278.

Caper, R. (2020). *Bion and Thoughts Too Deep for Words: Psychoanalysis, Suggestion, and the Language of the Unconscious.* New York: The Routledge Wilfred R. boon Studies Book Series.

Collingwood, R. G. (1994). *The Idea of History.* Oxford: Oxford University Press.

Corngold, S. (2022). *The Mind in Exile* (p. 189). Princeton: Princeton University Press.

Culbert-Koehn, J. (2011). An Analysis with Bion: An Interview with James Gooch. *Journal of Analytical Psychology*, 56, 76–91.

Dickinson, E. (2016). *The Collected Poems of Emily Dickinson*, Minneapolis: Lerner Publishing Group.

Eifermann, R. R. (1996). Uncovering, Covering, Discovering Analytic Truth: Personal and Professional Sources of Omission in Psychoanalytic Writing and Their Effects on Psychoanalytic Thinking and Practice. *Psychoanalytic Inquiry*, 16, 401–425.

Eissler, K. R. (1953). The Effect of the Structure of the Ego on Psychoanalytic Technique. *Journal of the American Psychoanalytic Association*, 1, 104–143.

Eissler, K. R. (1974). On Some Theoretical and Technical Problems Regarding the Payment of Fees for Psychoanalytic Treatment. *International Review of Psychoanalysis*, 1, 73–101.

Erikson, E. (1964). *Insight and Responsibility.* New York: W. W. Norton.

Ferenczi, S. (2018). *Final Contributions to the Problems and Methods of Psychoanalysis*, M. Balint (Ed.). New York: Routledge.

Freud, S. (1901). On Dreams. In: *The Standard Edition of the Complete Psychological Works of Sigmund Freud* (vol. 5, pp. 629–686).

Freud, S. (1933). Why War? *The Standard Edition of the Complete Psychological Works of Sigmund Freud* 22:195–216 p. 213.

Freud, S. (1981). *The Standard Edition of the Complete Psychological Works of Sigmund Freud*, J. Strachey (Ed.). London: Hogarth Press (Original works published 1886–1939).

Gabbard, G. O. (1982). The Exit Line: Heightened Transference-Countertransference Manifestations at the End of the Hour. *Journal of the American Psychoanalytic Association*, 30, 579–598.

Ghent, E. (1990). Masochism, Submission, Surrender – Masochism as a Perversion of Surrender. *Contemporary Psychoanalysis*, 26, 108–136.

Glover, E. (1926). A "Technical" Form of Resistance. *International Journal of Psychoanalysis*, 7, 377–380.

Green, A. (1983). The Dead Mother. In *On Private Madness.* London: Karnac, 2005.

Green, A. (1998). The Primordial Mind and the Work of the Negative. *International Journal of Psychoanalysis*, 79, 49–665.

Greenson, R. (1960). The Conflict Between Psychoanalysis and Religion. In R. A. Nemiroff, A. Sugarman and A. Robbins (Eds.), *On Loving Hating and Living Well – The Public Psychoanalytic Lectures of Ralph R. Greenson.* Madison, CT: Indiana University of Pennsylvania, 1992.

Heimann, P. (1956). Dynamics of Transference Interpretations. *International Journal of Psychoanalysis*, 37, 303–310.

Isaacs, S. (1939). Criteria for Interpretation. *International Journal of Psychoanalysis*, 20, 148–160.

Isakower, O. (1992). The Analyzing Instrument in the Teaching and Conduct of the Analytic Process. *Journal of Clinical Psychoanalysis*, 1, 181–222.

Jacobs, T. J. (1986). On Countertransference Enactments. *Journal of the American Psychoanalytic Association*, 34, 289–307.

Jacobs, T. J. (2018). On Countertransference Enactments. *PEP/UCL Top Authors Project Video Collection*, 1, 25.

James, W. (1929). *The Varieties of Religious Experience*. The Modern Library. New York: Random House.

Jones, E. (1953–1957). *The Life and Work of Sigmund Freud* (Vols. 1–3). London: Hogarth Press.

Joseph, B. (1983). On Understanding and not Understanding: Some Technical Issues. *International Journal of Psychoanalysis*, 64, 291–298.

Joseph, B. (2018). Ending Analysis. *International Journal of Psychoanalysis*, 99, 1427–1434.

King, P. and Steiner, R. (1991). *The Freud-Klein Controversies 1941–45*. New Library of Psycho-Analysis 11. London: Tavistock/Routledge.

Klein, M. (1937). Love, Guilt and Reparation. In M. Klein (Ed.), *Love Guilt and Reparation* (pp. 306–343). Vintage, 1998.

Loewald, H. W. (1988). Termination Analyzable and Unanalyzable. *Psychoanalytic Study of the Child*, 43, 155–166.

Lothane, Z. (1981). Listening with the Third Ear as an Instrument in Psychoanalysis: The Contributions of Reik and Isakower. *Psychoanalytic Review*, 68, 487–504.

Mason, A. (2000) Bion and Binocular Vision. *International Journal of Psychoanalysis*, 81, 983–988

Money-Kyrle, R. (1971). The Aims of Psychoanalysis. In D. Meltzer (Ed.), *The Collected Papers of Roger Money-Kyrle* (pp. 442–449). Strath Tay: Clunie, 1978.

Ogden, T. H. (1996). Reconsidering Three Aspects Of Psychoanalytic Technique. *International Journal of Psychoanalysis* 77:883–899.

Ohana, D. (2020). *The Fascist Temptation: Creating a Political Community of Experience*. New York: Routledge.

Poland, W. (2018). *Intimacy and Separateness in Psychoanalysis*. New-York: Routledge.

Rolnik, E. J. (2001). Between Memory and Desire: From History to Psychoanalysis and Back. *Psychoanalysis and History*, 3, 129–151.

Rolnik, E. J. (2008). Reading a 1933 Letter from Paula Heimann to Theodor Reik. *Journal of the American Psychoanalytic Association*, 56, 409–430.

Rolnik, E. J. (2009). *The Truth in Folds- Analysis of a Victim of a Munchhausen Syndrome by Proxy*. Paper presented at the Israel Psychoanalytic Society.

Rolnik, E. J. (2012). *Freud in Zion: Psychoanalysis and the Making of Modern Jewish Identity*. London: Karnac.

Rolnik, E. J. (2015). Before Babel: Reflections on Reading and Translating Freud. *Psychoanalytic Quarterly*, 84, 307–330.

Rolnik, E. J. (2019b). Listening to the Internal Psychoanalytic Objects. In: A. Fachler (Ed.), *Feeling the Elephant: Blind Spots of Psychoanalysis and Psychoanalytic Therapists* (pp. 41–65). Carmel Publishing House Jerusalem [Heb.].

Rolnik, E. J. (2020). Epistolary Epiphanies-Freud as a Letter Writer. In: D. Finzi (Ed.), *Sigmund Freud, Berggasse 19. The Origin of Psychoanalysis* (pp. 241–251). Wien-Hatje Cantz.

Rolnik, E. J. (2022). "The Jewish Offensive" – The Reception of Freud's *Moses and Monotheism* in Mandatory Jewish Palestine. In L. J. Brown (Ed.), *On Freud's Moses and Monotheism*. Routledge.

Rolnik, E. J. (2025). Dreams and Trauma: With Freud to Zion. In: S. Frosh & D. Baum (Eds.), *International Handbook for Psychoanalysis and Jewish Studies*. Forthcoming. Routledge.

Rosenfeld, H. (1978). Notes on the Psychopathology and Psychoanalytic Treatment of Some Borderline Patients. *International Journal of Psychoanalysis*, 59, 215–221.

Sandler, J. (1976). Countertransference and Role-Responsiveness. *International Review of Psychoanalysis*, 3, 43–47.

Sandler, J. (1983). Reflections on Some Relations Between Psychoanalytic Concepts and Psychoanalytic Practice. *International Journal of Psychoanalysis*, 64, 35–45.

Sedlak, V. (2000). The Dream Space and Counter-Transference. In: R. J. Perelberg (Ed.), *Dreaming and Thinking* (pp. 37–52). Karnac: London.

Segal, H. (2007). Symbolic equation and symbols. In *Yesterday, Today and Tomorrow* (pp. 111–113). London: Routledge.

Solan, R. (2015). *The Enigma of Childhood: The Profound Impact of the First Years of Life on Adults as Couples and Parents*. London: Routledge.

Spotnitz, H. (1969). *Modern Psychoanalysis of the Schizophrenic Patient*. New York: YBK Publishers.

Steiner, J. (1994). Patient-Centered and Analyst-Centered Interpretations: Some Implications of Containment and Countertransference. *Psychoanalytic Inquiry*, 14, 406–422.

Steiner, J. (2011). The Numbing Feeling of Reality. *Psychoanalytic Quarterly*, 80, 73–89.

Strachey, J. (1934). The Nature of the Therapeutic Action of Psycho-Analysis. *International Journal of Psychoanalysis*, 15, 127–159.

Weber, M. (1919). Science as a Vocation. In H. H. Gerth and C. Wright Mills (trans. and Eds.), *Max Weber: Essays in Sociology* (pp. 129–156). New York: Oxford University Press, 1946.

Weiss, E (1970). *Sigmund Freud as a Consultant: Recollections of a Pioneer in Psychoanalysis*. New York: Intercontinental Medical Book.

Weiss, H. (2021). The Conceptualization of Trauma in Psychoanalysis: An Introduction. *International Journal of Psychoanalysis*, 102, 755–764.

Whitehead, A. N. (1929). *The Aims of Education and Other Essays.* New York: Macmillan.

Wille, R. S. (2008). Psychoanalytic Identity: Psychoanalysis as an Internal Object. *Psychoanalytic Quarterly*, 77, 1193–1229.

Winnicott, D. W. (1953). Transitional Objects and Transitional Phenomena: A Study of the First Not-Me Possession. *International Journal of Psychoanalysis*, 34, 89–97.

Winnicott, D. W. (1960). Ego Distortion in Terms of True and False Self. In *The Maturational Processes and the Facilitating Environment* (pp. 140–152). New York: Indiana University of Pennsylvania, 1965.

Winnicott, D. W. (1965). The Value of the Therapeutic Consultation. In *Psycho-Analytic Explorations* (pp. 318–324). London: Karnac, 1989.

Winnicott, D. W. (1968). The Use of An Object. *International Journal of Psychoanalysis*, 50, 711–716.

Wittgenstein, L. (2012). *Tractatus Logico Philosophicus*, C. K. Ogden (trans.). New York: Dover Publication.

Woolf, V. (1982). *Orlando: A Biography*. London: Hogarth Press.

German sources

Bohleber, W. (1997). Trauma, Identifizierung und historischer Kontext. Über die Notwendigkeit, die NS-Vergangenheit in Den psychoanalytischen Deutungsprozeß einzubeziehen. *Psyche – Z Psychoanal*, 51, 958–995.

Eifermann, R. R. (1987). "Deutschland" und "die Deutschen": Agieren von Phantasien und deren Entdeckung in der Selbstanalyse. *Jahrbuch der Psychoanalyse*, 20, 165–206.

Fenichel, O. (1945). *Psychoanalytische Neurosenlehre. Bd 1–3*. Oltern/Freiburg i. Br.: Walter, 1974–1977.

Mann, T. (1939). *Der Zauberberg* (Einführung in den Zauberberg. Für Studenten der Universität Princeton. Als Vorwort.) In: *Thomas Mann Collected Works in XIII vols. Reden und Aufsätze*. Vol. IX. Frankfurt a.M. S. Fischer Verlag 1975.

Mitscherlich, A. M. (1967). *Die Unfähigkeit zu trauern. Grundlagen kollektiven Verhaltens*. München: Piper.

Sebald, W. G. (2003). Konstruktionen der Trauer. Zu Günter Grass "Tagebuch einer Schnecke" und Wolfgang Hildesheimer "Tynset". In *Campo Santo*. München: Hanser.

Index

For Product Safety Concerns and Information please contact our EU
representative GPSR@taylorandfrancis.com
Taylor & Francis Verlag GmbH, Kaufingerstraße 24, 80331 München, Germany

www.ingramcontent.com/pod-product-compliance
Lightning Source LLC
Chambersburg PA
CBHW050654280326
41932CB00015B/2903